Practical PC

7th Edition

June Jamrich Parsons • Dan Oja

CONTAINS A Digital Book FOR A FULLY INTERACTIVE LEARNING EXPERIENCE

CENGAGE
Learning®

Australia • Brazil • Mexico • Singapore • United Kingdom • United States

Practical PC, 7th Edition

June Jamrich Parsons, Dan Oja

Senior Director of Development:
 Marah Bellegarde

Senior Product Team Manager:
 Donna Gridley

Associate Product Manager: Amanda Lyons

Product Development Manager:
 Leigh Hefferon

Senior Content Developer: Kathy Finnegan

Content Developer: Julia Leroux-Lindsey

Product Assistant: Melissa Stehler

Marketing Director: Elinor Gregory

Senior Market Development Manager:
 Eric LaScola

Market Development Manager: Kristie Clark

Marketing Manager: Gretchen Swann

Marketing Coordinator: Elizabeth Murphy

Content Project Manager:
 Jennifer Feltri-George

Art Director: GEX Publishing Services

Manufacturing Planner: Fola Orekoya

Cover Art: (C) VLADGRIN/Shutterstock.com

Electronic Publishing Specialist:
 Tensi Parsons

Digital Book Technician: Keefe Crowley

Digital Book Development:
 MediaTechnics Corp.

Prepress Production: GEX Publishing Services

Copyeditor: Suzanne Huizenga

Indexer: Alexandra Nickerson

For product information and technology assistance, contact us at
Cengage Learning Customer & Sales Support, 1-800-354-9706

For permission to use material from this text or product,
submit all requests online at **www.cengage.com/permissions**.
Further permissions questions can be e-mailed to
permissionrequest@cengage.com.

Library of Congress Control Number: 2013948000
ISBN-13: 978-1-285-07677-5
ISBN-10: 1-285-07677-X

Cengage Learning
200 First Stamford Place, 4th Floor
Stamford, CT 06902
USA

Cengage Learning is a leading provider of customized learning solutions with office locations around the globe, including Singapore, the United Kingdom, Australia, Mexico, Brazil and Japan. Locate your local office at:
www.cengage.com/global

Cengage Learning products are represented in Canada by Nelson Education, Ltd.

To learn more about Cengage Learning, visit **www.cengage.com**

Purchase any of our products at your local college store or at our preferred online store **www.cengagebrain.com**

Printed in the United States of America
1 2 3 4 5 6 7 19 18 17 16 15 14 13

Preface

About this book

Practical PC provides a state-of-the-art introduction to Windows-based computers, written in an easy-to-read style. In addition to the printed book, you receive a multimedia version of the entire printed textbook that also includes videos and interactive elements such as pop-up definitions, software tutorials, and practice tests.

Each chapter of this book focuses on a specific topic. The first page introduces the chapter topic and lists the chapter contents. Chapter features include the following:

- **FAQs**, or "frequently asked questions," address key questions, provide background information, and give specific tips for becoming a more proficient computer user.

- A three-page **Technology** section in each chapter provides an inside look at key hardware and software elements of digital devices.

- **Issue** pages highlight an ethical or cultural controversy that's relevant to the chapter topic.

- A **Project** shows you how to explore and apply the concepts presented in each chapter.

- **Assessment activities** include two sets of QuickCheck questions and Get It? practice tests designed to gauge proficiency on the concepts and software skills presented in the chapter. Scores can be saved in a Tracking file and submitted to instructors.

About the digital book

The interactive, multimedia digital book is loaded with features to enhance and reinforce learning.

 Try It! buttons produce step-by-step interactive software tutorials, which give you a chance to quickly hone your software skills.

 Play It! buttons show videos that explain how digital devices work.

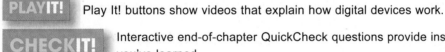 Interactive end-of-chapter QuickCheck questions provide instant feedback on what you've learned.

The Get It? button starts an interactive, auto-graded practice test containing ten questions randomly selected from the chapter test bank. Take a test more than once for a different set of questions. Results can be saved and delivered to instructors.

Pop-up Definitions & Glossary   Clickable boldface terms display pop-up definitions. A Glossary button provides easy access to all definitions from any page.

Projects

Each chapter includes a Project section with step-by-step instructions for applying the concepts covered in the chapter.

Explore your computer	Explore word processing software
Explore the Windows desktop	Explore spreadsheet software
Explore the user interface	Explore databases
Open and save files	Explore presentation software
Organize and find files	Explore digital sound
Explore file protection measures	Explore digital photos
Explore your Internet connection	Explore video editing
Explore browser security	Find the technical specifications for your PC
Explore e-mail	Get started with programming

Use this book because...

You want to learn about computers. *Practical PC* will help you understand enough "tech talk" so you can decipher computer ads and hold your own when the conversation turns to computers.

You want to learn Windows. *Practical PC* will show you how to use Windows controls and manage files so that you can use your computer to do neat stuff without frustration.

You want to learn how to use the Internet. *Practical PC* will show you how to get connected, use a browser, send e-mail, and launch a search engine.

You want to find out what a computer can do for you. You'll have a chance to experiment with all kinds of software applications, including software for word processing, art, video editing, music composition, and graphics.

Teaching tools

With **ExamView**, our powerful testing software package, instructors can generate printed tests, create LAN-based tests, or test over the Internet.

An **Instructor's Manual** outlines each chapter, and provides valuable teaching tips and solutions for projects.

WebTrack is a versatile tool that provides automated delivery of tracking data from any student directly to the instructor with minimal setup or administrative overhead.

Acknowledgments

When you think about how a textbook is created, you might envision a lone author who produces a manuscript that is copyedited, then sent to the printer. If that was the case, textbooks might be less expensive, but they would certainly be less effective and far less interesting.

Today, creating a textbook is more like developing a computer game than penning a novel. It is a process that requires designers, script writers, narrators, animators, videographers, photographers, photo researchers, desktop publishers, programmers, testers, indexers, editors, reviewers—and, yes, somewhere in the middle of all this creative effort are the authors.

The successful launch of this textbook was possible only because of an extraordinary and diverse team of dedicated specialists who collaborate from geographically dispersed locations using the Internet. It is a team of disciplined professionals who do what it takes to meet deadlines with high-quality work and cheeriness, even after working all weekend.

We would like to acknowledge the members of our incredible team who helped to bring you this colorful, interactive textbook:

Donna Mulder: Our animation and screentour expert, Donna, works from her office in Colorado to produce all the interactive software tours and animations that give this book its hands-on appeal.

Keefe Crowley: Multi-talented Keefe produces the digital book by linking together the text, photos, videos, software tours, animations, and computer-scored quizzes. He also ushers the digital book through the testing process and is responsible for producing many of the photos and video sequences. Keefe keeps in shape riding his mountain bike even during snowy northern winters.

Chris Robbert: The voice of the *Practical* series, Chris records narrations from his studio in the U.S. Virgin Islands, and he is a talented musician who specializes in classical and jazz guitar.

Tensi Parsons: Our layout and desktop publishing expert, Tensi, is responsible for tracking all the elements for the printed book. Each chapter goes through at least four revisions, and Tensi's job is to keep everything straight so the final product meets the highest standards. Tensi coaches community rowing teams in her spare time.

Testers, testers, testers: Kevin Lappi, Joseph Smit, Nikki Smit, Marilou Potter, Kelsey Schuch, Nora Heikkinen, Michael Crowley, and the Course Technology Software Quality Assurance Team; they test the digital book, they test the instructions, and they test the tests.

Julia Leroux-Lindsey: As our editorial product manager, Julia oversees the manuscript from inception to publication.

Jen Feltri-George: As our content project manager, Jen monitors the flow of chapters among the copyeditor, author, and desktop publisher. She makes sure that all the final copy is clean and error-free.

Sarah A. Fowler: Sarah is our project manager who keeps track of the detailed production schedule.

Suzanne Huizenga: With today's technology, spelling errors are few and far between. But there are still a million and one grammar and style issues for the copyeditor to address, and Suzanne is a perfectionist with an eagle eye.

And that's not all! We simply cannot omit the editorial staff at Cengage Learning who make the executive decisions and work with customers: Donna Gridley, Amanda Lyons, Kathy Finnegan, and Melissa Stehler. They are this product's fairy godmothers who make the pumpkin turn into a coach.

Brief Contents

Contents

Contents

Contents

Before You Begin

You are going to enjoy using *Practical PC* and the accompanying digital book. The answers to the FAQs (frequently asked questions) in this section will help you begin.

FAQ Will the digital book work on my computer?

The easiest way to find out if the digital book works on your computer is to try it! Just follow the steps below to start the CD. If it works, you're all set. Otherwise, check with your local technical support person.

To run the digital book, your computer needs the Windows operating system (Windows 8, 7, Vista, or XP) and screen resolution of 1024 x 768 or better. You'll also need a CD or DVD drive. If one is not built into your computer, you can use an external drive to access the digital book or transfer it to your computer's hard disk.

The instructions below explain how to use the digital book from the CD. If you prefer to transfer the digital book to your computer's hard drive, refer to the instructions at the end of this section.

FAQ How do I start the digital book?

The digital book is distributed on a CD, which is easy to use and requires no installation. Follow these simple steps to get started:

1. Make sure your computer is turned on.

2. Insert the CD into your computer's CD/DVD drive.

3. If your computer displays an AutoPlay window similar to the one shown below, select the Run BookOnReader.exe option.

© MediaTechnics

DVD RW Drive (E:) PPC7

Choose what to do with this disc.

Install or run program from your media

 Run BookOnReader.exe
Publisher not specified

Other choices

 Open folder to view files
File Explorer

 Take no action

Source: Microsoft Corporation

4. When you see the title screen below, your digital book is open and is waiting for you to select tracking options. For information on tracking options, continue to the FAQ on the next page of your textbook.

The length of time your computer takes to open the digital book depends on your security settings. If you have security set to conduct a virus check on software running from CDs, you will have to wait for that process to be completed before the digital book opens.

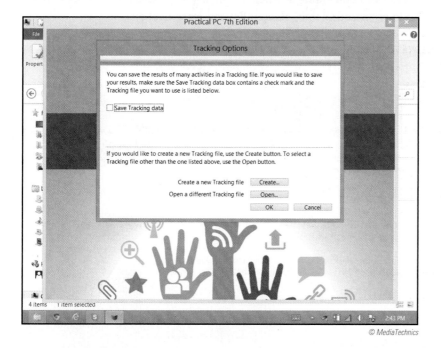

© MediaTechnics

Manual Start: Follow the instructions in the figure below only if you've waited a minute or two and the title screen has not appeared.

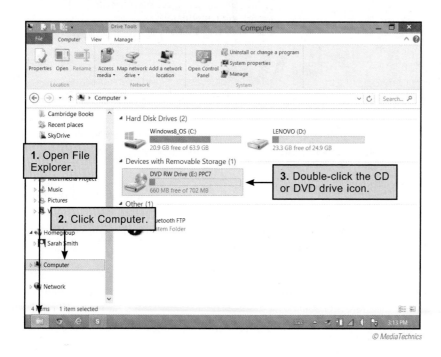

© MediaTechnics

FAQ How should I set my tracking options?

When the digital book opens, it displays the *Practical PC 7th Edition* title screen and a Tracking Options window. To proceed, you'll have to select your tracking settings.

A Tracking file records your progress by saving your scores on QuickChecks and Get It? practice tests at the end of each chapter. If you don't want to record your scores, simply make sure the *Save Tracking data* box is empty, then click the OK button to proceed straight to the first chapter.

If you prefer to track your scores, then you can create a Tracking file. It's easy! Click the Create button, then follow the on-screen prompts to enter your name, student ID, and class section.

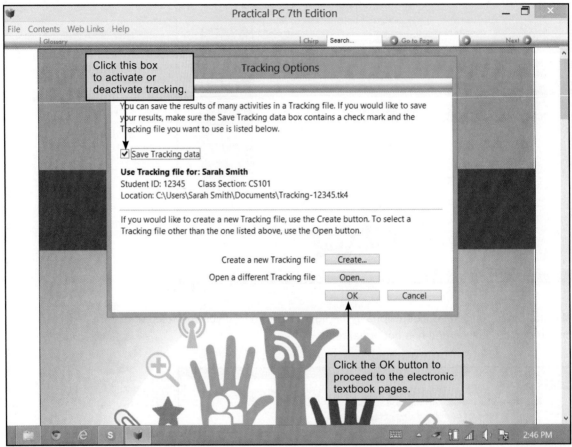

© MediaTechnics

When the Save As window appears, you can select the location for your Tracking file. If you are using your own computer, the default location in the Documents folder is a great place to store your Tracking file, so just click the Save button and you're all set!

If you are working on a public computer, such as one in a school lab, be aware that data stored on the hard disk might be erased or changed by other students unless you have a protected personal storage area. When working on a public computer or when you need to transport your data from one computer to another, a USB flash drive is a better option for storing your Tracking file.

To save your Tracking file in a location other than your computer's Documents folder, click the Computer icon, then double-click a storage location to select it. Click the Save button to finalize your storage selection.

FAQ How do I navigate through the digital book?

Each page of the digital book exactly duplicates a page from the printed book. Tools on the menu bar help you navigate from page to page. If your computer screen does not show an entire page, use the scroll bar.

Click Contents, then click any chapter to jump to the start of the chapter.

Enter a page number here, then click the > button to jump to a specific page.

Click here to go to the previous page.

Practical PC 7th Edition

File   Contents   Web Links   Help

| Glossary | Practice Test | Chirp   Search...   Go to Page   8   Back Next

Click File, then click Exit to close the digital book.

FAQ What is the boot process?

The power switch is located on your computer's system unit. Most power switches are labeled with a ⏻ symbol, and power lights indicate whether your computer is on or off. As soon as you switch on the power, your PC starts to "boot up." During the **boot process**, the PC performs diagnostic tests to make sure that the ke devices, RAM, and microprocessor are functioning correctly.

After testing the hardware, the boot program looks for the operating **operating system** is software that manages a computer's internal how you interact with the computer. You can use the operating syst files or start **application software** ("applications") that helps you p make calculations, draw pictures, or maintain your to-do list, for exa

Today's computers typically come with the operating system preins disk. The majority of computers run the **Microsoft Windows** operating system. Some computers also run other operating systems, such as OS X, iOS, Android, and Linux. Computers that run Windows are the main focus of this book.

hen the boot process is almost complete, you'll see the **Lock screen**, which displays time, date, and status icons. An **icon** is a small pictogram that represents a software plication, file, or tool that is accessible from the screen.

ck the Lock screen to continue to the login screen. If your computer has a touchscreen, you can swipe the Lock screen and use a picture password. Play the video for Figure 1-2 to see how.

Click here to go to the next page.

Drag the scroll box down or press the Page Down key to scroll down the page.

Drag the scroll box up or press the Page Up key to scroll back up a page.

Click a Try It! button to start a software tutorial.

TRY IT!

Figure 1-2

Lock screen

2:50 PM

© MediaTechnics

Before You Begin

FAQ What should I know about the Projects?

The Project section at the end of each chapter helps you consolidate and apply the concepts you've learned. All projects require a computer with the Windows 7 or 8 operating system. Other software that you'll need is listed at the beginning of each project.

If a project requires you to send an e-mail attachment to your instructor, use your usual e-mail software, such as Thunderbird, Microsoft Outlook, Windows Mail, Outlook.com, Gmail, or AOL Mail. First, make sure that you have saved the project file. Next, start your e-mail software. Then, follow your software's procedures for sending an e-mail attachment.

FAQ How does the interactive assessment page work?

Each chapter ends with an assessment page containing interactive activities. You can use these activities to evaluate how well you've mastered the concepts and skills covered in the chapter. If you do well on the QuickChecks and practice tests, then you're ready to move on to the next chapter. If you don't do well, you might want to review the material before continuing to the next chapter.

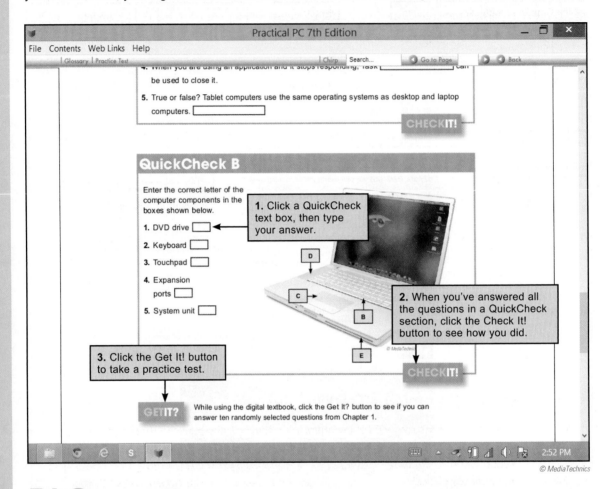

© MediaTechnics

FAQ Are all my scores tracked?

Your scores on QuickChecks and practice tests are tracked if you have activated tracking with a checkmark in the *Save Tracking data* box.

FAQ How can I change tracking options?

You can access the Tracking Options window at any time by clicking File on the menu bar, then selecting Change Tracking Options. When the Tracking Options window appears, you can activate or deactivate tracking, create a new Tracking file, or select a different Tracking file.

FAQ What if the Tracking Options window shows the wrong Tracking file?

When working in a computer lab or using a computer where other students are using the digital book, the Tracking Options window might show a Tracking file that belongs to another person because that person was the last one to use the computer. You can use the Open button on the Tracking Options window to select a different Tracking file. Tracking files are usually stored in the Documents folder.

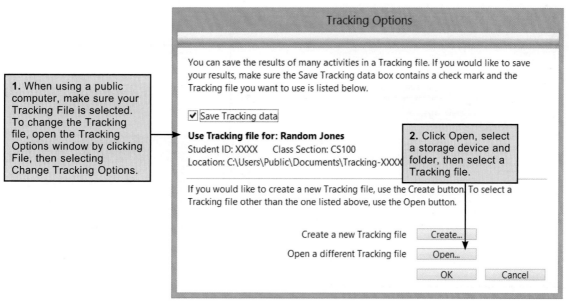

1. When using a public computer, make sure your Tracking File is selected. To change the Tracking file, open the Tracking Options window by clicking File, then selecting Change Tracking Options.

Tracking Options

You can save the results of many activities in a Tracking file. If you would like to save your results, make sure the Save Tracking data box contains a check mark and the Tracking file you want to use is listed below.

☑ Save Tracking data

Use Tracking file for: Random Jones
Student ID: XXXX   Class Section: CS100
Location: C:\Users\Public\Documents\Tracking-XXXX

2. Click Open, select a storage device and folder, then select a Tracking file.

If you would like to create a new Tracking file, use the Create button. To select a Tracking file other than the one listed above, use the Open button.

Create a new Tracking file   Create...
Open a different Tracking file   Open...

OK   Cancel

© MediaTechnics

FAQ How do I submit my Tracking file?

In an academic setting, your instructor might request your Tracking file data to monitor your progress. Your instructor will tell you if you should submit your Tracking file using the WebTrack system, if you should hand in your Tracking file on a USB drive, or if you should send the Tracking file as an e-mail attachment. To submit your Tracking file through WebTrack, select the File option, select Submit Tracking Data, then enter your instructor's WebTrack address.

FAQ How do I end a session?

You should leave the CD for *Practical PC* in the CD drive while you're using it, or you will encounter an error message. Before you remove the CD from the drive, you must exit the program by clicking File on the menu bar, then clicking Exit. You can also exit by clicking the Close button in the upper-right corner of the window.

FAQ What about sound?

If your computer is equipped for sound, you should hear narrations during the Try It! activities. If you don't hear anything, check the volume control on your computer by clicking the speaker icon in the lower-right corner of your screen. If you're working in a lab or an office where sound would be disruptive, consider using headphones.

Before You Begin

FAQ What if my computer has no CD drive?

The *Practical PC* digital book is distributed on a CD, but it can be transferred to your computer's hard disk. To do so, you will have to temporarily connect an external CD/DVD drive, which you can borrow from a friend, if necessary. Put the CD for *Practical PC* in the drive, then complete the following steps:

1. From the Windows 8 Start screen, click the Desktop tile. (For Windows 7, skip to Step 2.)

2. Select the ▦ File Explorer icon that's at the bottom of the desktop.

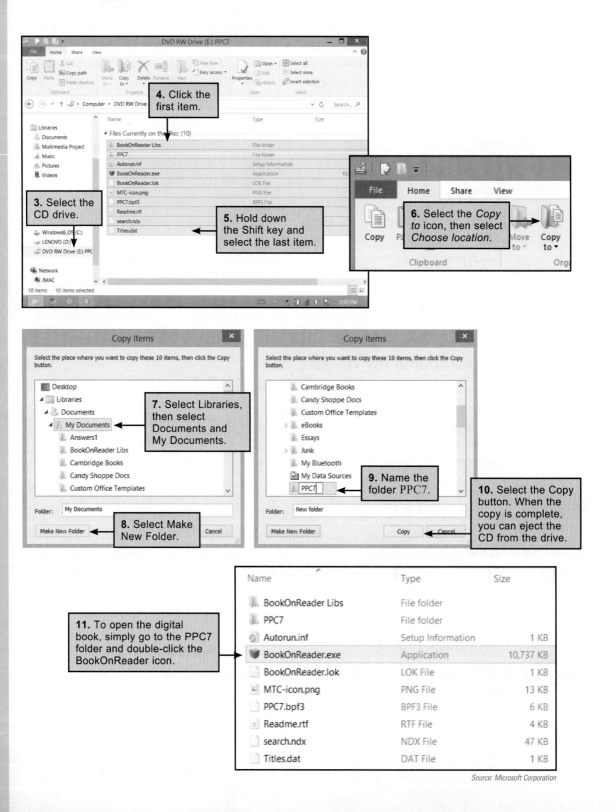

Source: Microsoft Corporation

Before You Begin

Practical PC
7th Edition

What's inside?

Chapter 1 provides an overview of your computer system, including the terminology and equipment you need to get started. Some of the material might be a review, but don't ignore the explanations that tell you *why* these things work the way they do.

● **FAQs:**

What's in the digital book?

Your digital textbook contains the entire text of the printed book. But that's not all! In the digital book, the figures "come to life" through videos and animations. To use the CD, simply insert it into your CD or DVD drive. After a few seconds, you should see the title page and the Tracking Options window. For more information about using the CD, refer to the Before You Begin section in the front of the book.

FAQ What are the basics?

Your **PC** (personal computer) is a collection of hardware and software components that help you accomplish many kinds of tasks. As you probably know, a computer and any equipment connected to it are called **hardware**. A set of instructions that a computer follows to perform a task is called a computer program or **software**.

The case that holds the computer's important hardware components is a **system unit**. It includes components to process, store, collect, and output data. The **microprocessor** is essentially the brain of the computer, which carries out commands that you issue when creating documents, drawing pictures, or manipulating numbers. Microprocessors work with **data** that represents words, numbers, and pictures. This data is held temporarily in memory chips called **RAM** (random access memory).

Data has a more permanent home on **storage media** such as hard disks, USB flash drives, CDs, and DVDs. Devices that are designed to store data on disks and other storage media are referred to as **storage devices**. The main storage device for most PCs is a high-capacity **hard disk drive** located inside the system unit.

Computers work with bits that represent data. A **bit** can have one of two states: 0 or 1. Eight bits are called a byte. One **byte** is used to represent one letter, numeral, or symbol. The capacity of storage devices is measured in megabytes, gigabytes, or terabytes. A **megabyte** (MB) is equivalent to approximately a million characters of data, a **gigabyte** (GB) is a billion characters, and a **terabyte** (TB) is a trillion characters.

Computers also include **input devices**, such as keyboards, mice, and touchpads, that are used to enter data for processing. **Output devices**, such as printers and display screens, show the results of processing. These devices can exchange data with the computer wirelessly, or they can be connected to a computer's **expansion ports** using a cable. A computer can connect to other computers and devices by means of a network. A computer network links computers together so that they can share data and devices. Figure 1-1 illustrates basic hardware components of a typical PC.

Figure
1-1

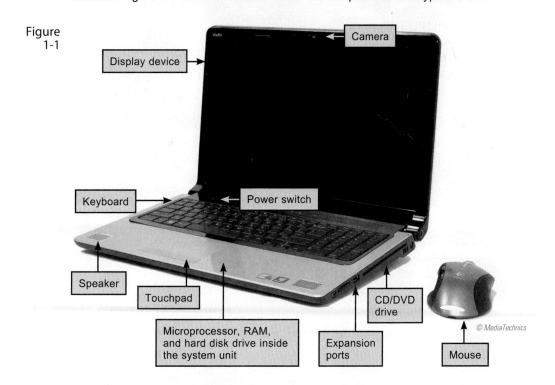

© MediaTechnics

FAQ What is the boot process?

The power switch is located on your computer's system unit. Most power switches are labeled with a ⏻ symbol, and power lights indicate whether your computer is on or off. As soon as you switch on the power, your PC starts to "boot up." During the **boot process**, the PC performs diagnostic tests to make sure that the keyboard, storage devices, RAM, and microprocessor are functioning correctly.

After testing the hardware, the boot program looks for the operating system. An **operating system** is software that manages a computer's internal operations and defines how you interact with the computer. You can use the operating system to organize your files or start **application software** ("applications") that helps you produce documents, make calculations, draw pictures, or maintain your to-do list, for example.

Today's computers typically come with the operating system preinstalled on the hard disk. The majority of computers run the **Microsoft Windows** operating system. Some computers also run other operating systems, such as OS X, iOS, Android, and Linux. Computers that run Windows are the main focus of this book.

When the boot process is almost complete, you'll see the **Lock screen**, which displays the time, date, and status icons. An **icon** is a small pictogram that represents a software application, file, or tool that is accessible from the screen.

Click the Lock screen to continue to the login screen. If your computer has a touchscreen, you can swipe the Lock screen and use a picture password. Play the video for Figure 1-2 to see how.

PLAYIT!

Figure 1-2

Lock screen

Time

Date

Network connection strength icon

Battery usage icon

Source: Microsoft Corporation

• What is the boot process? (continued)

As the boot process continues, you'll see the **Login screen**, which allows you to select a user account and log in to Windows. When you type your password, it usually appears as a series of dots as shown in Figure 1-3. This security measure hides your password from anyone who might be looking over your shoulder.

Figure 1-3

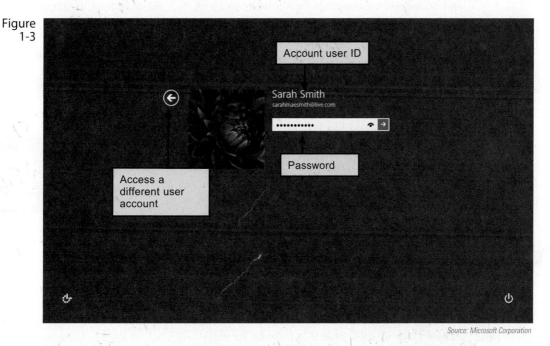

Source: Microsoft Corporation

After a successful login, Windows displays the **Start screen** that provides access to software applications, files, and settings for customizing your computer work environment. The Start screen shown in Figure 1-4 is typical, but yours might have a different color scheme and the rectangular tiles might have a different appearance.

Figure 1-4

Source: Microsoft Corporation

FAQ How do I make selections and issue commands?

When interacting with computers, you can use a mouse, touchpad, or touchscreen to select and manipulate screen-based objects. Whereas you might right-click an object to view a list of options when using a mouse, you would use the touch-and-hold gesture when using a touchscreen. "Touch and hold" means to hold your finger or stylus on the screen for the length of time it takes to count to 2. Basic mouse, touchpad, and touchscreen interactions are summarized in Figure 1-5.

Figure 1-5

	Mouse	Touchpad	Touchscreen
Select	Click	Tap	Touch
Activate	Double-click	Double-tap	Double-touch
Modify	Right-click	Tap lower-right corner	Touch and hold

© MediaTechnics

© MediaTechnics

Another handy tool for interacting with your computer is the ▢ **Windows key**. You can find the Windows key on the keyboard of desktop and laptop computers. Tablet computers without a keyboard have a Windows button instead. Use the Windows key or button to access the Start screen at any time while you are logged in.

The keys in the top row on a computer keyboard are called **function keys**. Each one is labeled with a small picture to indicate its purpose. Function keys can be used to control volume, screen brightness, wireless network connections, and multiple display devices.

Function keys are also labeled F1 through F12, to work in conjunction with the Fn key at the bottom of the keyboard. When you hold down the Fn key and press a function key, the application software you are using accepts it as a command. Function key commands vary from application to application. Consult the application's Help system to find out exactly what they do.

In addition to keys for typing letters, numbers, and symbols, computer keyboards also have several specialized keys for computer-related tasks.

The **CTRL key** (Control key) works in conjunction with other keys to perform keyboard shortcuts. For example, instead of locating the Copy command on a menu and clicking it, you can hold down the Ctrl key and press C to accomplish the same task.

The **Alt key** works in the same way as the Ctrl key for keyboard shortcuts.

The **Esc key** (Escape key) can be used to cancel an action or close a menu.

The **Enter key** (sometimes labeled Return) is used to move down a line when typing text for a document, but it can also be used at the end of an entry when you are ready to proceed to the next step.

The **Tab key** can be used to move to the next tab stop, but it is also used to move to the next field when entering data into a form on the screen.

FAQ How do I create and modify user accounts?

A **user account** includes a user ID and password, plus specifications about which files can be accessed and what settings can be adjusted. Windows offers two types of user accounts: administrator and standard user.

Administrator. An **administrator account** lets you change any Windows settings, change your account settings, access and change other users' accounts, install software, connect hardware, and access all the files on a computer. Certain activities, such as uninstalling software, cannot proceed unless you are logged in as an administrator or can enter an administrator account name and password. The first account that you set up on a new Windows computer automatically becomes an administrator account. You can use this account to set up additional user accounts.

Standard user. A **standard user account** allows you to access folders and files that you create, use most applications that are installed on the computer, and adjust settings that affect your personal view of the Windows desktop. With this type of account, however, you cannot install or uninstall software, configure hardware, or change settings that affect other users unless you know an administrator password.

In addition to the choice between an administrator and a standard user account, you can also choose whether to have a Microsoft account or a local account. A Microsoft account is essentially a global account that syncs your local computer to Internet-based services offered by Microsoft. This type of account gives you access to Microsoft downloads and online applications. A local account simply maintains your login credentials on one computer, allowing you to log in to that device.

Managing user accounts is easy. Figure 1-6 explains the options.

Swipe your touchscreen from the right or move the pointer to the lower-right corner of the screen, until the Charms menu appears, then select Settings.

TRYIT!

Figure 1-6

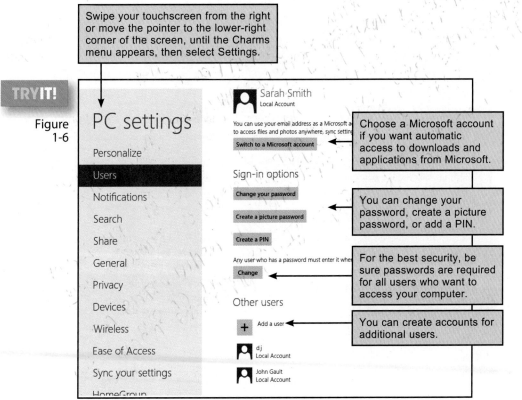

Source: Microsoft Corporation

FAQ What should I know about passwords?

A **password** is a series of letters and numbers associated with a user ID. In addition to using a password to log in to Windows, you also need a password to log in to your Facebook account, Twitter feed, and other Internet sites.

In movies, hackers can easily figure out a password by typing in a few names of the computer owner's favorite people. In reality, hackers employ password-cracking software that can try millions of possible passwords in a second.

When you create or modify a password, select one that is difficult for someone else to guess. Hackers can easily find information about you, such as your phone number, zip code, family members' names, and pets' names. Do not use them as passwords. Try not to use the same password at too many sites. Protect your financial information with a unique password that you do not use at your social networking sites.

A secure password is sometimes referred to as a "strong" password. Strong passwords are at least eight characters long. Adding more characters makes the password more difficult to crack. You should combine uppercase and lowercase letters, numbers, and special symbols such as @, #, and %. You can create a fairly secure password by replacing some of the letters with numbers and symbols in an easy-to-remember phrase such as MyP@ssw0rd.

Here's another technique for creating a strong password. Select a sentence that is at least eight words long and contains a number, such as "The first house I lived in was located on 522 Front Street." Combine the first letter of each word, maintaining its case, into a password string, as follows: Tfhlliwlo522FS.

Figure 1-7 sums up what you should know about creating strong passwords.

Figure 1-7

- Use passwords that are at least eight characters in length. The longer the password, the tougher it is to crack.
- Use a combination of letters, numbers, and special characters such as $ and #, if permitted.
- Use uppercase and lowercase letters.
- Use a passphrase based on several words or the first letters of a song, poem, or sentence.

- Do not use a password based on public information such as your phone number, Social Security number, driver's license number, or birthday.
- Avoid passwords that contain your entire user ID or part of it. A user ID of bjeffe coupled with a password of bjeffe123 is an easy target for password thieves.
- Steer clear of words that can be found in the dictionary, including words from other languages.
- Do not use common words spelled backwards. *Drowssap* (*password* spelled backwards) is not tricky enough to fool password-cracking software.

FAQ When should I sign out or switch users?

When you've finished using a computer or want to take a break, you have several options for logging off or shutting down. When you click your user account icon on the Start screen, a menu gives you a choice of locking your computer, signing out, or switching users.

- **Lock:** The Lock option displays the lock screen but keeps you logged in and keeps all of your applications and files open. To get back to work, simply enter your password at the Lock screen. Use this option when you are taking a break and want to get back to work quickly.

- **Sign out:** When you use the *Sign out* option, the files you were using are closed, but the computer is not turned off. Other users with valid accounts can then log on without restarting the computer and waiting for the computer to complete the boot process. Logging off is a good security practice when ending a computer session on any computer that is used by multiple people, such as computers in school labs and Internet cafés.

- **Switch user:** If you have more than one user account on your computer, the switch user option allows another person to log on without requiring you to log off or close your files. Use this option with care. If you leave unsaved files open and switch to a user who then shuts down the computer, your files might become damaged.

Selecting your account icon produces a list of options that lets you lock the computer, sign out, or switch users.

Figure 1-8

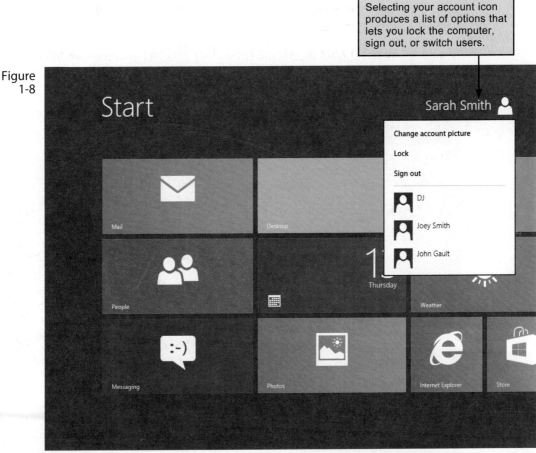

Source: Microsoft Corporation

FAQ How do I turn off my computer?

When you've completed a computing session, you might be tempted to simply hold down the power switch until the computer turns off. If you do so, however, your files might not close properly before the data in memory disappears when the power is cut. Instead of pressing the power switch, you should initiate the Windows **shut down** procedure. There are several ways to shut down Windows. An easy method is to type Off at the Start screen, then choose the option *Turn off your PC*.

If occasionally you forget to use the shut down procedure, don't panic. Many types of application software, such as word processors, have autosave routines that can restore files that might not have closed properly. The risk of losing data is there, however, so use the shut down procedure whenever possible.

You should shut down your computer when you don't intend to use it for several days. Shutting down is the best way to conserve power and prevent battery drain. You should always use the shut down procedure before unplugging a non-battery-powered computer. You can use the shut down menu's Restart option if Windows starts to behave erratically. Restarting usually resolves operational problems because it reloads the operating system.

Computer software sometimes has "bugs" or errors that cause your computer to "freeze up" or "hang" so you can't access the Shut Down option. Before you press the power switch, try holding down the Ctrl, Shift, and Esc keys at the same time. This key combination opens **Task Manager**, which enables you to close any non-responding applications. If only one application has frozen, you'll normally be able to close just that one application. You can then retry the Shut Down option to see if it works correctly.

Figure 1-9 shows how to access the *Shut down* option. Click the Try It! button to find out how to use Task Manager if an application is not responding.

TRYIT!

Figure 1-9

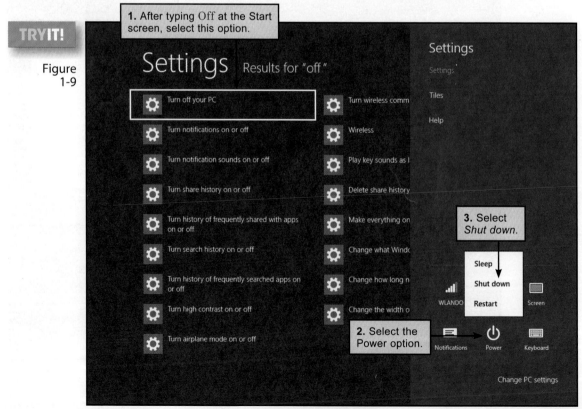

Source: Microsoft Corporation

FAQ When should I use sleep and hibernate modes?

When powering up your computer, you have to wait for the lengthy boot process to be completed. You also have to manually reopen all applications and files that you want to work with. Sleep and hibernate modes enable you to resume your work where you left off without having to wait for the boot process. When your computer is in these modes, you can wake it up by opening the lid, pressing a key, or moving the mouse.

When you put your computer into **sleep mode**, Windows keeps all your work in memory and puts your computer in a low-power, energy-saving state. Sleep mode is a good option if you use your computer intermittently throughout the day. Password-protecting your account ensures that your files are inaccessible to unauthorized people who wake up your computer.

When your computer enters **hibernate mode**, Windows saves all your work in progress to your hard disk and turns off your computer, but still remembers what you were working on the next time you start a new session. Hibernate uses slightly less power than sleep mode, but it takes a bit longer to get all your files and applications loaded up.

Your computer might automatically go into sleep or hibernate mode after a period of inactivity. You can manually put your computer into sleep or hibernate modes, too. You can initiate Sleep mode from the same menu used to shut down your computer. Your laptop computer might sleep or hibernate when you shut the lid. Briefly pressing the power switch might also initiate sleep or hibernate.

Sleep and hibernate modes are fully customizable using Power Options settings, as shown in Figure 1-10.

TRY IT!

Figure
1-10

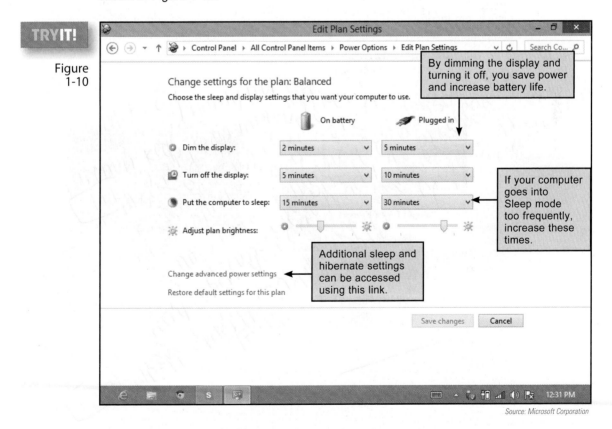

Source: Microsoft Corporation

Technology

Personal computers

The term **computer system** usually refers to a computer and all the components that are connected to it, such as a mouse, a printer, a scanner, and any external storage devices. At the core of a computer system is the computer itself, which can come in several configurations that fit on your desk or in your backpack. Each has advantages—you might find that you need more than one computer!

A **desktop computer** is designed to be a fairly permanent fixture on your desk. Key hardware components include the system unit, mouse, keyboard, and display device. You'll tend not to move a desktop computer very frequently because it takes some time to disconnect and then reconnect all the components. In addition, it requires power from a wall outlet.

Although they are rather large and not very portable, desktop computers provide the most expansion capability and the most computing power for your dollar. You can purchase a very serviceable desktop computer with a basic set of software tools for less than $500, although a high-performance computer with the latest processor and components can cost as much as $5,000.

Traditionally styled desktop computers are housed in a large, vertical tower case, which offers space inside for adding expansion cards and additional storage devices. The system unit, display device, and keyboard are usually separate components. Additional devices can be added using cable connections or wireless signals.

All-in-one computers offer another desktop option designed to be used on a desk and run on power supplied by a wall outlet. The processor, memory, storage devices, and display are incorporated into the system unit, but the keyboard and mouse are separate components. All-in-one computers do not offer space for adding expansion cards, so they cannot be easily upgraded with faster or higher capacity components.

Figure
1-11

All © MediaTechnics

Traditionally styled desktop computer   All-in-one desktop computer

Technology
(continued)

In contrast to desktop computers, a **portable computer** has the ability to operate on battery power. Its screen, keyboard, camera, storage devices, and speakers are fully contained in a single case so that the device can be easily transported from one place to another. Portable computers include laptops, netbooks, tablets, and smartphones.

A **laptop computer** (or notebook computer) is a small, lightweight personal computer designed like a clamshell with a keyboard on the base, and a display screen on the hinged cover. Laptops typically include a built-in touchpad that takes the place of a mouse for pointing and clicking. You can plug a laptop into a wall outlet or run it from an internal rechargeable battery.

Most laptops weigh between two and ten pounds and cost between $300 and $4,000. You can expect to pay about $450 for a mid-range current model laptop.

Most laptops provide expansion ports to which you can attach external devices such as mice, CD or DVD drives, and hard disk drives. Some laptops also include expansion slots into which you can insert memory cards that hold photos from digital cameras.

Small laptop computers are sometimes called netbooks. A netbook is useful for checking e-mail and social networking sites when you don't want to tote around a large laptop, but you'd like a usable keyboard. The price of an entry-level netbook computer starts at about $250.

Figure
1-12

© MediaTechnics

Laptop

© MediaTechnics

Netbook

Technology
(continued)

Portable computers come in several styles besides notebooks and netbooks. A **tablet computer** is a portable computing device featuring a touch-sensitive screen that can be used for input as well as output.

Tablet computers use different operating systems than those used for desktop, laptop, and netbook computers, which means that they may not run all the same software. Consumers need to be aware of this difference. Don't expect to install a software application on your laptop and then also install it on your tablet computer. You might, however, be able to purchase and install different versions of the software for the two devices.

Tablet computers are available in several configurations. A **slate tablet** configuration resembles a high-tech clipboard and lacks a built-in keyboard (although one can be attached). Popularized by the Apple iPad, tablet computers running Microsoft operating systems are also available.

A **convertible tablet** includes a keyboard that can be folded out of the way or detached. Convertibles are a bit larger and heavier than tablets, but prices for the two configurations are similar.

Tablet computers are great when you want a portable device for accessing the Internet, sending e-mail, and interacting with social networking sites. When tablet computers were first introduced in 2002, they were priced significantly higher than laptop computers with similar processors and memory capacity. Currently, however, tablet computers are priced only slightly higher than equivalent laptops.

Figure
1-13

© MediaTechnics
Slate tablet

Convertible tablet © MediaTechnics

Figure
1-14

© MediaTechnics

A **smartphone** features a small keyboard or touch-sensitive screen and is designed to fit into a pocket, run on batteries, and be used while you are holding it. Today's smartphones can be classified as personal computers because they are programmable, so they can download, store, and run software.

Smartphones can connect to cell phone networks to make voice calls, send text messages, and access the Internet. GPS capability gives applications the ability to provide location-based services, such as a list of nearby restaurants. Many smartphones also feature built-in speech recognition that allows you to ask questions and control the device using verbal commands. The operating systems for smartphones are similar to those used for tablet computers.

Project

Explore your computer

Whether you own a portable or desktop model, a computer is an important investment that you must protect. You realize the significant role a computer plays in your life when your system crashes and you're unable to complete important tasks. It is therefore essential that you have basic information about your computer at your fingertips in case you need technical support.

Knowing your PC's brand, model, and serial number is helpful if your computer is lost or stolen. In addition, a strong, secure password helps prevent others from tampering with your files, which is especially important if the files contain confidential information.

When you have completed this project, you should be able to:

- Locate basic system information about your computer, such as the brand, model, and serial number.

- Change your account picture.

- Identify the purpose of each function key on your computer's keyboard.

- Evaluate the security of your password.

- Identify the applications or tasks running on your account.

Requirements: This project requires Microsoft Windows 8, an Internet connection, and a browser such as Internet Explorer or Chrome. A word processor and e-mail are also required if you are submitting the deliverable electronically.

The deliverable for Project 1 is a document containing the following information:

1. The type of computer you own or regularly use, plus the brand and model

2. Your computer's serial number

3. Your computer's service tag, if there is one

4. A description of the function keys on your computer's keyboard

5. A list of the applications running on your account

6. An evaluation of your password's strength

7. Your account picture and the new picture you used to replace it

1. Write down the type of computer you own or regularly use (e.g., desktop, laptop, tablet). Also note your computer's brand and model. For example, Dell Inspiron 15r is the brand and model of a popular laptop computer. You should be able to find your computer's brand and model printed on the system unit.

2. Write down your computer's serial number. If you have a desktop model, this information is most likely on the side or back of your system unit. For laptops and tablets, look at the underside of the system unit.

• Explore your computer (continued)

3. Some computer manufacturers provide a service tag number, which is typically located near the serial number of your computer. This number, which is usually required for technical support, is associated with the warranty that comes with your computer. Jot down your computer's service tag, if there is one.

4. Take a look at the function keys on your computer keyboard. Make a list of each key's purpose. If you're skilled at drawing, make a sketch of the pictures on each function key.

© MediaTechnics

5. Use the Windows Task Manager to view the applications that are running on your account. Hold the Ctrl, Shift, and Esc keys at the same time. Write down the applications (Apps) that are listed. Which application is using the most memory? Are any applications not responding? Close Task Manager by clicking the [×] Close button.

Open Task Manager by holding down the Ctrl, Shift, and Esc keys.

Task Manager			2%	57%	0%	0%	
File Options View							
Processes Performance App history Startup Users Details Services							
Name		Status	CPU	Memory	Disk	Network	
Apps (8)							
Internet Explorer			0%	55.2 MB	0 MB/s	0 Mbps	
Internet Explorer			0%	100.3 MB	0 MB/s	0 Mbps	
Mail			0%	58.8 MB	0 MB/s	0 Mbps	
Paint			0%	16.6 MB	0 MB/s	0 Mbps	
PC settings			0%	8.8 MB	0 MB/s	0 Mbps	
People			0%	56.7 MB	0 MB/s		
Skype (32 bit)			2.7%	113.4 MB			
Task Manager			0%	19.2 MB			
Background processes (68)							
Adobe Acrobat Update Service (32 bit)			0%	0.7 MB	0 MB/s	0 Mbps	
Adobe Reader and Acrobat Manager (32 bit)			0%	2.3 MB	0 MB/s	0 Mbps	
Adobe® Flash® Player Utility			0%	1.8 MB	0 MB/s	0 Mbps	
Ask Updater (32 bit)			0%	2.8 MB	0 MB/s	0 Mbps	
BACK Monitor Application (32 bit)			0%	1.2 MB	0 MB/s	0 Mbps	
Bonjour Service			0%	1.3 MB	0 MB/s	0 Mbps	
COM Surrogate			0%	1.0 MB	0 MB/s	0 Mbps	
COM Surrogate			0%	0.9 MB	0 MB/s	0 Mbps	
Communications Service			0%	13.6 MB	0 MB/s	0 Mbps	
Fewer details						End task	

Use this button to close Task Manager.

Make a note of the apps running on your computer.

Find the app that uses the most memory.

4:54 PM

Source: Microsoft Corporation

• Explore your computer (continued)

6.   Modify your account picture. From the Start screen, select your user name. Click *Change account picture*. You can use the Browse link to select a photo stored on your computer, or you can use the Camera link to take a new photo. Make sketches of your previous account picture and the new picture that you selected.

7.   Check the strength of your current Windows password at the Microsoft Web site. To accomplish this step:

Go to the Windows desktop by selecting the Desktop tile on the Start screen.

Select the ⬭ Internet Explorer or ⬤ Chrome button at the bottom of the screen.

When the browser opens, enter www.microsoft.com in the address bar.

In the Search box, enter Password Checker, press the Enter key, then select the Password Checker link.

Enter the password that you use to log in to your Windows computer.

Write down your password score.

If your current password strength is less than medium, find a stronger password.

Close your browser.

Update your password, if necessary, by selecting your account icon on the Start screen and using the *Change your password* link.v

Source: Microsoft Corporation

8.   To submit this project, consolidate the information you gathered into a written document, a document created with word processing software, or an e-mail message as specified by your instructor.

Issue

Is the digital divide growing?

Some people have access to information technologies, such as computers, cell phones, and the Internet. Other people have limited or no access. This disparity between technology "haves" and "have nots" is referred to as the digital divide. It is also called the technology gap.

Researchers have determined that factors such as gender, race, income, age, education, and location contribute to the digital divide. As you might expect, technology use in developing countries lags behind use in developed countries. Within countries, low-income households tend to own fewer technology tools than middle-income and high-income households. In rural areas, technology use is not as prevalent as in metropolitan areas.

Are technology tools really that important? One way to answer that question is to imagine your life without a computer or Internet access. Certainly that deficit would limit your educational and employment opportunities. So within the context of our society, computers and the Internet are important economic tools and the digital divide may be depriving "have nots" of important opportunities.

The effect of the digital divide is controversial. Those who cannot afford computers and Internet connections are not necessarily cut off from using those technologies. Many libraries and community organizations provide public access to computers and technology tools. Further, although at first glance it might appear that technology "haves" benefit from a disproportionate amount of computer and Internet access, much of the time this equipment is used for entertainment and has no significant impact on economic opportunities.

Some data indicates that the digital divide is closing. Falling computer prices, government initiatives, and programs sponsored by private organizations are succeeding in their efforts to provide technology tools to "have nots."

Increased smartphone use is also bridging the digital divide. In the U.S., approximately half of the adult population has a smartphone. That percentage is about the same regardless of ethnicity or gender. Yet smartphone ownership is not common among individuals who are over age 65, who earn less than $30,000 a year, or who have no high school diploma. To find more statistics about computer and Internet use, refer to the Pew Research Center and the United States Census Bureau.

What do you think?

1. Do you think the digital divide is closing?   ○ Yes   ○ No   ○ Not sure

2. Do you think that smartphones provide sufficient access to the Internet and other tools for improving economic status?   ○ Yes   ○ No   ○ Not sure

3. Do you favor spending tax dollars to make computers available in public libraries?   ○ Yes   ○ No   ○ Not sure

4. Would you favor allowing college students to spend their financial aid money on computers?   ○ Yes   ○ No   ○ Not sure

QuickCheck A

1. A(n) [＿＿＿＿＿＿＿] is the "brain" of your PC, which carries out the commands you issue on data that represents words, numbers, and pictures.

2. Microsoft Windows is an operating system that the computer starts during the [＿＿＿＿＿＿＿] process.

3. True or false? The password ez2guess is more secure than easyguess. [＿＿＿＿]

4. When you are using an application and it stops responding, Task [＿＿＿＿＿＿＿] can be used to close it.

5. True or false? Tablet computers use the same operating systems as desktop and laptop computers. [＿＿＿＿＿＿]

CHECKIT!

QuickCheck B

Enter the correct letter of the computer components in the boxes shown below.

1. DVD drive [＿＿]

2. Keyboard [＿＿]

3. Touchpad [＿＿]

4. Expansion ports [＿＿]

5. System unit [＿＿]

A
D
C
B
F
G
E

© MediaTechnics

CHECKIT!

 GETIT?   While using the digital textbook, click the Get It? button to see if you can answer ten randomly selected questions from Chapter 1.

Working with Windows

What's inside?

In Chapter 2, you'll discover why the operating system is the core piece of software on your PC. Plus, you'll find out how to start your applications and how to use the tools provided by Windows. You'll get the scoop on the Windows 8 Start screen and find out how it differs from the desktop. And you'll have an opportunity to compare the Control Panel to the PC Settings panel.

What's in the digital book?

The tours in Chapter 2 are all about getting familiar with the tools Windows offers for customizing your work area and keeping your digital devices operating efficiently.

FAQ How do I use the Start screen?

Once you're logged in, Windows displays the Start screen with its array of colorful tiles. **Start screen tiles** represent applications, storage areas, and links to social media sites. The Start screen is optimized for a touch interface, so tiles can be dragged or selected using a mouse, your finger, or a stylus. Clicking a tile starts the corresponding application. When using a touchscreen, simply touch a tile to access its contents. Figure 2-1 explains the elements of the Start screen.

Figure 2-1

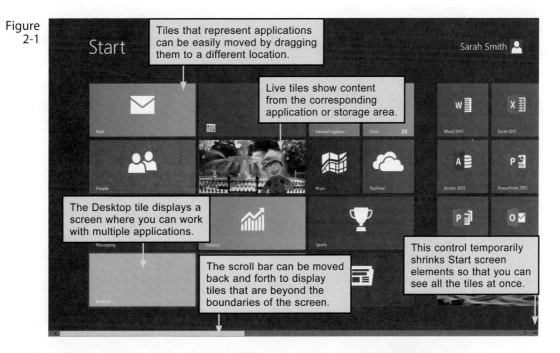

- To return to the Start screen from any application, press the ⊞ Windows key on your computer keyboard or the Windows button on a tablet computer's case.

- If your computer has a touchscreen, you can scroll by swiping right or left. You can also use pinch and zoom gestures to increase or decrease the size of the Start screen tiles.

- **Live tiles** pull content from applications or storage areas and display it within the tile. For example, activating live tiles for the Photos tile displays a slide show of photos stored in your Pictures folder. When the Mail tile is live, it displays incoming e-mail messages. Figure 2-2 illustrates how to turn on live tiles.

Figure 2-2

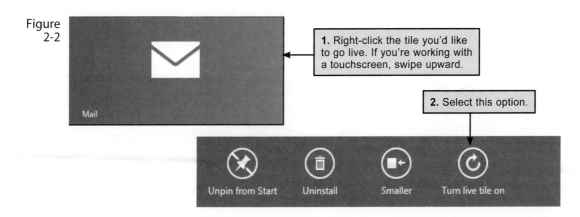

• How do I use the Start screen? (continued)

The Start screen includes a built-in Search function. While looking at the Start screen, you can activate the Search box by typing the first few letters of the item you're looking for. Windows displays a list of matching items, which you can select and access with a mouse click or touch. Figure 2-3 illustrates the screen that appears when you type word while the Start screen is displayed.

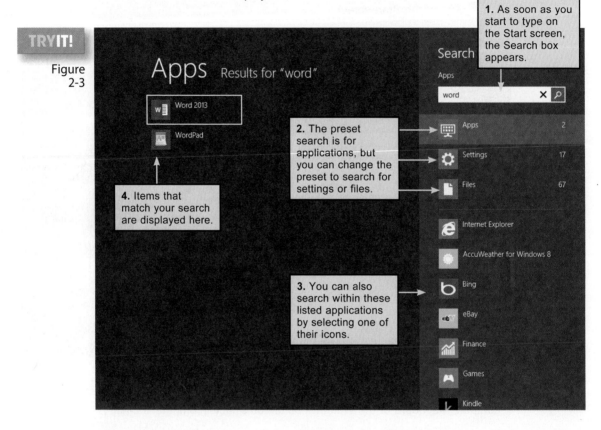

Figure
2-3

When using the Search box, keep in mind that you can alter the search for the following specific categories:

- **Apps.** The preset search for apps is useful if you want to start an application or a utility for which there is no tile. Math Input Panel, Character Map, Magnifier, Steps Recorder, and QuickTime Player are just a few apps that you might want to access using Search.

- **Settings.** When you search in Settings, you can find useful system utilities for customizing your computer's display, printers, security, and more. Use the Search box to enter one or more keywords, such as change password, to access a utility that will help you view and change settings.

- **Files.** When you search in Files, you can find specific documents that you've created based on their titles or their contents. You can also locate photos, graphics, music, and other media by their titles.

- **Listed applications.** The Search box also works with listed applications, such as Internet Explorer, AccuWeather, and Bing. For example, if you enter a search for Savannah, GA and click the AccuWeather icon, you'll see the current temperature in that city. Selecting the IE or Bing icon displays links to information about Savannah and its tourist attractions.

FAQ What is the Windows desktop?

The **Windows desktop** is the backdrop for many of the tasks you perform on your computer. You can easily access the desktop by selecting the Desktop tile from the Start screen. The desktop can display application windows, message windows called **dialog boxes**, and icons.

When several windows are open on the desktop, you can manipulate them in a variety of ways to arrange your desktop for maximum efficiency. You can maximize a window so that it fills the screen and provides the largest amount of working space. When working back and forth between two windows, you might want to size them to fit side by side. Click the Try It! button in Figure 2-4 to explore ways to organize your desktop.

Figure
2-4

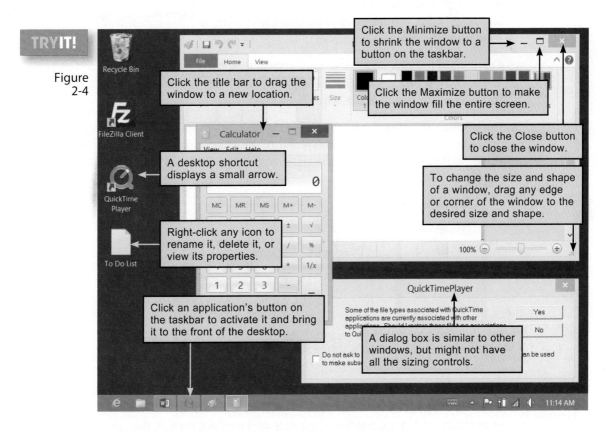

It is simple to rearrange desktop icons so that those you use most often are easy to find. You can also create new folder and file icons for quick access to documents you frequently use.

- To create a new icon on the Windows desktop, right-click any empty area of the desktop and select New. Select an icon type from the list, then assign it a name.

- A **desktop shortcut** is an icon that displays a small arrow to indicate that it is simply a link to an application or a file. If you delete a desktop shortcut, you are only deleting the icon, not the application or the file it represents.

- To delete an icon from the desktop, right-click it and click Delete.

- To rename an icon, right-click the icon and select Rename.

- To display the properties of an icon, right-click the icon and select Properties.

- Before dragging icons to a new location, right-click anywhere on the desktop and choose View. Make sure that *Auto arrange* and *Align to grid* are not checked.

FAQ How do I use the desktop taskbar?

The **taskbar** is located at the bottom of the Windows desktop and holds a variety of useful controls as shown in Figure 2-5.

Figure 2-5

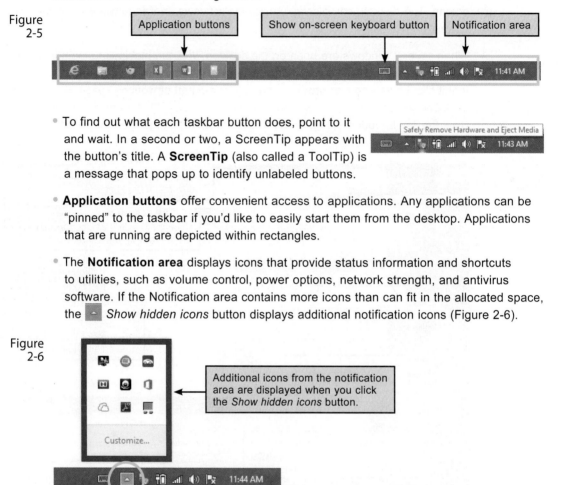

- To find out what each taskbar button does, point to it and wait. In a second or two, a ScreenTip appears with the button's title. A **ScreenTip** (also called a ToolTip) is a message that pops up to identify unlabeled buttons.

- **Application buttons** offer convenient access to applications. Any applications can be "pinned" to the taskbar if you'd like to easily start them from the desktop. Applications that are running are depicted within rectangles.

- The **Notification area** displays icons that provide status information and shortcuts to utilities, such as volume control, power options, network strength, and antivirus software. If the Notification area contains more icons than can fit in the allocated space, the ▲ *Show hidden icons* button displays additional notification icons (Figure 2-6).

Figure 2-6

Additional icons from the notification area are displayed when you click the *Show hidden icons* button.

- A computer keeps track of the current date and time using a battery-operated internal clock. Your computer uses the clock to record the date and time when files are created or modified, so it is important that the date and time are correct. Because the clock syncs with a standard clock on the Internet, the time is usually correct except for some discrepancies that result from daylight saving time. To change the time or date, right-click the displayed time and select Adjust Date/Time.

- The taskbar's 🔊 Volume icon lets you quickly adjust the sound level emitted by your computer's speakers. Click the Volume icon to display the adjustment control.

- The taskbar's 📶 Internet access icon displays the strength of your wireless connection. Selecting it lets you connect to or disconnect from a network.

- On some computers, the taskbar is set to disappear when it is not in use. To reveal it, pass the mouse pointer off the bottom edge of the screen. You can also change the size of the taskbar to display more or fewer application buttons.

- To customize the taskbar, right-click it and select Properties from the shortcut menu.

FAQ How do I access the PC Settings panel?

PC Settings is a panel of options for modifying and customizing the way Windows looks and works. PC Settings can be accessed from the **Charms menu** that appears when you move the pointer to one of the corners of the screen, or when you swipe in from the right edge of a touchscreen (Figure 2-7).

Figure
2-7

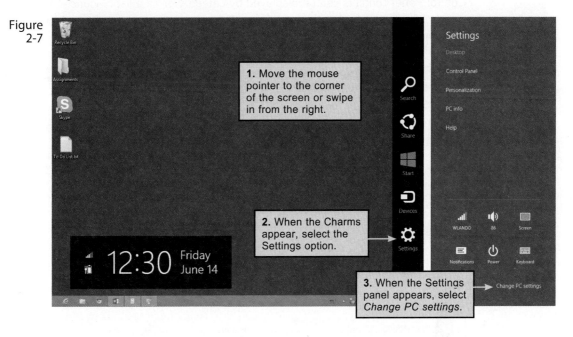

The options offered by the PC Settings panel are most relevant for tablet users, for customizing the Start screen, and for changing the password. Select the Try It! button in Figure 2-8 to get acquainted with the PC settings list.

TRYIT!

Figure
2-8

PC settings

- Personalize
- Users
- Notifications
- Search
- Share
- General
- Privacy
- Devices
- Wireless
- Ease of Access
- Sync your settings
- HomeGroup

Lock screen   Start screen   Account picture

FAQ What is the Control Panel?

The **Control Panel** is a collection of tools for customizing Windows system settings so that you can work more efficiently. When you're at the Start screen, you can open the Control Panel by typing control and then selecting Control Panel from the Search list.

Control Panel contents can be displayed by category or as a list of icons. The list of icons is easiest to navigate. As shown in Figure 2-9, you can view the list by selecting the *Large icons* view.

Figure
2-9

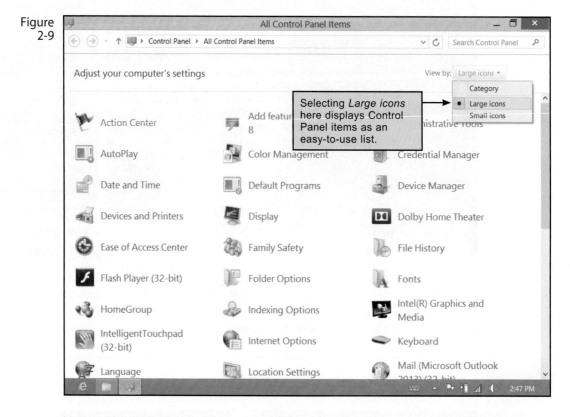

You can search within the Control Panel using the Search box at the top of the screen. This search feature is useful if you can't figure out which icon leads to the settings you want to change. Suppose you want to find out if a device driver is up to date. There is no icon labeled "Device Driver" in the Control Panel. Figure 2-10 illustrates the results of a search for driver.

Figure
2-10

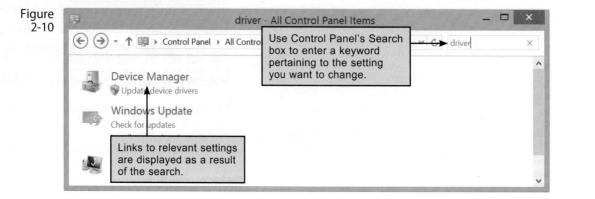

FAQ Does it matter if I'm using a touchscreen?

Windows 8 has a dual personality that affects the way you work with it. On the one hand, Windows 8 offers a flexible desktop originally designed for use with a keyboard and mouse. On the other hand, Windows also includes elements designed for touchscreen devices, such as tablet computers and smartphones. Both aspects of Windows can be useful, depending on the task you're trying to accomplish and the device that you are using.

The Windows desktop is inherited from earlier versions of Windows. It lets you spread out multiple application windows to work on several projects at the same time. On devices with large screens, this feature is useful. On small screen devices, however, multiple windows may be too small to use effectively. If you have a computer with a large screen, be sure to take advantage of the desktop's ability to display multiple application windows as shown in Figure 2-11.

Figure 2-11

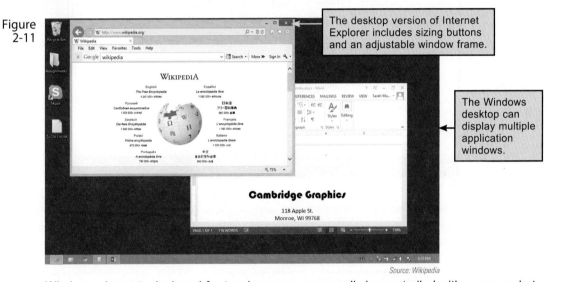

The desktop version of Internet Explorer includes sizing buttons and an adjustable window frame.

The Windows desktop can display multiple application windows.

Source: Wikipedia

Windows elements designed for touchscreens can usually be controlled with a mouse, but they are sometimes tricky to access. For example, the Charms menu is easy to access with one swipe on a touchscreen. When using a mouse, however, the Charms menu can be frustratingly elusive to capture. Figure 2-12 offers some tips for using Windows when your device has a large display, mouse, and keyboard, but no touchscreen.

Figure 2-12

- Type the first few characters of an application's name to access it from the Start screen.

- Learn which tiles open up touchscreen applications so you don't expect them to appear on the desktop along with other applications.

- Use the Control Panel to customize settings.

- Skip the Charms menu and go directly to the PC Settings panel by typing PC Settings at the Start screen.

- Switch back and forth from the Start screen to the desktop using the Desktop tile or the Windows key.

- Type off at the Start screen to shut down your computer.

• Does it matter if I'm using a touchscreen? (continued)

Windows 8 offers a set of elements optimized for touchscreen devices. Sometimes referred to as RT or Metro, touchscreen elements of Windows feature large icons, well-spaced menus, and applications that are used one at a time.

Tablet applications fill the screen when they are open, so you can work with only one application at a time. Applications designed for these devices may not include Maximize, Minimize, or Restore buttons. Figure 2-13 illustrates the touchscreen version of Internet Explorer.

Figure
2-13

The touchscreen version of Internet Explorer has no sizing buttons and can only be displayed in full-screen mode.

Source: Wikipedia

The Start screen, Charms menu, and PC Settings panel are part of the touchscreen toolkit because of their large format controls. Figure 2-14 offers some tips for using Windows when your device has a touchscreen.

Figure
2-14

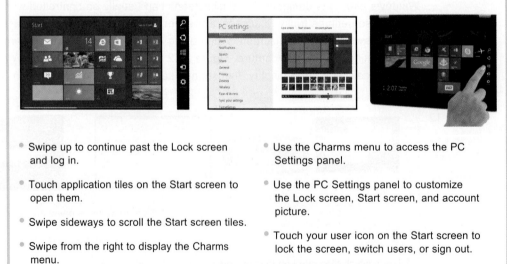

- Swipe up to continue past the Lock screen and log in.

- Touch application tiles on the Start screen to open them.

- Swipe sideways to scroll the Start screen tiles.

- Swipe from the right to display the Charms menu.

- Display the Start screen by pressing the Windows button.

- Use the Charms menu to access the PC Settings panel.

- Use the PC Settings panel to customize the Lock screen, Start screen, and account picture.

- Touch your user icon on the Start screen to lock the screen, switch users, or sign out.

- Tap the Settings option on the Charms menu, then touch the power button to shut down your tablet device.

FAQ How do I access Windows Help?

The Windows Help and Support Center is your gateway to Windows manuals, FAQs, and troubleshooting wizards. Basic help information is stored on your computer as part of Windows; additional help is supplied by Microsoft's online support center. To access information about Windows features, type Help at the Start screen.

Computer manufacturers sometimes customize the Help and Support Center to include specific information about a particular brand of computer. This information can include troubleshooting tips, links to Internet-based help systems, and even links to brand-specific message boards and forums. Figure 2-15 explains basic tools for using Windows Help.

Figure
2-15

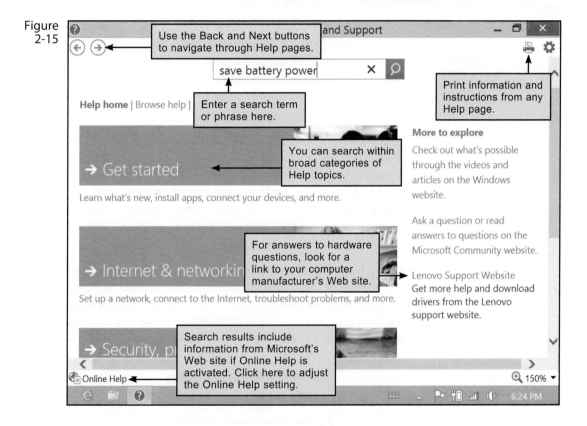

- If the Help and Support Center does not supply the information you need, use a search engine, such as Google, to hunt for user groups, online forums, or articles containing relevant information. Be cautious, however, about information from public online forums. Participants are not necessarily experts and they might provide inaccurate or misleading advice.

- When you need help, you might consider asking local experts. For example, you might have a friend who has extensive Windows experience; your school might provide a student help desk; or your workplace might employ a staff of IT technicians.

- Help is a two-way street. As you gain expertise, consider sharing your knowledge in return for the help you received from others.

Technology

System software

Operating systems, such as Microsoft Windows, are examples of **system software**, which works behind the scenes to help a computer keep tabs on itself in order to function efficiently. System software is different from application software. Whereas application software is designed to help a person carry out a task such as word processing or sending e-mail, system software is dedicated to the computer's internal operation.

System software can be divided into two categories: operating systems and system utilities. As you know, an operating system is foundational software that acts as the master controller for all activities that take place within a computer system.

The operating system is the core piece of software on your PC. You work with it directly to start applications and organize files stored on your disks. The operating system sets the standard for the on-screen controls displayed by all your application software. In addition, the operating system works behind the scenes to detect equipment failure, maintain security, manage storage space, and communicate with all the devices connected to your computer.

Operating systems are available for all types of computers. In addition to Microsoft Windows, OS X and Linux are also used on desktop and laptop computers. OS X is installed exclusively on Apple computers. Linux is primarily an operating system used for servers that handle network communications, e-mail systems, and Web sites. Microsoft Windows RT, iOS, and Android are used on tablet computers and smartphones. You can think of them as spin-offs from their desktop counterparts, Microsoft Windows, OS X, and Linux.

A **system utility** is a type of software that can be used to add functionality to the operating system, customize your screen-based work environment, set up communication between the computer and other devices, and enhance your computer's security. When adjusting settings from the Control Panel or PC Settings panel, you are using system utilities designed to modify and customize the way the computer operates.

Figure
2-16

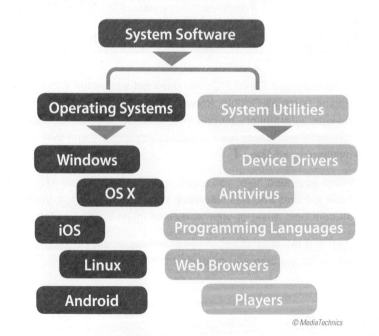

© MediaTechnics

Technology
(continued)

Microsoft Windows is one of today's most popular operating systems. It was originally designed for desktop computers and has evolved through several generations, each one slightly different from the others in terms of features and appearance. Of the Windows generations listed in the time line in Figure 2-17, the last four remain in widespread use today.

Figure
2-17

Windows Time Line							
Windows 3.1 1992	Windows 95 1995	Windows 98 1998	Windows Me 2000	Windows XP 2001	Windows Vista 2007	Windows 7 2009	Windows 8 2012

© MediaTechnics

Windows 8 is available in several editions including Standard, Pro, Enterprise, and RT. Standard and Pro editions work well for individuals and small businesses using desktop and laptop computers. The Enterprise edition is designed to meet the needs of businesses that have in-house and remote workers. Windows RT is optimized for tablet computers.

Windows is also available in 32-bit and 64-bit editions. Most of today's computers have 64-bit microprocessors, so they typically use the 64-bit edition of Windows.

Knowing which edition of Windows is installed on your computer is useful, especially when troubleshooting hardware and software problems. To discover which edition of Windows you're using, type System in the Start menu's Search box, then select Settings. Choose *Show which operating system your computer is running* to view the System window shown in Figure 2-18.

Figure
2-18

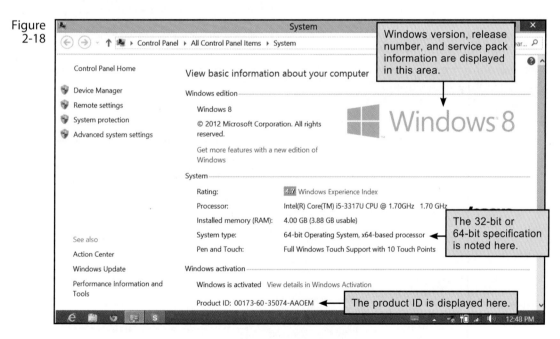

Technology
(continued)

A **device driver** is software that helps devices establish communication with a computer. This type of system software is used by printers, monitors, wired network devices, modems, storage devices, mice, videogame controllers, and scanners. Once installed, a device driver automatically starts when it is needed. Device drivers usually run in the background without opening a window on the screen.

Suppose you connect a new printer to your computer. You might also have to install a printer driver or select a preinstalled driver. After the device driver is installed, it runs in the background to send data to the printer whenever you initiate a print job. The printer driver alerts you only if it runs into a problem, such as if the printer is not connected or it runs out of paper.

Devices can sometimes malfunction. Suppose, for example, that your laptop's built-in camera stops working. The problem could be caused by a hardware failure, but sometimes the device driver malfunctions or no longer works after your computer receives an operating system update. When a device malfunctions, first make sure it is plugged in, then check its status in Device Manager and determine if you have the most current version of its device driver.

On a PC, you can check the status of a device, change its settings, and check for updated device drivers by typing device driver at the Start screen and selecting Settings. Choose Device Manager to view a list of your computer system hardware and corresponding device drivers, as shown in Figure 2-19.

Type device driver at the Start screen, then select Settings. Choose Device Manager to display this window.

Figure 2-19

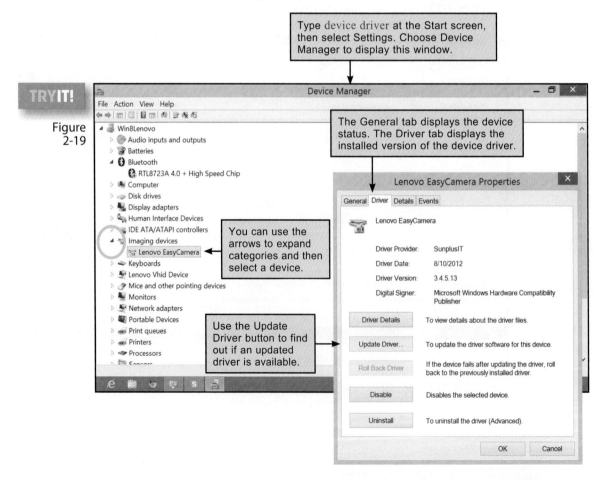

The General tab displays the device status. The Driver tab displays the installed version of the device driver.

You can use the arrows to expand categories and then select a device.

Use the Update Driver button to find out if an updated driver is available.

Project

Explore the Windows desktop

In this chapter, you were introduced to Windows 8. You learned about elements of the Start screen and the Windows desktop. You also learned about the Control Panel and PC Settings, two collections of system utilities that offer a range of tools for customizing your desktop and maintaining your computer system.

In this project, you will learn how to customize the Windows Start screen and desktop. When you have completed this project, you should be able to:

● Customize your Start screen using the PC Settings panel.

● Customize your desktop using the Control Panel.

● Use the taskbar.

● Create a desktop icon

● Take a snapshot of your screen using the Print Screen key and the Paint application.

Requirements: This project requires Microsoft Windows 8 and Paint. Word processing software or e-mail are optional for submitting deliverables electronically.

Deliverables:

1. A list of your computer's notification icons and their status

2. A list of applications pinned to the left side of the taskbar

3. A description of differences between items pinned on the right and left sides of the taskbar

4. A list of two applications that might be useful to pin to the taskbar

5. A snapshot of your customized Windows desktop

6. A snapshot of your customized Start screen

1. Change the color and background of the Start screen by completing the following steps:

    Swipe from the right side of the screen or point to the lower-right corner to display the Charms menu.

    Select Settings.

    Select *Change PC settings*.

    With Personalize selected, choose the *Start screen* option.

    Choose a background and a color scheme.

    Return to the Start screen when you're satisfied with your choices.

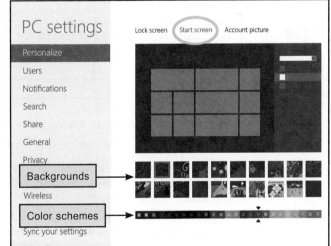

• Explore the Windows desktop (continued)

2. Customize the background and theme for your desktop by completing the following steps:

At the Start screen, type Control Panel and then select it from the list of results.

At the Control Panel screen, make sure the view is set to *Large icons*.

Select Personalization.

Experiment with the Desktop Background option and the Color option. Consider using a photo for the background.

When you are satisfied with your desktop design, use the *Save theme* link to give it a name.

Close the Personalization window.

3. List the status of all your computer's notification icons by completing the following steps:

Hover the mouse pointer over each notification icon to display its name.

Click the ⏶ button in the notification area.

Select Customize.

List the name of each icon and its status (shown in the Behaviors column).

Make sure that the Windows Explorer icon for *Safely Remove Hardware and Eject Media* is set to *Show icon and notifications*.

Close the Notification Area Icons window.

Icons	Behaviors	
🖳 Windows Explorer Safely Remove Hardware and Eject Media	Show icon and notifications	⌄
🔋 Power 95% available (plugged in, not charging)	Show icon and notifications	⌄
📶 Network WLANDO Internet access	Show icon and notifications	⌄

4. Examine the buttons on the left side of the taskbar and complete the following steps:

List the names of the applications that are pinned to the taskbar.

When you hover the pointer over these buttons, a small window called a thumbnail appears. What happens if you move the pointer off the thumbnail? What happens if you click the thumbnail?

Summarize what you've learned about pinned applications and thumbnails in a sentence or two.

Based on your observations, write down differences and similarities between the kinds of items that are pinned to the left side of the taskbar, and those that are pinned to the notification area.

Jot down two applications that you frequently use that you might want to pin to the taskbar.

• Explore the Windows desktop (continued)

5. Create a desktop icon for a file that you name My To-Do List. Complete the following steps:

    Right-click (or touch and hold) any empty area of the desktop.

    Select New from the pop-up menu.

    Select Microsoft Word Document or Text Document.

    When the icon appears, name it My To-Do List.

    Double-click the icon to open the blank document you just created.

    Enter a few tasks, then save the document.

    Close the document window.

6. Take a snapshot of your customized desktop by completing the following steps:

    Make sure the Windows desktop is displayed.

    Press the PrtSc (or Print Screen) key on the computer keyboard. Doing so places a copy of the screen on the Clipboard.

    Open Paint by going to the Start screen, typing Paint, then choosing the Paint option.

    Paste the Clipboard contents into Paint. To do so, hold down the Ctrl key and press C. Alternatively, you can select the Paste button on Paint's ribbon bar.

    Save the file and name it [Your Name]'s Desktop. To do so, select File, then select Save As. Select a file format; PNG or JPEG are the best options. You can put the screenshot in the Pictures library.

    To print the screenshot (if assigned), select the File tab, then select Print. When the Print window opens, choose the desired printer, then select the Print button.

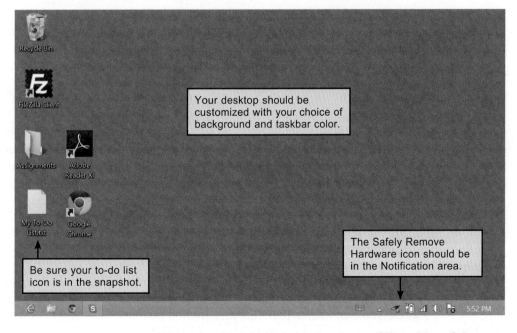

7. Take a snapshot of your customized Start screen and name it [Your Name] Start Screen.

8. Consolidate the deliverables for Project 2 into printed format, a document file, or an e-mail message as specified by your instructor.

Issue

Does technology rule your life?

Walk down any street, or ride in any bus, train, or airplane. Walk into a supermarket or coffee shop. People everywhere are interacting with digital devices. Some are engaged in earnest conversations, with cell phones glued to their ears. Others with busy thumbs are texting. Some are grinning into their smartphone cameras, playing video games, or Yelping the best nearby restaurant. Many others continuously check their screens for incoming messages.

Although is difficult to imagine life without that connected buzz, but sophomores at the Catelleja School in Palo Alto signed a pledge to go without digital devices for 48 hours. They were allowed to use a cell phone or landline for making voice calls, but they were not allowed to text. They could not use a computer except to do assigned homework. They could not watch television, listen to the radio, or play recorded music.

Most students reported a similar pattern: their digitally unconnected weekend began with frustration and boredom. Friday night was the low point, but by Saturday afternoon students had discovered other activities to fill their time. By Sunday, many students had adjusted to life without constant connectivity.

But some students found it difficult to adjust to an unplugged lifestyle. They were stressed, irritable, and restless. They had trouble concentrating and felt isolated. These students had developed digital dependency. Studies have found that receiving messages and other online goodies triggers the release in your brain of a chemical called dopamine that can lead to addictive behavior.

Becoming aware of your level of dependency on a constant feed of digital info is the first step toward maintaining a balance between cyberspace and the real world. Signs that your digital dependency is nearing the danger zone include:

- You are compelled to respond immediately to texts and e-mails.
- You have the sensation that your phone is vibrating or ringing when it is not doing so.
- You scroll obsessively through Facebook and Twitter feeds.
- You feel restless when away from your digital devices.
- You pay more attention to what's happening on your digital device than what's going on around you.

Life is all about what you pay attention to and what you ignore. Technology can be a distraction or it can be a tool for intentional and meaningful interaction. It is your choice. For more information on this topic, you can go online and search for information about technology addiction, or you can look around you and see for yourself how technology is used and misused.

What do you think?

1. Does a day ever go by when you don't check your phone or computer for calls and texts?　　○Yes ○ No ○ Not sure

2. Do you sometimes feel that your friends pay too much attention to their digital devices?　　○Yes ○ No ○ Not sure

3. Have you ever heard of Slow Tech?　　○Yes ○ No ○ Not sure

QuickCheck A

1. The Windows _____ offers an area where you can open multiple application windows to work on several projects at the same time.

2. The PC _____ panel provides options for customizing the Lock screen and the Start screen.

3. The Control Panel links to a collection of system _____ that can be used to customize various Windows settings so that you can work more effectively.

4. True or false? The Charms menu and Control Panel are optimized for touchscreen use. _____

5. When a device malfunctions, you might need an updated device _____ to get it working again.

CHECKIT!

QuickCheck B

Identify the desktop element by typing the letter corresponding to it.

1. Charms menu _____

2. Desktop shortcut _____

3. A pinned item _____

4. Dialog box _____

5. Taskbar notification area _____

CHECKIT!

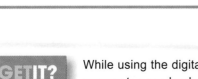 **GETIT?**   While using the digital textbook, click the Get It? button to see if you can answer ten randomly selected questions from Chapter 2.

Getting Started with Software

What's inside?

Chapter 3 provides some handy tips for figuring out how to use the software you currently have and for installing new software on your PC. The term **Windows software** refers to applications that are designed to run on computers that have the Microsoft Windows operating system installed. The terminology can be a bit confusing. Windows software does not mean Microsoft Windows, but rather applications that run on Windows computers. This chapter focuses on Windows software applications, but also covers Web apps and mobile apps that can be used on a variety of devices.

What's in the digital book?

Chapter 3 videos and software tours show you how to download, install, and remove software.

FAQ How do I know which software will work on my computer?

Computers—and that includes desktops, laptops, tablets, and smartphones—usually come with a variety of preinstalled software. Your device has an operating system and some system utilities. Some application software might also be included. That's great for a start. But if you're like the majority of digital device owners, you want more applications and utilities than those supplied out of the box.

You'll find applications in a variety of places. Electronics stores carry a small selection of boxed application software for desktop and laptop computers. Software for these computers can also be found on software publishers' Web sites and download sites, such as Tucows and CNET Download.com. Tablet and smartphone owners usually obtain software from online app stores, such as iTunes, Amazon Appstore, and Google Play.

To discover if an application will work on your digital device, you can check the software's system requirements. **System requirements** specify the operating system and minimum hardware capacities necessary for a software product to work correctly. To find the system requirements, look on the software product box, on the software's download page, or in its app store description.

Figure 3-1

System Requirements

Operating Systems: Windows 8/7/Vista/XP
Processor: Intel Core or equivalent
Memory: 1 GB or more
Hard Disk Space: 50 MB for installation
Screen Resolution: 1024 x 768 or better
Internet Connection

eCourse Internet Works
2014 eCourseWare Corp. All rights reserved. eCourse is a registered trademark of eCourseWare Corp.

• **Operating system.** First, check whether the software is designed for your device's operating system: Windows, OS X, iOS, Android, or Linux.

• **Check Windows version and bit specs.** For Windows software, make sure the system specs are compatible with your version of Windows. An application designed for Windows 8 might not work on a device running Windows RT. If given a choice between a 32-bit and 64-bit version of the software, choose the one that corresponds to your version of Windows.

• **Storage.** Applications installed on permanent storage within a device require storage space. System requirements usually specify how much space is required. Check your device to find out how much space is available. Even if you have enough space, you might decide not to install a big app that uses all the remaining storage space.

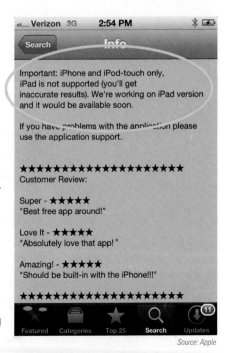

Source: Apple

• **Mobile devices.** Apps from an app store don't necessarily work on all devices with a compatible operating system. For example, an app from the iTunes Store might work on an iPhone, but not on an iPad. Read the app store description carefully before you buy.

FAQ How do I install local software?

Some software applications must be installed on your computer before you can use them. A software product that's installed on your computer's hard disk is referred to as **local software**. Local software requires hard disk space, but it tends to be full-featured and respond quickly to your commands. Local software is self-contained and does not require a network connection for operation.

Two categories of software—Web apps and portable apps—do not require installation on your computer's hard disk. A **portable app** is designed to run from removable storage devices, such as USB flash drives and CDs. A **Web app** runs on a remote Web server and is accessed using a browser.

For local software on a computer running Windows, the **installation process** copies files from a download site or distribution CD to your computer's hard disk, adds the software's name to the Start screen, and provides Windows with technical information needed to efficiently run the new software. When files are copied from a network or Internet site to your computer, the process is called downloading and files that you copy are referred to as a **download**. An **upload** is the reverse and refers to files that are copied from your computer to a network site.

Information about newly installed software is stored on the hard disk in a special file called the **Windows Registry** that keeps track of all the hardware and software installed on your computer. You can envision the Registry as a hotel register that keeps track of guests who check in and check out.

For most Windows software, the installation process is easy. Click the Try It! button in Figure 3-2 to step through the process of downloading and installing a local application.

TRYIT!

Figure 3-2

1. Download the distribution file containing the software.   **DOWNLOAD** Ⓥ

2. If the download site is trustworthy, select Run when prompted.

Do you want to run or save **windows-movie-maker_2012-Build-16.4.3....exe** (648 KB) from **fast.findmysoft.com**? ✕   Run   Save ▼   Cancel

3. Windows will scan the software for viruses. You might be asked to approve the download to verify that you, rather than a remote hacker, initiated the installation.

4. The first item downloaded is usually an installer that will handle any additional downloads and the installation process. Follow the instructions presented on your screen to download the remaining files.

5. You might be asked to select a location for the new software. You can simply select the location suggested by the installer.

6. When the setup is complete, look for it on the Start screen.

7. You might be required to activate the product by entering an activation code or product key. Cut and paste the code if possible; otherwise, type it carefully.

• How do I install local software? (continued)

A lot of action goes on behind the scenes when you install software on a Windows computer. Understanding the nuts and bolts of the installation process can help you troubleshoot problems and deal with older software that might not include automated installation routines.

1. Download. The first step in the process is to download the software's files to your computer. If you must download a file manually, be sure to make a note of its file name and the folder in which you save it.

2. Find the download. Downloaded files are generally stored in the Downloads folder on your computer's hard disk. If you need to find a download to unzip it, install it, or reinstall it, that is the place to look.

3. Extract. Software at download sites is usually compressed to make it as small as possible so that it downloads quickly. As part of the installation process, the software must be "extracted" to restore it to its original form. Extraction can be carried out manually if there is not an automated installation process.

4. Set up. Once extracted, the software is moved to its own folder, usually one that is within the Program Files folder. This process is typically handled by an installer or a setup routine included in the download. When installing from a CD, insert the disc and wait a few seconds for the setup routine to begin. If you're installing downloaded software, look for a file named Setup in the Downloads folder on your hard disk. During the setup process, you might be given options, such as the one shown in Figure 3-3.

Figure 3-3

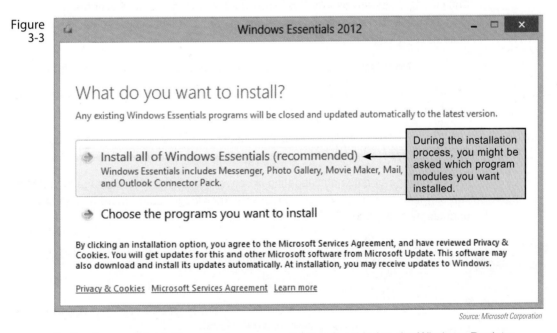

Source: Microsoft Corporation

5. Configure. Information about a new application is added to the Windows Registry. The configuration process is handled by the installer and is not commonly carried out manually.

6. Access. Links are created to make it easy for users to start the new application. These links could appear as icons on the desktop or as tiles on the Windows Start screen. Icons and tiles can be created manually if the installer does not create them or if additional startup links are desired.

FAQ What about software upgrades and updates?

Periodically, software publishers produce **software upgrades** designed to replace older versions. Upgrades are often designated by a **version number** (also referred to as a revision number), such as version 1.1 or version 2.0. A software upgrade usually offers enhanced features and performance. Upgrading to a new version normally involves a fee, but is typically less costly than purchasing a completely new version.

If you've registered your current software, you're likely to receive e-mail notifications when new versions are available. Otherwise, you can keep informed about upgrades by periodically visiting the publisher's Web site. Before you decide to upgrade, make sure that you understand its features, purpose, and installation procedures. Although an upgrade usually fixes some bugs, it might introduce new bugs. Upgrades can also introduce hardware or software compatibility problems, so make sure you have a recent backup of your computer files before proceeding.

The procedure for installing an upgrade for a local application is usually similar to the process of installing the original version. The installation routine copies the upgrade to your computer's hard disk, extracts it, and makes the necessary modifications to the Windows Registry. The upgrade generally overwrites the old version of the application, but does not affect data files that you've created.

In between major new software upgrades, publishers often release **software updates**, sometimes referred to as patches, designed to fix bugs and update security. It is always a good idea to install updates when they become available.

Software updates are usually free. They are typically distributed over the Internet. Using the software's Preferences or Options menu, you can select how you'd like to handle updates:

• Manual. No updates are collected or installed until you manually check for them.

• Notification. The software notifies you when an update is available, and then you decide if and when you want to install it.

• Automatic. The software periodically checks its publisher's Web site for updates, downloads updates automatically, and installs them without user intervention.

The advantage of automatic updating is convenience. The disadvantage is that changes can be made to your computer without your knowledge. Learn more about software updates by clicking the Try It! button in Figure 3-4.

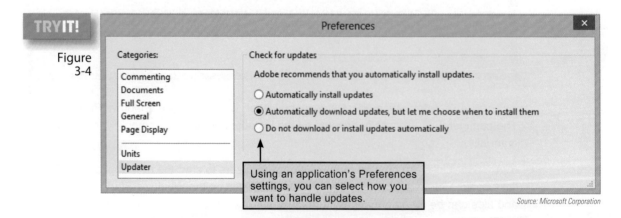

TRYIT!

Figure 3-4

Using an application's Preferences settings, you can select how you want to handle updates.

Source: Microsoft Corporation

FAQ How do I remove local software?

At some point, you might choose to remove a local software application from your computer, a process sometimes called uninstalling. You might want to remove an application to make room on the hard disk for other programs, documents, or graphics. You might no longer need some of your software or expired demoware. You might want to replace an application with one that has a better collection of features.

On some computers, it is possible to remove an application simply by tracking down the program file and deleting it. With Windows, however, the process is different because applications may consist of several program modules housed in various folders. Finding these modules is difficult because they may not have names associated with the application.

Another characteristic of program modules is that they can be shared by multiple applications. For example, both your word processing application and your graphics application might use the same program module containing a collection of clip art pictures. If you uninstall the graphics application, should your computer delete the clip art module from the disk and remove its entry from the Registry? The answer is no—because then the clip art would not be available when you use your word processor. Generally, your computer should not delete shared program modules when you uninstall software. When in doubt, don't delete!

In addition to the problem of shared program modules, removing software is complicated by the necessity of keeping the Windows Registry up to date. Remember that the Registry keeps track of all hardware and software in a computer system. When software is removed, the Registry files must be modified accordingly.

To correctly uninstall a local application on a Windows computer, it is essential to use an uninstall utility. Windows offers an uninstall utility that can be used to remove software from your computer. To access this utility, go to the Control Panel, then select Uninstall a Program. When you see the list of programs, choose the one you want to remove (Figure 3-5).

TRYIT!

Figure 3-5

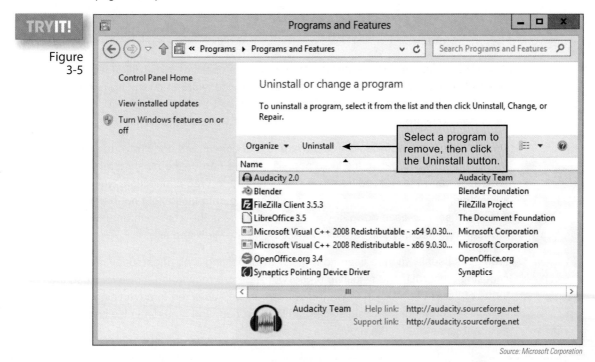

Source: Microsoft Corporation

FAQ How do I get started with Web apps?

A Web app (or Web application) is software that is accessed with a Web browser. Instead of running locally, the program code for the software runs on a remote computer connected to the Internet or another computer network. The concept of using software supplied over the Internet from a remote server is sometimes referred to as **cloud computing**.

Web apps are available for many of the same applications that run locally, such as e-mail, photo sharing, project management, maps, and games. In addition, Google, Microsoft, Zoho, and other software vendors offer popular spreadsheet and word processing Web apps that allow participants in multiple locations to collaborate on projects.

Many Web apps, such as Gmail and Facebook, require no installation at all on your local computer. Your device must, however, have a Web browser and remain connected to the Internet while using the app. Web apps sometimes offer local versions that you can install and use when an Internet connection is not available. Google Docs (Figure 3-6) is an example of a Web application that has a corresponding client program for offline use.

TRYIT!

Figure 3-6

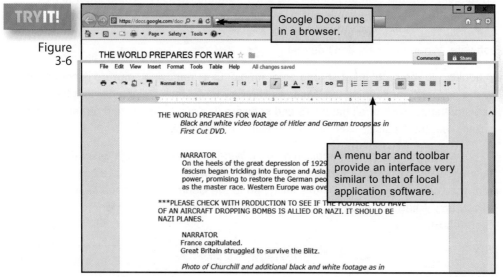

Google Docs runs in a browser.

A menu bar and toolbar provide an interface very similar to that of local application software.

Source: Google

Some Web apps are free, whereas others require a one-time registration fee or ongoing monthly usage fees. Companies supplying software that runs from the Internet are referred to as **application service providers** (ASPs). The process of deploying fee-based software over the Internet is termed **Software as a Service** (SaaS).

One advantage of Web-deployed software is that consumers don't have to worry about installing updates because the Web app site always carries the most current version. Web apps can be accessed from any computer with a Web connection, which is another advantage. However, Web apps and corresponding data files might not be accessible if the ASP service goes down, if you attempt to access the apps with an unsupported browser, or if security software blocks access to the Web app site.

Web apps usually require users to register by supplying a bit of personal information, choosing a user ID, and selecting a password. Before registering, however, read the terms of use and privacy policy. Find out if you'll be subjected to advertising, if your personal information can be disclosed to third parties, and if anyone else can access data files that you store on the provider's site.

FAQ What about apps for mobile devices?

A **mobile app** is designed for a handheld device, such as a smartphone, a tablet computer, or an enhanced media player. This category of software consists of small, focused applications that are sold through an online app store. Many apps are free or cost just a few dollars. There are lots of them, ranging from games to medical diagnostic tools used by health professionals. Some apps transform your device, turning your iPhone into a tape measure, for example, or your iPad into a piano.

Most handheld devices can use both Web apps and mobile apps. The difference between the two is that Web apps run on a remote computer, whereas mobile apps run from the handheld device, so they must be downloaded and installed. There are also some hybrid apps that run locally but access data stored on the Web. Mapping applications and apps that display your local weather operate in this way.

Figure 3-7

An icon provides access to the app store for a mobile device. The icon might also indicate if updates are available.

© MediaTechnics

To install a mobile app, the first step is to visit the app store for your device. iPhone, iPad, and iPod Touch owners can find apps for their devices at the online iTunes App Store; Droid owners can go to Google Play. Most handheld devices have an icon that takes you directly to the app store for your device's platform (Figure 3-7).

At the app store, log in, select an app, and pay for it, if necessary. Touching the Download button retrieves the file and installs it automatically. The installation process places the app's program file on the storage device and creates an icon that you can use to launch the app.

Updates are accessed from an Updates button on the app store screen. Touching the button displays a list of updates. You might be asked for your user ID and password before continuing to a screen where you can touch the Update button. Some updates are large and take a few minutes to download and install.

The process of removing software on mobile devices varies by device. On the iPhone and iPad, touch and hold the application's icon until it jiggles. Then touch the ⊗ and select the Delete option.

iPads, iPhones, and iPods are only allowed to download apps from the official iTunes App Store. Apps are available from other sources, but using them requires an unauthorized change to the device's software called a **jailbreak**.

Software that helps you jailbreak a device is available from several Web sites. After downloading and installing the jailbreak software, your device will be able to install apps from a variety of sources other than the iTunes App Store. The jailbreak lasts until you accept a software update from Apple. Updates wipe out the jailbreak software, forcing you to reinstall it.

Android phones are not limited to a single app store, so there is no need to jailbreak them to access more apps. There are various ways to make unauthorized modifications to any mobile device to overcome limitations imposed by mobile service providers. The process is called **rooting**, but most consumers have no need to root their mobile devices.

FAQ What's the significance of software copyrights and licenses?

After you purchase software, you might assume that you can install it and use it in any way you like. However, your purchase entitles you to use the software only in specifically prescribed ways. In most countries, computer software, like a book or movie, is protected by a copyright.

A **copyright** is a form of legal protection that grants the author of an original work an exclusive right to copy, distribute, sell, and modify that work. Purchasers do not have this right except under the following special circumstances described by copyright laws:

- The purchaser has the right to copy software from distribution media or a Web site to a computer's hard disk in order to install it.

- The purchaser can make an extra, or backup, copy of the software in case the original copy becomes erased or damaged, unless the process of making the backup requires the purchaser to defeat a copy protection mechanism designed to prohibit copying.

- The purchaser is allowed to copy and distribute sections of a software program for use in critical reviews and teaching.

Most software displays a copyright notice, such as © 2014 eCourse Corporation, on one of its screens. This notice is not required by law, however, so software without a copyright notice is still protected by copyright law.

In addition to copyright protection, computer software is often protected by the terms of a software license. A **software license**, or license agreement, is a legal contract that defines the ways in which you may use a computer program.

Figure
3-8

© MediaTechnics

A **EULA** (end-user license agreement) is displayed on the screen when you first install software. After reading the software license on the screen, you can indicate that you accept the terms of the license by clicking a designated button—usually labeled OK, I agree, or I accept (Figure 3-8). If you do not accept the terms, the software does not load and you will not be able to use it.

From a legal perspective, there are two categories of software: public domain and proprietary. **Public domain software** is not protected by copyright because the copyright has expired, or the author has placed the program in the public domain, making it available without restriction. Public domain software may be freely copied, distributed, and even resold. The primary restriction on public domain software is that you are not allowed to apply for a copyright on it.

•What's the significance of software copyrights and licenses? (continued)

Proprietary software has restrictions on its use that are delineated by copyright, patents, or license agreements. Some proprietary software is distributed commercially, whereas some of it is free. Based on licensing rights, proprietary software is distributed as commercial software, demoware, shareware, freeware, and open source software.

Commercial software is typically sold in computer stores, on Web sites, and at app stores. Although you "buy" this software, you actually purchase only the right to use it under the terms of the software license. Commercial software is also available as a rental for which you pay a monthly fee. Most licenses for commercial software adhere closely to the limitations provided by copyright law, although they might give you permission to install the software on multiple devices provided that you are the primary user.

Demoware is a version of commercial software that is distributed as a trial version. Demoware often comes preinstalled on new computers, but it is limited in some way until you pay for the full version. Commonly, demoware use is free for a limited period of time. At the end of the trial period, the software stops working if you don't pay for it. Most demoware alerts you when the trial period is coming to a close.

Shareware is another type of software licensed for free use during a trial period, after which users are supposed to pay a registration fee. Payment is on the honor system, however, so shareware authors collect only a fraction of the money they deserve for their programming efforts. Shareware users are encouraged to make copies of the software and distribute them to others. These shared copies provide a low-cost marketing and distribution channel.

Freeware is copyrighted software that—as you might expect—is available for free. Because the software is protected by copyright, you cannot do anything with it that is not expressly allowed by copyright law or by the author. Typically, the license for freeware permits you to use the software, copy it, and give it away, but does not permit you to alter it or sell it. Many utility programs and device drivers as well as some games are available as freeware. Some freeware displays annoying ads, which can be discontinued by purchasing an ad-free version of the app.

Open source software is often developed as a public, collaborative effort of volunteers. It is distributed for free or for a nominal charge under a license that permits users to view the source code, improve it, and redistribute the software. **Source code** is a series of instructions, written in a human-readable programming language, that are executed by the computer when you run an application. Linux is an example of open source software, as are LibreOffice, Thunderbird e-mail, and the Firefox browser.

Software vendors have a variety of ways to prevent unauthorized use of applications. The use of registration keys is common. A **registration key** is a unique set of letters and numbers used to activate a product. When you purchase software, you may be provided with a registration key on the screen or in an e-mail message. During the installation process, you'll be asked to enter your registration key. Only valid keys are accepted. They are usually checked against an online database of registration keys to make sure that keys are not passed around and shared by multiple users.

Technology

User interfaces

The combination of audio, visual, and mechanical tools that you use to interact with a computer is called the **user interface**. On traditional desktop computers, that interface consists of screen-based graphical elements, a keyboard, and a mouse. The user interface for laptops usually includes a touchpad. For tablets and smartphones, the user interface revolves around a touchscreen.

Originally, computer software had text-based user interfaces. A **command-line user interface** requires users to type memorized commands to start applications and accomplish tasks. Text-based menus are a bit easier to use. They provide a list of commands to choose from. Figure 3-9 illustrates how to format a worksheet number when using a spreadsheet application that has a vintage text-based menu.

Figure 3-9

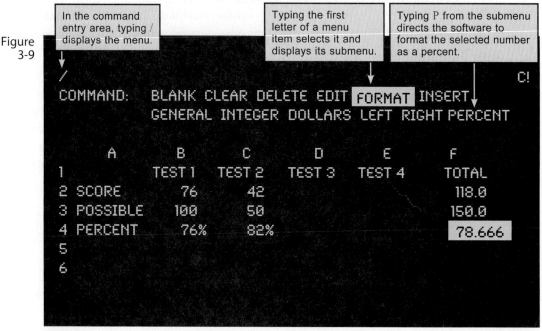

© MediaTechnics

Most computers today feature a graphical user interface, abbreviated as GUI and pronounced as "gooey" or "gee you eye." A **graphical user interface** provides a way to select menu options and manipulate graphical objects displayed on the screen using a mouse or gesture. Each graphical object represents a computer task, command, or real-world object.

Icons, buttons, and tiles. An icon is a small picture that represents an application, a file, or a hardware device. Icons can be displayed on the desktop, and they can be incorporated into buttons or tiles on the Start screen, toolbars, or taskbars (Figure 3-10).

Figure 3-10

Source: Apple   Source: Apple   © MediaTechnics   Source: Apple   Source: Microsoft Corporation

Technology
(continued)

Toolbars, taskbars, docks, menus, and ribbons. Buttons and icons can be grouped together to keep them organized. These groups are called taskbars and docks when they are part of the operating system's desktop. They are generally located at the bottom of the screen but might be movable to other locations. Figure 3-11 illustrates the dock from an Apple device and the Windows taskbar.

Figure 3-11

iPad dock

Source: Apple

Windows taskbar

Source: Microsoft Corporation

Strips of icons and buttons in application windows are referred to as toolbars, menu bars, or ribbons. These interface elements are popular because you simply choose the command you want from a list. Also, because all the command choices are valid, it is not possible to invoke invalid commands that generate errors.

Figure 3-12

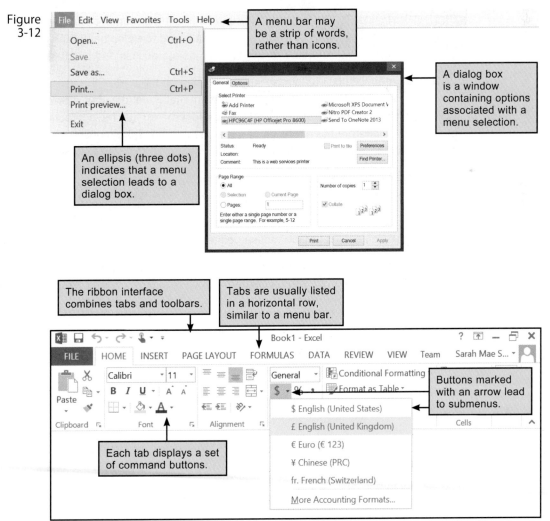

A menu bar may be a strip of words, rather than icons.

A dialog box is a window containing options associated with a menu selection.

An ellipsis (three dots) indicates that a menu selection leads to a dialog box.

The ribbon interface combines tabs and toolbars.

Tabs are usually listed in a horizontal row, similar to a menu bar.

Buttons marked with an arrow lead to submenus.

Each tab displays a set of command buttons.

Source: Microsoft Corporation

Technology
(continued)

Applications can be grouped into several functional categories, and there tend to be similarities in the user interfaces of applications within a category.

Figure 3-13

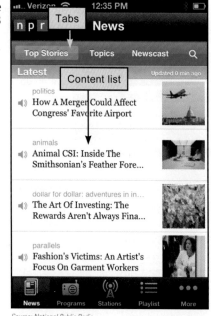

Source: National Public Radio

Applications designed to help you access content, such as videos, music, ebooks, or news stories, typically display a list as the central interface element. Buttons or tabs may be used to provide different views of the list (Figure 3-13).

Applications designed to help you create content, such as documents, spreadsheets, and artwork, tend to provide a work area surrounded by menus and toolbars. The work area may initially be blank or it might display a selected template or theme.

User interfaces can also be classified as explicit or implicit. An explicit user interface provides clearly labeled controls and all of them are accessible using a standard access method, such as clicking a menu or tab. Every command option is linked to an object on the screen, so it is clear how to access and use it.

Implicit user interfaces call for some experimentation on the part of the user. The Charms menu is an example of a user interface component that is not obvious. There is no icon, button, or menu on the screen to indicate its presence. You just have to somehow know that you can swipe from the right side of the screen or move the mouse pointer to the lower-right corner of the screen to get the Charms menu to appear.

Using an implicit interface can be frustrating. The following tips can help you locate commands when some are hidden:

- When using a mouse, you can try clicking, double-clicking, and right-clicking any screen-based object. Hover the mouse pointer over an object to view its ScreenTip.

- Remain aware of the mouse pointer shape. When the pointer changes shape, an object on the screen can usually be manipulated in some way.

- When using a touchscreen, swiping from the sides, top, or bottom of the screen may reveal a set of controls.

- You can hold or double-tap screen-based objects in addition to tapping them once. Sometimes swiping an object produces a list of commands or options.

- Watch the demo if your application supplies one. Demos provide a quick overview showing how to use key elements of the user interface.

- Check help if you are unable to figure out how to access a command.

- Don't forget about online user groups. Use a search engine to find the commands necessary to accomplish a task.

Project

Explore the user interface

In this chapter, you learned about selecting and installing application software. You also learned about basic user interface elements. Are there common elements among user interfaces? Let's find out.

When you have completed this project, you should be able to:

* Identify the elements in a word processor's user interface.

* Compare and contrast the user interfaces of various applications.

* Identify hidden interface elements.

Requirements: This project requires Windows 8, Paint, and Microsoft Office Word or any other word processor. You will need access to Adobe Reader, which you can download in Step 6. The project also requires access to three additional applications, which can be installed on your computer or on your smartphone.

The deliverable for Project 3 is a document containing the following:

1. Your word processor's name

2. A list of your word processor's menu titles or the ribbon's tab titles

3. A list of five word-processing tasks and the control used to accomplish each task

4. A screenshot of your word processing window illustrating its user interface in action

5. A screenshot of Adobe Reader illustrating its user interface in action

6. A list of three similarities and three differences in between the user interfaces for your word processor and Adobe Reader

7. A paragraph describing the user interfaces for three desktop or mobile content applications

8. A description of hidden interface elements that you find in the desktop or mobile applications from item 7

1. Open the word processing software you use most frequently and start a new document with the title Project 3 [Your Name].

2. Type your name, then record the name of your word processing software on the next line.

3. Examine the user interface for your word processing software. If it has a menu bar, add a list of the menu titles to the Project 3 document. If the user interface has a ribbon, list the tab titles.

4. Consider how intuitive your word processing software is to use. For example, if you want to adjust the margins, is it easy to guess which menu or tab to use? List five word processing tasks that you typically use. For each task, describe the menu, toolbar button, or ribbon control that you use.

• Explore the user interface (continued)

5.   Take a screenshot of your word processing application window, showing a submenu or dialog box. To take a screenshot of the word processor window, press the PrtSc or Print Screen key on your keyboard. Paste the screenshot into the Project 3 document.

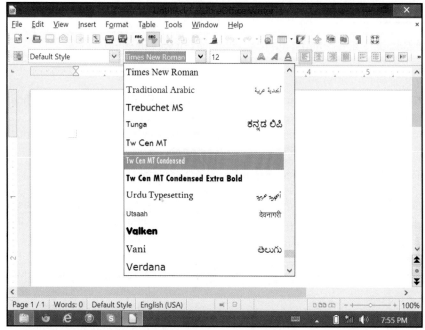

Source: The Document Foundation

6.   Start Adobe Reader. To do so, type Adobe on the Start screen, then select it from the list of apps. If Adobe Reader is not installed on your computer, do the following:

Use a browser to connect to get.adobe.com/reader.

Select the download button, then select Run when prompted.

Follow the instructions on the screen to complete the installation and start Adobe Reader.

7.   Explore the Adobe Reader user interface menus, toolbars, and other controls. Can you open a PDF file?

Explore the user interface (continued)

8. Take a screenshot of Adobe Reader showing its user interface in action.

Source: Adobe/Microsoft Corporation

9. Compare the user interface for Adobe Reader to your word processor's user interface. Find three similarities and three differences between the two interfaces. If your word processor allows you to overlay callouts or text on images, you can indicate similarities and differences directly on the screenshots. As an alternative, you can simply list the similarities and differences under the screenshots.

10. Identify three desktop or mobile applications that are designed to help you locate and consume content. List the names of these applications and their primary purpose. Write a paragraph that describes the user interface elements on the main screen of each application.

11. Work with the three content applications you've selected to discover if there are any hidden elements. You can go online and check demos, tutorials, and YouTube videos for the application, too. Record your findings in the Project 3 document.

12. Save the Project 3 document as Project 3 [Your Name]. To submit the project, print the document or send it electronically as specified by your instructor.

Issue

To buy or subscribe?

Back in the day when consumers purchased software on floppy disks or CDs, once the software was installed on a hard disk, it could be used just about forever without incurring additional costs or fees. The perpetual software licenses for these software products had the advantage of longevity. Disadvantages of this licensing model included a high price tag and an excuse for software counterfeiting and piracy.

Microsoft Office Professional retailed at $579 when it was released in 1990. Business owners had no choice but to pay the price. Productivity gains made the cost acceptable, even including the price of purchasing upgrades when new versions were released. For students and individuals, however, the high price of software was prohibitive. Piracy increased at an alarming rate despite special student pricing and aggressive anti-piracy measures.

Counterfeit software was—and still is—sold in retail stores and through online auctions. Often the packaging looks so authentic that buyers have no idea they have purchased illegal goods, though the low prices should have offered a clue to the software's illegal origins.

Internet pirates use the Web as a way to illegally distribute software. In Net jargon, the terms "appz" and "warez" (pronounced as "wares" or "war EZ") refer to pirated software. Some warez have been modified to eliminate serial numbers, registration requirements, expiration dates, or other forms of copy protection.

Web sites and peer-to-peer file-sharing networks sell or distribute hundreds of thousands of pirated software products. Some of these products contain malicious software that can infect your computer and steal your personal data.

Software subscriptions offer an alternative to perpetual licenses. A subscription is paid for on a month-to-month basis, much like renting an apartment. Your subscription gives you access to the software and any updates that occur while you are subscribed.

Software publishers such as Microsoft and Adobe are encouraging customers to try subscriptions. Office 365, the subscription equivalent to Microsoft Office 2013, costs $100 per year or $10 per month for a household license, which allows you to install the software on up to five devices and there is no limit on the number of users who can use those five devices.

Is it more economical to purchase a perpetual license or pay for a subscription? The answer depends on the software. You can only answer this question if you compare the prices, features, and licenses for both options.

What do you think?

1. Is the subscription model for you?   ◯ Yes ◯ No ◯ Not sure

2. Do you think most people try to comply with the terms of software license agreements?   ◯ Yes ◯ No ◯ Not sure

3. Have you ever used pirated software?   ◯ Yes ◯ No ◯ Not sure

QuickCheck A

1. The Windows [＿＿＿＿＿＿] is a file that keeps track of all installed hardware and software within a computer system.

2. True or false? For best results, on a Windows computer, you should uninstall software by locating the main program file, selecting it, then pressing the Delete key. [＿＿＿＿＿]

3. True or false? Portable software products, also referred to as Web apps, are supplied by companies called application service providers (ASPs). [＿＿＿＿＿]

4. Software [＿＿＿＿＿＿] are designed to fix bugs and decrease security problems of existing software programs.

5. Two types of software allow you to "try before you buy": demoware and [＿＿＿＿＿＿].

CHECKIT!

QuickCheck B

Answer each question with Y (yes) or N (no), based on the information provided in the software license agreement on the right:

1. Can I install the software and then decide if I agree to the license? [＿＿＿]

2. Can I rent the software to my friends? [＿＿＿]

3. Can I sell the software at my Web site? [＿＿＿]

4. Can I install the software on three of my computers? [＿＿＿]

5. If I sell my computer, can the buyer legally use the software if I no longer use it? [＿＿＿]

Software License Agreement

Important - READ CAREFULLY: This License Agreement ("Agreement") is a legal agreement between you and eCourse Corporation for the software product, eCourse GraphWare ("The SOFTWARE"). By installing, copying, or otherwise using the SOFTWARE, you agree to be bound by the terms of this Agreement. The SOFTWARE is protected by copyright laws and international copyright treaties. The SOFTWARE is licensed, not sold.

GRANT OF LICENSE. This Agreement gives you the right to install and use one copy of the SOFTWARE on a single computer. The primary user of the computer on which the SOFTWARE is installed may make a second copy for his or her exclusive use on a portable computer.

OTHER RIGHTS AND LIMITATIONS. You may not reverse engineer, decompile, or disassemble the SOFTWARE except and only to the extent that such activity is expressly permitted by applicable law.

The SOFTWARE is licensed as a single product; its components may not be separated for use on more than one computer. You may not rent, lease, or lend the SOFTWARE.

You may permanently transfer all of your rights under this Agreement, provided you retain no copies, you transfer all of the SOFTWARE, and the recipient agrees to the terms of this Agreement. If the software product is an upgrade, any transfer must include all prior versions of the SOFTWARE. You may receive the SOFTWARE in more than one medium. Regardless of the type of medium you receive, you may use only one medium that is appropriate for your single computer. You may not use or install the other medium on another computer.

CHECKIT!

 GETIT?   While using the digital textbook, click the Get It? button to see if you can answer ten randomly selected questions from Chapter 3.

What's inside?

All of the documents, pictures, and music that you download or create with your PC are stored as files. Chapter 4 helps you understand how to best name your files, how to store them, and how to open them.

What's in the digital book?

Don't miss the Chapter 4 screen tours that provide all the basics about files and storage technologies.

FAQ What is a computer file?

A **computer file** (usually just referred to as a file) is a collection of data that has a name and is stored on a hard disk, CD, DVD, USB flash drive, network drive, or cloud storage device. Virtually all the information you can access from your computer is stored as files. Each document, graph, or picture you create with application software is stored as a file. The Web pages you view from the Internet are also stored as files, as are the applications that you download. Computer files can be divided into two categories: executable files and data files.

An **executable file** is a computer program containing instructions written in a computer programming language. Your computer "executes" these instructions to complete tasks such as sorting lists, searching for information, printing, or making calculations. For example, the word processing program that tells your computer how to display and print text is an executable file. When you select an application from the Start screen, the computer runs the application's executable file.

A **data file** contains words, numbers, and pictures you can manipulate. For example, a document created using word processing software is a data file. You have several ways to access a data file, including the Open option on your application software's File menu and the Windows file management utility.

Files are stored in a variety of ways, based on whether they contain text, music, graphics, or computer programs. As shown in Figure 4-1, files often include additional embedded information that helps your computer identify, reconstruct, and display the file correctly.

Figure 4-1

Files can contain text, music, graphics, or computer programs. This file contains text.

Old Coasters Never Die

Who wants to save an old roller coaster? Leap-the-Dips is the world's oldest roller coaster and, according to a spokesperson for the Leap-the-Dips Preservation Foundation, one of the most historically significant. Built in 19...

Hidden information stored at the beginning of a file provides your computer with specifications needed to display it correctly.

```
{\rtf1\ansi\ansicpg1252\deff0\nouicompat\deflang1033{\fonttbl{\f0\fnil
\fprq8\fcharset0 Times New Roman;}{\f1\fnil\fcharset0 Calibri;}}
{\*\generator Riched20 6.2.9200}\viewkind4\uc1
\pard\qc\b\f0\fs32\lang9 Old Coasters Never Die\par

\pard\b0\i\fs24 Who wants to save an old roller coaster?\i0  Leap-the-Dips is
the world's oldest roller coaster and, according to a spokesperson for the
                    ndation, one of the most historically
                    ap-the-Dips is \ldblquote the sole survivor of
                    s represented in more an 250 parks in North
                    ars of the amusement industry. \par
LaMarcus Adna Thompson patented the first coaster in 1885. Using an idea
borrowed from the Mauch Chunk gravity railroad in Summit Hill, Pennsylvania,
Thompson built a gravity-based Switchback Railway at Coney Island.
According to an article by Scott Rutherford, passengers climbed to the top of
a platform and rode a bench-like car down a 600\~ft track and up to the top
of another tower. There the vehicle was switched to another track and
passengers took the return trip. The ride was later modified so that it
completed an oval circuit. \par
```

Old Coasters - WordPad

Old Coasters - RTF - Notepad

FAQ What are file properties and tags?

File properties describe file characteristics such as name, type, location, and size. A file's properties also include the dates when the file was created, modified, and last accessed.

Additional properties are assigned to certain types of files. For example, JPEG graphics files have a Dimensions property that indicates the picture's resolution, such as 1024 x 768. Music files don't have the Dimensions property, but they do have a Length property that indicates the music run time in minutes and seconds.

Some file properties, such as date and size, are assigned by Windows and cannot be directly changed by users. Other properties can be user-modified with customized **tags** that describe and categorize files. For example, a student might assign a tag such as "Downloaded from e-Course Web site" to an image file in order to remember its original source.

Properties and tags can generally be viewed from the operating system's file manager. The utility included with Windows 8 for managing files is called **File Explorer**. You can open this utility by selecting the icon located on the taskbar of the Windows desktop. Figure 4-2 explains how to view file properties and tags in File Explorer's Details pane.

Figure
4-2

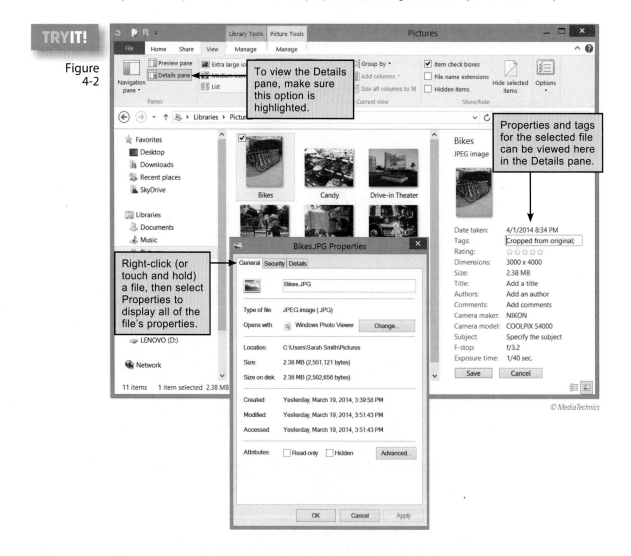

© MediaTechnics

FAQ What do I need to know about file names and extensions?

Every computer file has a **file name** that is used to locate it from among the hundreds or thousands of files on a storage device. Effective file names describe their contents. Names can include multiple words, numbers, and spaces. Most people tend to apply the same capitalization for file names as they would for titles, using uppercase for the first letter of every word except articles and prepositions.

Although some computing tasks are **case sensitive**, which means they distinguish between uppercase and lowercase letters, Windows file naming is not case sensitive. You can use uppercase and lowercase letters, and Windows will maintain the case you specify. However, if you name a file "Sage" you cannot name another file "SAGE" because Windows considers those file names to be the same.

Some words are not allowed as file names and some symbols cannot be used. When naming files, keep the following file naming conventions in mind.

Figure 4-3

Symbols Not Allowed	File Names Not Allowed	Maximum Length
/ < > " \ : | * ?	Aux, Com1, Com2, Com3, Com4, Con, Lpt1, Lpt2, Prn, Nul	256

© MediaTechnics

When a file is created, a file extension is typically added to the file name. A **file extension** is a set of characters added to a file name to indicate the file's contents and origin. For example, Microsoft Word adds .docx extensions to the file names of documents. OpenOffice Writer adds .odt extensions. A file extension is separated from the main file name with a period but no spaces, as in Sage.docx. File extensions are typically three or four characters in length.

Hundreds of file extensions exist, and the situation would be pretty grim if you had to remember the extension for each application you use. Happily, you don't generally have to memorize file extensions—instead, your software automatically adds the correct one when you save a file. The type of file created by an application is sometimes referred to as the application's **native file format**. For example, DOCX is Microsoft Word's native file format.

Even though you don't have to manually add the correct file extension to a file name, identifying the contents of files based on the extensions in the table below can be handy when looking at file lists.

Figure 4-4

File Contents	File Extensions
Documents	.doc or .docx (Microsoft Word) .odt (LibreOffice Writer) .txt .rtf .wpd .wps
Databases	.mdb or .accdb (Microsoft Access) .dbf .odb (LibreOffice Base)
Spreadsheets	.xls or .xlsx (Microsoft Excel) .ods (LibreOffice Calc)
Graphics	.bmp .tif .gif .jpg .png .swf
Sound	.wav .mid .aif .mp3 .m4p .m4a .ogg
Video	.wmv .mpg .mov .avi .flv .WebM
Web pages	.htm .html
Computer programs	.exe .com .sys .dll .drv .ocx .app

© MediaTechnics

• What do I need to know about file names and extensions? (continued)

Operating systems tend to be configured to hide file extensions because novice users find them confusing, but file extensions are handy for identifying the contents of files and identifying malware that may have two extensions. A file such as PreRelease.mp3.com is likely to contain a virus. You can easily reveal file extensions. Figure 4-5 illustrates how.

Figure
4-5

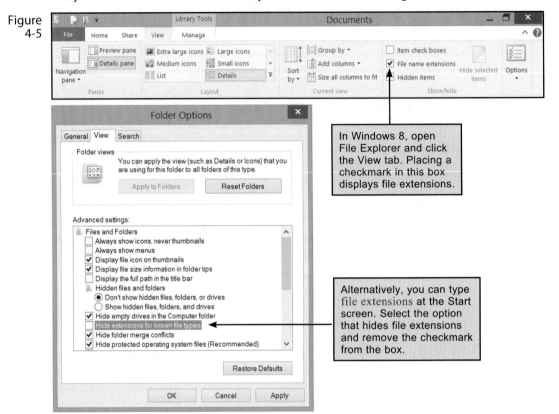

Regardless of whether extensions are hidden or shown, Windows displays a **file type** (also called a file format) based on the extension. A document created with Microsoft Word 2013 is labeled Microsoft Word Document. A document created with LibreOffice Writer would be classified as an OpenDocument Text file based on its .odt file extension. Before you open a file, pay attention to the file type to get an idea of what a file contains and which application is required to work with it.

Figure
4-6

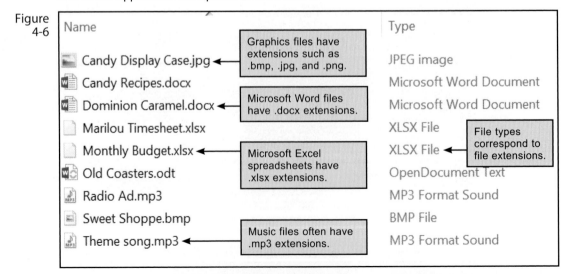

FAQ How do I open data files?

To view or modify an existing file, you must open it first. You can open files from the Start screen, the desktop, applications, or File Explorer.

- **Start screen.** At the Start screen, you can type all or part of a file name and then select the File option. Windows displays the names of matching files, and you can choose the one you want. Windows automatically starts the corresponding application software.

Figure 4-7

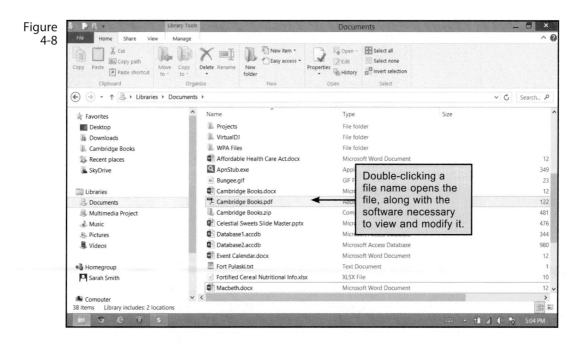

- **Windows desktop.** If you have saved a file, such as a to-do list, on the Windows desktop, double-click its icon to open the file. As with the Start screen, Windows automatically starts the application software required to view and revise the file.

- **Application software.** Most application software includes an Open command that helps you locate a file by choosing the storage device and folder in which the file is stored. Once you've selected a location, your application displays a list of files that have compatible file types. For example, Microsoft Word's Open command lists only DOCX files, so you don't have to sift through a long list that includes graphics, spreadsheets, and music files.

- **File Explorer.** Double-clicking a file from the list displayed by File Explorer starts the application software and opens the selected file.

Figure 4-8

FAQ How does Windows know which application to use when I open a file?

When you double-click a file name, Windows opens an application that you can use to view and modify the file contents. This process is possible because Windows keeps a list of file types and their corresponding default programs. A **default application** is the one that Windows uses when you open a particular file type. The link between a file type and its default application is sometimes called a **file association**.

Often, the default application is the program that was used to create a file. So, as you might expect, Microsoft Excel is the default application for the XLSX file type. Whenever you open an XLSX file, Windows automatically opens Microsoft Excel so that you can view and edit the file.

You might wonder what happens if a file can be opened by more than one application. For example, you can use Paint, Photoshop, Photo Viewer, and many other graphics applications to work with JPEG image file types. If you have several of these applications installed on your computer, how does Windows know which one to use? It uses the application from the default application list.

In some cases, however, the default application is not the one you'd like to use. You can open files using an application other than the one in the default application list in the following ways:

- Right-click (or touch and hold) the file name and select the *Open with* option. Windows displays a list of applications, and you can choose the one you want to use to view and edit your file. This method works well for occasional use.

- You can open the default applications list and change the application that Windows automatically opens for a specific file type.

Click the Try It! button to find out more about changing the application that Windows uses to open various file types.

Figure 4-9

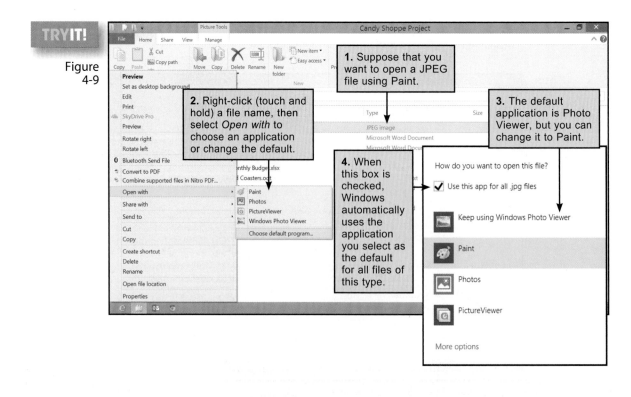

FAQ How do I create and save files?

The most common way to create files is by using application software; for example, using Microsoft Word to create a document. Most applications have a New option that opens a work area where—depending on the application—you can enter text, numbers, shapes, or musical notes. As you create content, your computer holds the data in memory.

When you're ready to save a file by transferring it to more permanent disk or USB flash drive storage, use the Save or Save As command. These commands can usually be accessed from the File menu or tab.

Figure 4-10

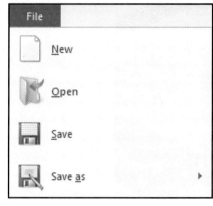

Save As. The Save As option allows you to select a name and storage device for a file. The first time you save a file, you use the Save As option. You can also use the Save As option when you've revised a file and want to save the original version in addition to the newly revised version. Select Save As and give the file a new name or designate a different storage location for it.

Save. The Save option simply saves the file you're working with under its current name and at its current location. Use this option as you work, to periodically save the latest version. Also, use the Save option before you close a file.

The first time you save a file, regardless of whether you use Save or Save As, you'll be directed to the Save As screen. Click the Try It! button in Figure 4-11 to walk through the process of saving a newly created document.

Figure 4-11

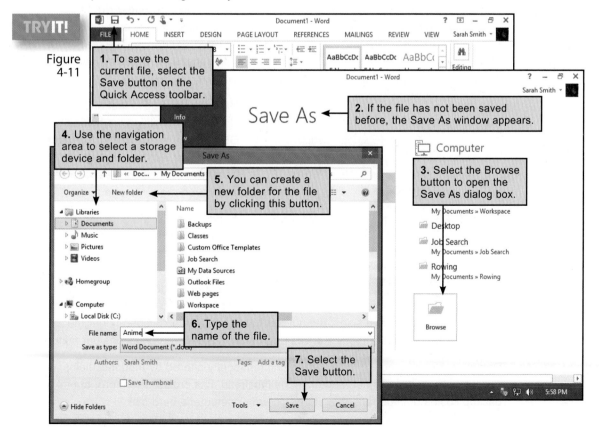

1. To save the current file, select the Save button on the Quick Access toolbar.

2. If the file has not been saved before, the Save As window appears.

3. Select the Browse button to open the Save As dialog box.

4. Use the navigation area to select a storage device and folder.

5. You can create a new folder for the file by clicking this button.

6. Type the name of the file.

7. Select the Save button.

Technology

Hard disk drives

In this chapter, you've learned about creating, saving, and opening files. Desktop and laptop computers have a hard disk as the primary storage device. A **hard disk** is a circular, rigid storage medium that is typically made of aluminum or glass and coated with metallic particles. One or more of these disks and their corresponding read-write heads are sealed inside a hard disk drive. The hard disks inside the drive are also called **platters**. A typical PC hard disk drive contains two to four platters. See a hard disk in action by clicking the Play It! button for Figure 4-12.

PLAYIT!

Figure
4-12

© MediaTechnics

Figure
4-13

With horizontal storage, particles are arranged end to end, and use of the disk surface is not optimized.

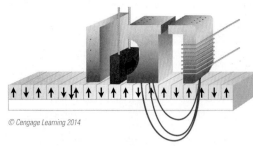

© Cengage Learning 2014

With vertical storage, particles stand on end so that many more can be packed on the disk surface.

Hard disks use **magnetic storage technology**, in which an electronic device called a **read-write head** magnetizes microscopic metallic particles on the disk surface. The read-write head also senses the particles' polarity to retrieve data (Figure 4-13).

Magnetic storage is fast and inexpensive. A typical hard disk drive holds 500 GB of data—that's 500 billion letters, numbers, or symbols. Drives with 1–2 TB (terabyte) capacities are available if you need even more storage space.

Access time is the time necessary for the read-write heads to locate and collect data from the disk. Access times average about 9 ms (milliseconds). That's only nine thousandths of a second! Drive access is also measured by rotational speed. The faster a drive spins, the quicker it can get data positioned under the read-write head. Most of today's drives operate at 7,200 rpm (revolutions per minute).

Data stored on magnetic media can be unintentionally altered by magnetic fields, dust, mold, smoke particles, heat, and drive malfunctions. It is crucial, therefore, to make backup copies of important data stored on your computer's hard disk.

Technology
(continued)

Hard disk drives have massive storage capacity, but they fill up fast. To find out how much space remains on your computer's hard disk, you can right-click a drive icon to display its Properties window, as shown in Figure 4-14.

Figure
4-14

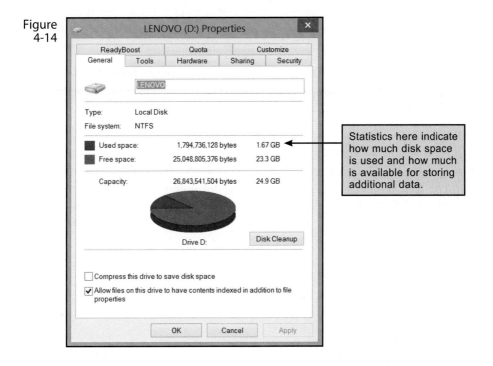

LENOVO (D:) Properties

| ReadyBoost | Quota | Customize |
| General | Tools | Hardware | Sharing | Security |

LENOVO

Type: Local Disk
File system: NTFS

■ Used space: 1,794,736,128 bytes   1.67 GB
■ Free space: 25,048,805,376 bytes   23.3 GB

Capacity: 26,843,541,504 bytes   24.9 GB

Drive D: Disk Cleanup

☐ Compress this drive to save disk space
☑ Allow files on this drive to have contents indexed in addition to file properties

OK   Cancel   Apply

Statistics here indicate how much disk space is used and how much is available for storing additional data.

If you run out of space on your original hard disk, for less than $100 you can add a second hard disk drive inside the tower unit of traditionally styled desktop computer systems.

Another option is an **external hard disk drive**, such as the one in Figure 4-15. These drives connect to a USB port on your computer. They are the best option for portable and all-in-one computers, but can also be connected to desktop tower units. External hard drives are available in capacities similar to internal hard drives, but they normally cost just a bit more.

Figure
4-15

© MediaTechnics

In addition to providing extra storage space, an external hard disk drive can be used to transport large data files from computer to computer. They can also be used as backup devices. You simply back up or copy your data to the external hard disk drive, unplug the drive from your computer, and then store it in a safe location. If your computer is hit by lightning or otherwise damaged, the backup copy of your data should still be safe on the disconnected external hard disk drive.

Technology
(continued)

In the course of adding, modifying, and deleting files, the efficiency of your PC's hard disk drive begins to decrease so that it takes longer to store, find, and retrieve files. Why does this happen and what can you do about it?

A hard disk is divided into concentric circles called **tracks**. Each track is divided into **sectors**. Each sector is a fixed size and can hold a certain amount of data. Although a file does not have to fill a sector, your PC must use more than one sector for a large file.

For the most efficient hard disk operation, your PC should place the data for a large file in adjacent sectors so that the read-write head can quickly move from one part of the file to the next. Your files are not always stored so efficiently. In the course of revising your files, the sectors in which they are stored can become scattered all over the disk.

In tech speak, a file that is stored in nonadjacent sectors is referred to as a **fragmented file**. A disk containing many fragmented files is called a **fragmented disk** and is not operating at peak efficiency. Windows provides a **defragmentation utility** that reorganizes the disk and puts the data for each file in adjacent sectors. Defragmentation works behind the scenes so it does not affect the structure of files and folders that you've created. After defragmenting the hard disk, your computer should retrieve and store files more quickly.

Windows 8 is configured for automated defragmentation to take place weekly. Select the Try It! button in Figure 4-16 to see how to access defragmentation settings and how to defragment a disk manually.

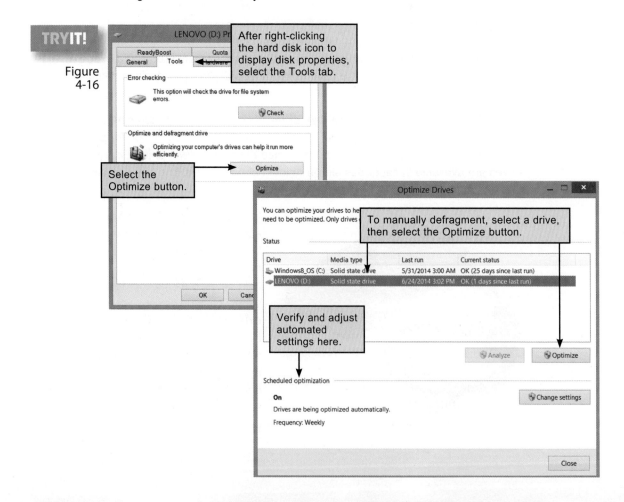

Figure 4-16

Project

Open and save files

You can create files using several different techniques, but the process typically begins with opening the application that you'll use to enter your text, graphics, or sounds for the new file. In this chapter, you learned how to save the files you create. You also discovered various ways of opening files. You were introduced to the concept of file types, which are associated with default applications.

When you have completed this project, you should be able to:

• Identify an application's native file type.

• Create and save new files.

• Use different methods to open files from within an application.

Requirements: This project requires Microsoft Windows 8, Notepad, WordPad, Paint, and three other applications of your choice. E-mail is optional for submitting deliverables.

Deliverables:

1. A document listing Notepad's default file type and file name extension, WordPad's default file type and file name extension, a list of WordPad's alternative file types, and the default file types of three applications of your choice

2. A file or printout of Drawing Second Draft

1. Find the native file format for the Notepad application. To do so, complete these steps:

    Use the Start menu's Search box to open the Notepad application.

    Type a sentence or two.

    Select the File menu and select Save.

    Write down Notepad's standard file type shown in the *Save as type* box.

    Select the Cancel button, then close the Notepad application without saving your work.

2. Find the native file format for the WordPad application and write it down.

3. List the alternative file formats that you can use with WordPad. To complete this step, do the following:

    With WordPad's Save As dialog box open from the previous step, select the down-arrow button of the *Save as type* box.

    Record the file types listed.

    Click the Cancel button, then close the WordPad application.

4. Open three other applications and write down their standard file types.

• Open and save files (continued)

5.   Create a simple graphic using the Paint application. To begin:

Open the Paint application.

Choose the *Rounded rectangle* button located on the ribbon near the top of the screen.

Toward the upper-left corner of the window, draw a rectangular box that's approximately 1 x 2 inches.

6.   Save your drawing by completing the following steps:

Select the File tab and select Save As.

Choose *PNG picture* as the file type.

Type Drawing First Draft for the file name.

Select the Save button. The file should automatically be saved in your Pictures folder.

Close the Paint application.

7.   Complete the following steps to modify your drawing:

Open the Paint application.

Select the File tab and select Open.

Double-click the file named Drawing First Draft.

Choose the red box in the color palette at the top of the Paint window.

Select the 🔲 *Fill with color* button on the ribbon.

Click anywhere within the rectangle. The rectangular box should turn red.

Select the File tab, then select the Save option.

Close the Paint application.

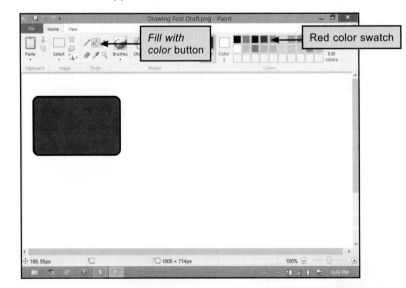

• Open and save files (continued)

8. Modify your drawing again and save it as a second file:

   Open Paint and open Drawing First Draft.

   Use the Oval button to draw a circle next to the rectangle.

   Color the circle yellow. Your drawing should look like the example below.

   Select the File tab, then select Save As.

   Choose PNG as the file type.

   Name the file Drawing Second Draft [Your Name]. Close the Paint window.

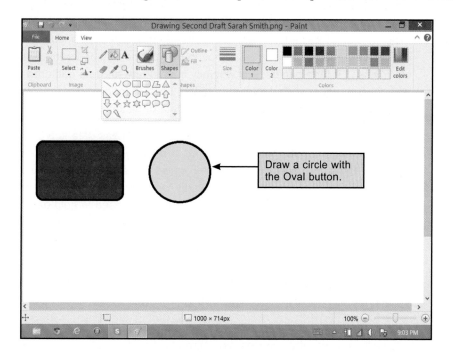

9. Find out which application on your computer is associated with the PNG file type:

   At the Start screen, type associate, then select the Settings option.

   Select *Change the file type associated with a file extension*.

   Scroll down the list to .png.

   Write down the name of the application listed in the Current Default column.

10. Verify that Windows uses the default application to open PNG files by doing the following:

    Open the Start screen and type drawing in the Search box.

    Select the File option. Your two drafts should appear in the list.

    Double-click Drawing First Draft to open it.

    Confirm which application opened your drawing to be sure it corresponds with the default application you found in Step 9.

11. Consolidate the deliverables for Project 4 into printed format, a document file, or an e-mail message as specified by your instructor.

Issue

How permanent are electronic files?

Conventional wisdom might lead you to believe that files stored on computers must be far safer than their nonelectronic counterparts scattered in filing cabinets, ledgers, and laboratory notebooks. Surely, the data stored on computers must have a longer life expectancy than records stored on flimsy paper.

The unsettling answer is that electronic data has a relatively short lifespan. Several factors are to blame, including media deterioration and, surprisingly, advances in storage technologies.

Electronic storage media can hold data for a limited period of time before they begin to deteriorate, lose data, and become unreadable. Solid state and magnetic media have life expectancies of about ten years. Data stored on optical media, such as CDs and DVDs, might last for 30 years or more. Although that period of time seems ample for storing your old English Lit term papers, it is woefully inadequate for data gathered by private, public, and government agencies related to births, deaths, marriages, land ownership, military service, business transactions, and other data of historical interest.

In today's computerized world, government and business data is typically archived onto a set of discs or computer tapes and stored in a safe, climate-controlled place. Periodically, that data might be moved to a fresh set of discs or tapes to offset gradual deterioration. New storage technologies with increasingly long life spans are being developed. For example, a DVD crafted from synthetic stone is supposed to hold data for 1,000 years!

As data sits in its archival vaults, however, computer equipment is constantly changing. Even if the data itself does not deteriorate, after a point, the devices necessary to access that data might no longer exist. And suppose you cleverly store the device with the data. You still might not be able to access the data if future operating systems no longer include the device drivers necessary to interact with those old storage devices.

And what about cloud storage? Even though photo sharing and cloud backup are relatively new, several services have already shut down after giving subscribers only a couple of weeks' notice to retrieve their files before everything on the site was erased.

Various solutions to the archival storage problem exist, but they all require proactive planning and execution. Whereas the Dead Sea Scrolls could be read thousands of years after they were written, archeologists who come across a cache of USB flash drives a thousand years from now may not have the technology to access their contents.

What do you think?

1. Do you have any electronic files that you would want to access 30 or 40 years from now?   ◗ Yes ◯ No ◯ Not sure

2. Can you think of any business or government agency that might have a problem accessing archival data in the future?   ◯ Yes ◯ No ◯ Not sure

3. Do you think most people are aware of the potential problem related to accessing archival data?   ◯ Yes ◯ No ◯ Not sure

QuickCheck A

1. In the example Budget.xlsx, the file name extension is [   ] .

2. The [   ] application for DOCX files is Microsoft Word.

3. Hard disk drives are an example of [   ] storage technology.

4. True or false? Windows can be configured to hide file extensions. [   ]

5. True or false? You should use the Save As command when you would like to save a version of an existing file under a different name. [   ]

CHECKIT!

QuickCheck B

Based on the information shown, fill in the boxes below.

1. The application with the most associations [   ]

2. The extension of files opened by Windows Media Player [   ]

3. The extension with no default application [   ]

4. The application that opens PNG files [   ]

5. The application that opens PDF files [   ]

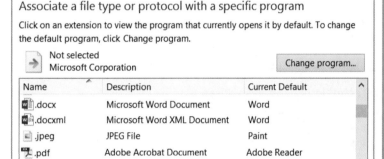

Associate a file type or protocol with a specific program

Click on an extension to view the program that currently opens it by default. To change the default program, click Change program.

Not selected
Microsoft Corporation

Change program...

Name	Description	Current Default
.docx	Microsoft Word Document	Word
.docxml	Microsoft Word XML Document	Word
.jpeg	JPEG File	Paint
.pdf	Adobe Acrobat Document	Adobe Reader
.mp3	MP3 Format Sound	Windows Media Player
.dothtml	Microsoft Word HTML Template	Word
.png	PNG File	Paint
.dotx	DOTX File	Not selected

CHECKIT!

GETIT?   While using the digital textbook, click the Get It? button to see if you can answer ten randomly selected questions from Chapter 4.

Organizing Files and Folders

What's inside?

When using a tablet computer or smartphone, consumers don't pay much attention to files. But when using desktop and laptop computers to create content, such as compositions, essays, and worksheets, a well organized set of files can eliminate frustrating sessions spent locating misplaced files or working with outdated files. Chapter 5 provides tips on organizing files, folders, and libraries so that you can easily locate them and the information they contain. The Technology section focuses on USB flash drives.

What's in the digital book?

In Chapter 5, you'll take an in-depth look at how to use File Explorer and practice skills that will help you keep your files organized.

FAQ What's in the File Explorer window?

You can get the big picture of files stored in all your computer's libraries and folders using File Explorer. Files are stored in a hierarchical arrangement of folders and subfolders. A **folder** (sometimes called a directory) groups files to keep them organized. Folders can hold other folders called **subfolders**. Windows groups folders into **libraries**, including four predefined libraries: Documents, Music, Pictures, and Videos.

The File Explorer window is divided into several components. Understanding these components helps you find files and keep them organized. Study Figure 5-1 to familiarize yourself with File Explorer's Navigation pane, file list, toolbar, and Details pane. Then click the Try It! button to learn how to sort the file list and change views.

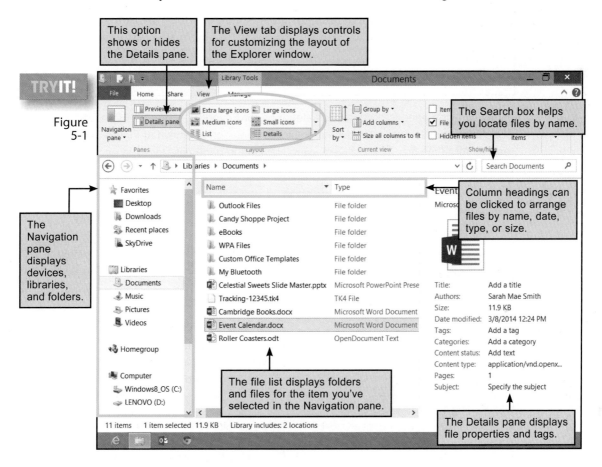

Figure 5-1

• You can use the View tab to change the way the file list is displayed. Icon views display a picture to represent each file along with its name. **List view** displays the name of each file along with a small icon that indicates its type. **Details view** displays the file name, size, type, and date modified. The example above shows the Details view.

• **Hidden files**, such as many of the system files essential for running Windows, are not displayed in the file list. To display hidden files in Windows 8, select the View tab, then put a checkmark in the *Hidden items* checkbox.

• There is no need to go to the Start screen to find files. A Search box is located in the upper-right corner of the File Explorer window.

FAQ How are files categorized?

The Navigation pane on the left side of the Explorer window categorizes devices and folders for easy access. When you select a device, folder, or library from the Navigation pane, the contents of the item you've selected are shown in the file list.

Figure 5-2

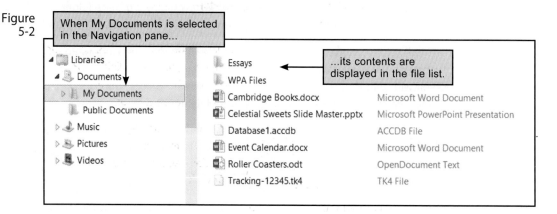

The Navigation pane is divided into categories for Favorites, Libraries, Homegroup, Computer, and Network. Review the navigation categories shown in Figure 5-3 and then read on for some tips on effectively using Navigation pane categories to access and organize files.

Figure 5-3

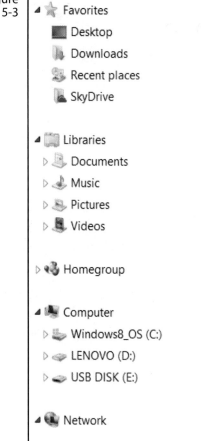

Favorites give you fast access to folders you use frequently. Simply drag a folder or file to the Favorites list, and you won't have to click through layers of folders to reach it. The Favorites list includes **SkyDrive**, an Internet-based storage location for saving files in the cloud.

Libraries are virtual folders that contain links to folders and files. Windows is preconfigured with four libraries, but you can make your own, for example, to hold a set of links to family history material that's stored in document and photo folders.

Homegroup offers access to shared folders, files, and printers on computers in a home network. When your computer joins a homegroup, the computers for other members of the group are listed under the Homegroup option.

Computer gives you access to folders on all devices connected to your computer. When accessing files stored on CDs or USB flash drives, use the Computer link.

Network provides a link to folders stored on local area network file servers and other network users' computers that you have permission to access.

FAQ How do I navigate to various folders and storage devices?

Most files are stored on your computer's hard disk. To transport a file, however, you might store it on a USB flash drive or CD. To share a file with others, you might store it on a network drive or a cloud storage drive. As you work with files, it is important to keep track of the device where a particular file is stored.

Figure 5-4

As shown in Figure 5-4, Windows displays a unique icon for each type of storage device, including your hard disk, USB flash drive, network file server, cloud storage (SkyDrive), and local area network folders.

Each local storage device on a Windows-based computer is identified by a unique **device letter**. The device letter for the hard disk drive is usually C.

Some hard disk drives are divided into sections. Each section is called a **disk partition** and it is treated like a separate drive. A common use of partitions is to divide the hard disk into a C: drive containing the operating system and a D: drive containing data files.

Another common partition scheme places the operating system and data files on drive C:, while device drivers and other utilities supplied by the computer manufacturer are stored on the D: partition as shown in Figure 5-5.

Figure 5-5

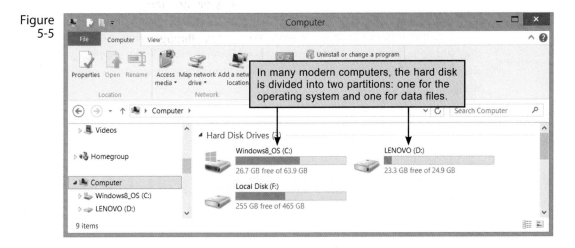

Remaining aware of partitions is important when working with files. For example, when your computer's hard disk has two partitions and you are searching for a file, you might need to carry out two searches; one on each partition.

In addition, when a hard disk is partitioned, you'll want to know which partition contains data files so that you can store new files there.

How do I navigate to various folders and storage devices? (continued)

Folders in the Navigation pane are arranged in a hierarchy. You can expand the hierarchy to show subfolders, or you can collapse the hierarchy to hide subfolders using the following techniques:

• Click (or touch) a device or folder icon to display its contents in the file list.

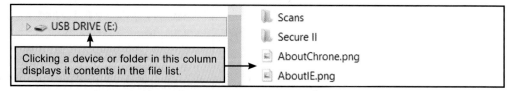

• Double-click (or touch and hold) an icon or select the small ▷ arrow to display additional levels of folders in the Navigation pane, rather than the file list.

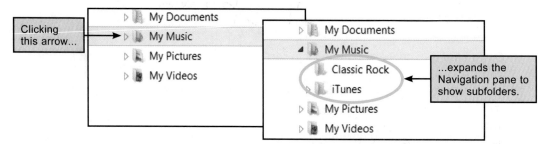

• To hide levels of folders, select the ◢ angled arrow.

A device letter, folder, file name, and extension specify a file's location. This specification is sometimes referred to as a **file path**. When subfolders are written out in a file path, they are separated from folders with a \ backslash symbol. If you create a subfolder called Essays in the My Documents folder and use it to store a file called Macbeth, its path would be written like this:

C:\Users\YourName\Libraries\Documents\My Documents\Essays\Macbeth.docx

The Try It! for Figure 5-6 shows how to navigate a file's path by expanding and collapsing the file hierarchy.

TRY IT!

Figure 5-6

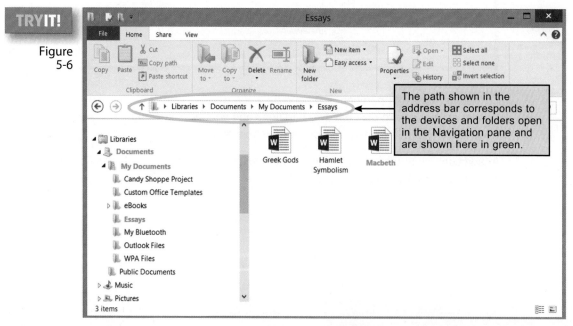

FAQ Can I create my own libraries and folders?

Windows provides each user account with a set of folders and libraries. To maintain well organized storage, you will certainly want to create additional folders. You might also decide to create additional libraries.

Let's consider folders first. Your predefined folders include My Documents, My Music, My Pictures, My Videos, and Downloads. That's a good start, but these folders can quickly accumulate many files that eventually become unwieldy to work with.

You can create subfolders and use them to divide files into more manageable groups. To do so, simply right-click a folder, select New, then select Folder. Enter a name for the subfolder. Once the subfolder is created, you can move files into it.

Next, consider libraries. Windows provides four predefined libraries: Documents, Music, Pictures, and Videos. These library names are deceptively similar to the names of your predefined folders, but libraries and folders are not the same.

A library is similar to a folder only in the sense that it can be used to group similar files; however, a library doesn't actually store files. Instead, it contains a set of links to files that are stored on various devices and in various folders.

To understand how you might use libraries, suppose you're working on a project that uses a variety of documents and music. You can create a library for the project that includes folders from My Documents and Public Music. These folders remain in their original locations, but the files they contain all appear in the listing for the new library.

The concept to understand is that a library such as Music is not a "real" location; it is more like an index in a book. If you try to create a subfolder by right-clicking the Music library, the subfolder will actually be created under My Music, which is a "real" folder. Click the Try It! button to learn more about creating and using libraries and folders.

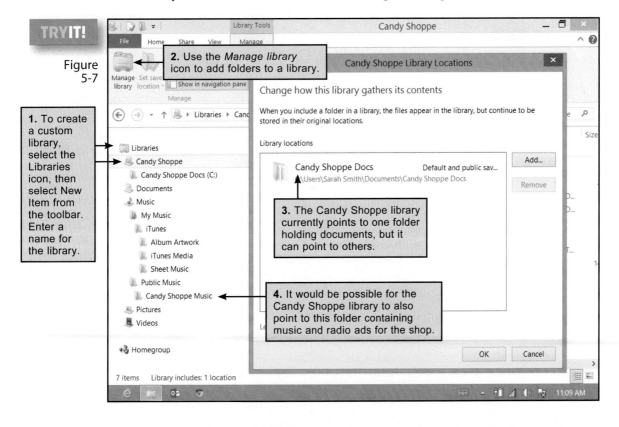

Figure 5-7

TRY IT!

1. To create a custom library, select the Libraries icon, then select New Item from the toolbar. Enter a name for the library.

2. Use the *Manage library* icon to add folders to a library.

3. The Candy Shoppe library currently points to one folder holding documents, but it can point to others.

4. It would be possible for the Candy Shoppe library to also point to this folder containing music and radio ads for the shop.

FAQ How do I change the name of a file or folder?

Once you have located a file or folder, it's easy to **rename** it so that its name better describes its contents. You can also use the Rename command to standardize the names of similar files, such as Playoff 2013, Playoff 2014, and Playoff 2015, so that they appear in sequence.

Renaming files is fairly straightforward, except for a little twist involving file extensions. When file extensions are hidden, it is not necessary to worry about them. As you rename a file, Windows automatically retains the old file extension for the new file name.

When file extensions are visible, however, you should be careful not to change them. Windows uses a file's extension to determine the application that opens it. If the extension is changed, Windows might not be able to open the selected file. For example, if you were to inadvertently change a document's extension from .docx to .bmp, Windows would no longer try to open it with Microsoft Word. Instead, it would try to open the file with Paint, and that would produce an error because the file does not contain a graphic.

Windows offers several ways to change the name of a file:

• Right-click (or touch and hold) the file name, then select Rename from the shortcut menu.

• Click the file name, then click it again. After a brief pause, you'll be able to type the new name.

• Select the file name, then select the Rename button on the Home tab.

Renaming a folder follows the same general procedures as renaming a file. Figure 5-8 illustrates the right-click procedure for renaming a file and shows the location of the Rename button on the Home tab.

Figure 5-8

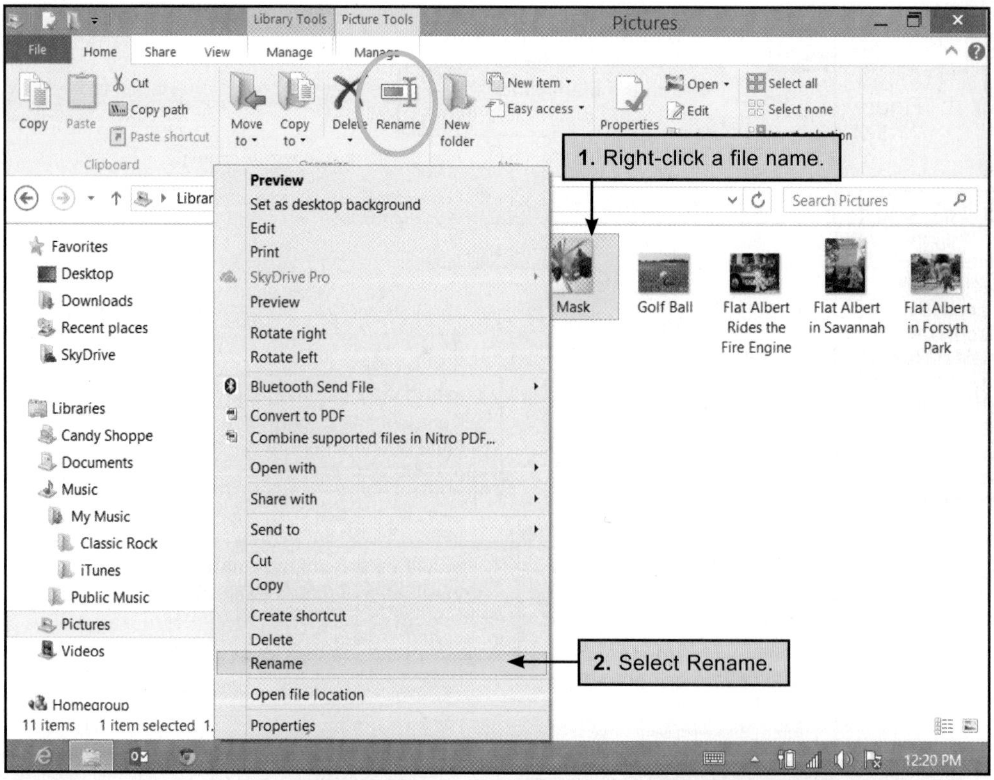

© MediaTechnics

FAQ How do I keep my files organized?

The key to organizing your files is to create a clearly structured set of folders. Here are a few hints to help you improve the organization of your files:

- Use descriptive names for files and folders.

- Always store your data files in a folder. The first level under a device should contain only folders, not files.

- Whenever possible, store your files in your personal folders: My Documents, My Music, and so on.

- Create subfolders of your personal folders as necessary to group files logically by project or by type.

- Try not to store your data files in the folders that contain program modules for your application software.

- Delete unneeded files and folders.

In order to maintain logical groupings of files in your folders, you can move files from one folder to another. Consider moving files as necessary to group similar files into folders where you can easily find them.

You can move a file simply by dragging it from the File list to a folder in the Navigation pane. This procedure sometimes misfires, however. If you don't carefully position the file on the destination folder, the file can drop into an unintended folder where it could be difficult to find. To avoid this problem, use the cut and paste method.

When you use the cut and paste method to move a file, Windows removes or "cuts" the file from its current location and places it on the **Windows Clipboard**, which is a temporary holding area in your computer's memory. After you select a new location for the file, you can paste the selected folder or file from the Clipboard to its new location. Associating the process of moving files with "cut and paste" can help you remember the sequence of commands needed to move a file. Click the Try It! button to practice moving a few files.

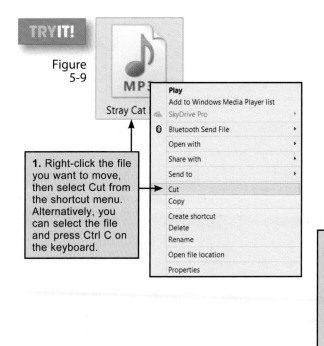

Figure 5-9

1. Right-click the file you want to move, then select Cut from the shortcut menu. Alternatively, you can select the file and press Ctrl C on the keyboard.

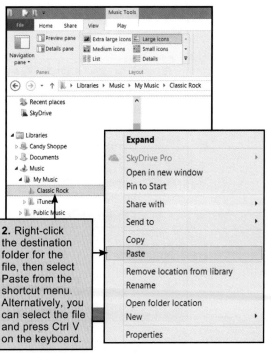

2. Right-click the destination folder for the file, then select Paste from the shortcut menu. Alternatively, you can select the file and press Ctrl V on the keyboard.

• How do I keep my files organized? (continued)

Whereas you move files to improve their organization on a drive, you copy a file when you want to create a duplicate. You can copy a file into another folder before modifying it. You might copy a group of important files to a CD, which you could store in a secure location. You can also copy files to a USB flash drive if you want to access them on a computer other than your own. You can even copy files to an Internet-based cloud storage site to access them from a public computer while you're traveling.

To copy a file, Windows places a duplicate of the file on the Clipboard. The original file remains in its original location. After you select a location for the copy, you can paste the file from the Clipboard to the new location. Think of copying files as "copy and paste" to remember this sequence of commands.

In addition to copying a single file, you can copy groups of files using these techniques:

- To select a series of files, click the first file and then hold down the Shift key as you click the last file. All of the files in between will be selected. Continue holding down the Shift key as you right-click to view the shortcut menu, then select Copy.

- If you want to select files that aren't listed consecutively, hold down the Ctrl key while you select each file. The Shift key and Ctrl key procedures work for moving files as well as copying them.

- You can use the *Select all* or *Select none* buttons on the toolbar to select all of the files in a folder or deselect them.

- The *Invert selection* button deselects the files that you've selected and selects the files that you did not select.

Figure 5-10

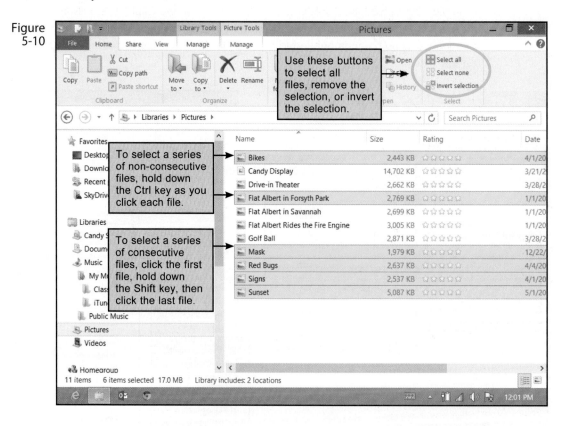

FAQ How do I delete files and folders?

When you no longer need files or folders, you should delete them so that your computer's hard disk drive works more efficiently. Deleting unneeded files also pares down directory listings to avoid clutter. Deleting old versions of files helps you avoid revising an outdated version of a file when you meant to revise the current version.

To delete a file, select it and click the Delete button on the Home tab. Alternatively, you can right-click a file and select Delete from the shortcut menu. You can delete a folder using the same procedure; but be aware that when you delete a folder, you delete all the files it contains. You can use the Ctrl key, Shift key, or Select All option to delete more than one file or folder at a time.

If you run out of disk space, Windows displays a "Disk Full" message. This message usually means it's time for some PC housecleaning. If your hard disk is full, you might eventually have to delete old files and unneeded software. When removing software, remember to use an uninstall procedure rather than manually deleting program files.

Before you delete files and software, you can usually regain space by emptying your computer's Recycle Bin. The **Recycle Bin** is a holding area for the files you've deleted from your PC's hard disk. When you delete a file from the hard disk, its name is removed from Explorer's file list, but the file itself remains on the disk and continues to occupy disk space. This space is not released until you empty the Recycle Bin.

It is nice to know that a deleted file is not gone forever until you empty the Recycle Bin. You can retrieve files from the Recycle Bin and restore them to their previous folders. This feature is an excellent safety net if you mistakenly delete a file. Remember, however, that the Recycle Bin holds only hard disk files. It doesn't retain files you've deleted from USB flash drives and other storage devices. Select the Try It! button to find out how to delete a file and how to use the Recycle Bin.

TRYIT!

Figure
5-11

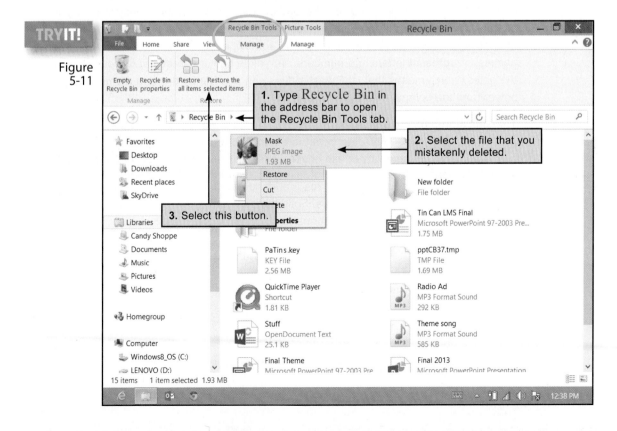

Technology

USB flash drives

A **USB flash drive** is a compact and portable solid state storage device that makes it easy to carry files and programs with you for use on computers at home, school, work, and libraries or other public access sites. USB flash drives are also referred to as UFDs, thumb drives, keychain drives, and jump drives. Typically about two inches long and less than an inch wide, USB flash drives come in a rainbow of colors and styles as shown in Figure 5-12.

Figure
5-12

© MediaTechnics

USB flash drives have capacities ranging from 16 MB to 256 GB. USB drives are no match, however, for the storage capacity and speed of a hard disk drive. When working with a USB drive to access large files, you might notice a performance lag.

Technically, USB flash drives are not drives at all. Unlike hard disk drives, USB flash drives contain no mechanical parts. Instead, USB drives use **solid state technology**, which holds data in erasable, rewritable circuitry, rather than on spinning disks.

Solid state chips contain a grid of cells, and each cell contains two transistors that act as gates. Each gate can be open or closed. Your computer uses various combinations of open and closed gates to represent data, somewhat like Morse code uses dots and dashes to represent letters and numbers. Very little power is required to open and close the gates, which means that USB flash drives can operate by drawing a small amount of power from the computer.

The data stored on a USB drive is retained without the need for additional power, even when the device is disconnected from the computer. Because they don't need batteries or an external power cable, USB flash drives can be small and very portable.

Without moving parts, USB flash drives are immune to the mechanical failures that affect CD, DVD, and hard disk drives. Solid state technology is durable and impervious to vibrations, magnetic fields, and normal temperature variations. However, USB flash drives have a limited number of erase-write cycles, which means that you can't change the data they contain an infinite number of times. Inexpensive USB drives are rated for about 10,000 cycles. As insurance against losing data, you should store copies of the files on your USB flash drive in a backup location, such as on your computer's hard disk.

Technology
(continued)

USB flash drives plug into a computer's **USB port**, a rectangular socket positioned on the front, side, or back of the system unit. These ports are typically labeled with the ⟜ USB symbol.

When inserting a USB flash drive, make sure it is correctly aligned with the port. If the ⟜ logo is printed or embossed on the USB device, the logo should be oriented up or toward you. As soon as you insert the USB device, Windows detects it and opens a window similar to the one in Figure 5-13 that you can quickly use to run applications and access files.

Figure
5-13

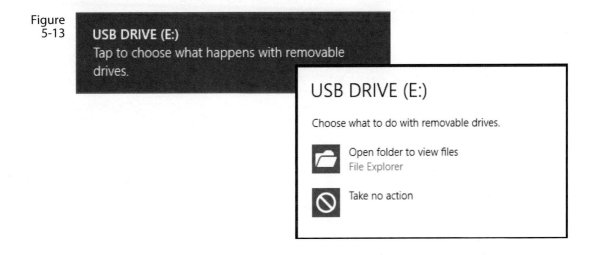

You can use File Explorer to check the contents of a USB flash drive, and you can open files directly from it. You can also copy files from your hard disk to a USB drive if you'd like to transfer a file to a different computer, or when you want to use a file while working at a public computer.

Figure
5-14

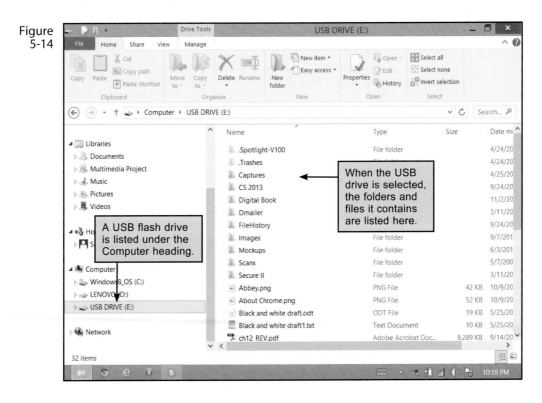

Technology
(continued)

When you are ready to remove a USB flash drive from a computer, you should first click the eject icon in the notification area and wait for Windows to give you the Safe To Remove Hardware message shown in Figure 5-15.

Figure
5-15

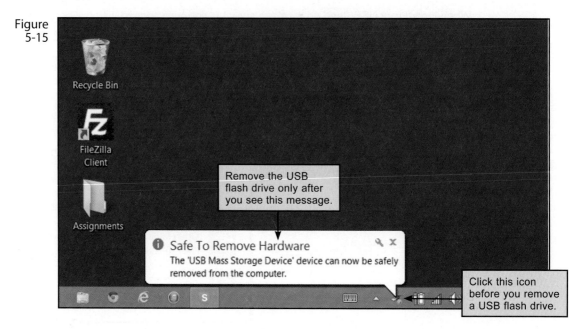

Remove the USB flash drive only after you see this message.

Safe To Remove Hardware
The 'USB Mass Storage Device' device can now be safely removed from the computer.

Click this icon before you remove a USB flash drive.

Occasionally, Windows displays a message indicating that you should not remove the USB flash drive. Make sure that you have closed all the files that are stored on the USB drive. You might also have to close any programs that you used during your current computing session. If all else fails, you can shut down the computer and remove the USB flash drive while the computer is off.

Project

Organize and find files

In addition to your PC's performance, the way you manage and organize your files is an important factor in how quickly you can accomplish tasks with your computer. This chapter covered a wide range of file management topics, such as creating folders; renaming, moving, copying, and deleting files; and various shortcuts to finding your files.

When you have completed this project, you should be able to:

- Catalog the storage devices connected to your computer.

- Locate files using the File Explorer Search box.

- Identify all your personal folders.

- Create new folders.

- Move files from one folder to another.

- Sort files by name, type, date, or size.

- Improve the organization of your files.

Requirements: This project requires Microsoft Windows 8 and Paint. A word processor and e-mail are optional for submitting deliverables.

Deliverables:

1 Answers to the questions in Steps 1–3, 5, 7–11, and 13

2 A screenshot entitled Project 5 Original [Your Name] from Step 12

3 A screenshot entitled Project 5 Improved [Your Name] from Step 15

1. Catalog all the storage devices connected to your computer by doing the following:

   Open File Explorer.

   Expand the Computer option so that you see all the devices connected to your computer.

   List the storage devices attached to your computer and take note of the icons that represent them.

2. List the names of the files stored on your computer that contain the word "sample" in the file name. To complete this step, do the following:

   Enter sample in File Explorer's Search box.

   (Hint: If your hard disk is partitioned into Drive C: and Drive D:, search both drives.)

• Organize and find files (continued)

3. Select the Pictures library and display its subfolders in the Navigation pane. How many folders are included in the library, and what are their names?

4. Create a new folder by clicking the *New folder* button on the Explorer toolbar. Name the folder Project 5 Pictures.

5. Which folder now holds the Project 5 Pictures subfolder? To answer this question, click each of the folders in the Pictures library until you find the Project 5 Pictures folder.

6. Take a screenshot of the Pictures library. Save the file as Project 5 Pictures Library [Your Name]. Close the Paint window. Where does Windows automatically save the file?

7. Move the screenshot file that you created in Step 6 to the Project 5 Pictures folder by dragging it to the folder, or by cutting and pasting it into the folder. Does the file appear in the Pictures library list?

• Organize and find files (continued)

8. Open the Documents library so that its subfolders and files are displayed in the Files pane. Make sure the View is set to Details. How many subfolders are in the My Documents folder? (Hint: Look at the Details pane.)

9. Make sure the Documents library is displayed in the Files pane, then arrange its contents by type. How many files of each type are there?

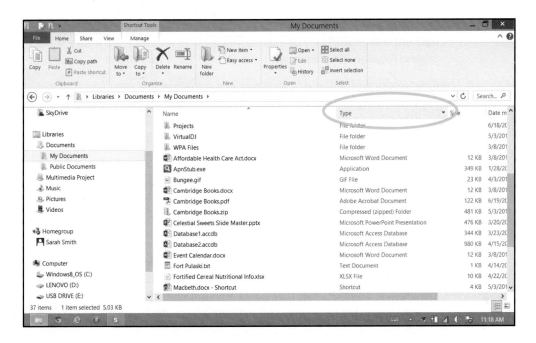

10. Arrange the files by size. What are the name and size of the largest file? What are the name and size of the smallest file?

11. Arrange the files by date. What are the name and date of the most recent file? What are the name and date of the oldest file?

12. Take a screenshot showing the subfolders for My Documents. Name the file Project 5 Original [Your Name].

13. List three ways you could improve the folder structure.

14. Carry out your plan from the previous step. Create, rename, and delete folders as necessary, then move files into them.

15. Take a screenshot of the new directory structure. Save the screenshot and name it Project 5 Improved [Your Name].

16. Compile your answers for the questions in Steps 1–3, 5, 7–11, and 13, plus the Original and Improved screenshots from Steps 12 and 15. Submit this material in the format specified by your instructor.

Issue

Are deleted files legally garbage?

In a highly publicized drug case, police searched through trash bags left on the curb by a suspected cocaine dealer. The evidence they collected led to a conviction, which was appealed because the police had not obtained a search warrant. The conviction was upheld by the U.S. Supreme Court, which ruled that garbage left on the curb is in the public domain and police can search it without a warrant.

What does this case have to do with computers? Files you delete from your PC's hard disk are marked for deletion and transferred to the Recycle Bin. The data remains on the hard disk, however, just in case you want to restore a file from the Recycle Bin to its original location. Files in the Recycle Bin are easy for anyone to access.

Even emptying the Recycle Bin does not actually erase your files from the disk. The sectors holding the data are simply marked as available, which allows data to be stored in them at some point in the future. The old "deleted" file data remains on the disk until the operating system needs those sectors for new data. Only then is the data in those sectors overwritten.

Deleted data might remain on a disk for years. New data might overwrite some of the sectors with new data, but the bits and bytes of data from old files commonly remain on sectors scattered across the disk—a Social Security number here, a bank account number there. Anyone who is sophisticated in the use of computers can rummage through this file garbage, but is it legal and ethical to do so?

Your computer is not on the curb, so it is not in the public domain. The files it contains are protected by laws that make it illegal for high-tech thieves to gain unauthorized access, and that prevent law enforcement agents from search and seizure without a search warrant. But what if you donate your computer to a school or take it to a recycling plant? What if your hard drive fails and you have to send it in for repair or replacement? Even if you go through your file list, carefully delete your personal data, and empty the Recycle Bin, parts of your files remain in sectors marked for deletion. With special software, it is easy to search for and view the sectors that contain deleted files.

To avoid identity theft from your discarded computer equipment, you can run **file shredder software** to overwrite all hard disk sectors with random bits. This software does a pretty good job of making your old data inaccessible. Computer forensic tools, however, can sometimes retrieve data from disks that have been overwritten with file shredder software. To be very sure that your data cannot be retrieved, open the hard drive assembly, remove the platters, and use sandpaper to rough up the surfaces.

What do you think?

1. Have you ever used file shredder software?   ◯ Yes   ◯ No   ◯ Not sure

2. Do you agree with the U.S. Supreme Court ruling that curbside garbage is in the public domain?   ◯ Yes   ◯ No   ◯ Not sure

3. Are you familiar with the laws in your country or state that limit access to the data on your computer?   ◯ Yes   ◯ No   ◯ Not sure

QuickCheck A

1. C:\JobSearch\Resume.doc would be referred to as a file [＿＿＿＿＿＿＿＿] .

2. A(n) [＿＿＿＿＿＿＿＿] is a virtual folder that contains links to other folders and files.

3. To select several files listed consecutively, click the first file, then hold down the [＿＿＿＿＿＿＿＿] key and click the last file.

4. True or false? The Recycle Bin allows you to recover files that you have mistakenly deleted from a hard disk. [＿＿＿＿＿]

5. When you rename a file, you should make sure that you maintain the same file [＿＿＿＿＿＿＿＿] .

CHECKIT!

QuickCheck B

For each description below, enter the letter of the corresponding object.

1. The selected library [＿＿＿]

2. The selected file [＿＿＿]

3. Click to sort by type [＿＿＿]

4. The selected file's path [＿＿＿]

5. A library that is not expanded [＿＿＿]

CHECKIT!

 GETIT? While using the digital textbook, click the Get It? button to see if you can answer ten randomly selected questions from Chapter 5.

6 Protecting Your Files

What's inside?

Chapter 6 presents the gruesome details on the disasters that might befall your important data files—fires, floods, hurricanes, tornadoes, viruses, head crashes, and hard drive failures. It includes tips for avoiding some disasters and recovering from those disasters that you can't prevent.

What's in the digital book?

Losing files can cost you time and money. Chapter 6 not only exposes you to possible ways you can lose your data, but also teaches you precautionary measures that you can take before disaster strikes. View these screen tours to see how you can protect your data.

FAQ What should I know about losing data?

Hardware failures, human error, fires and floods, power spikes, and power outages can damage files to the point where the data they contain is no longer accessible. If you understand where risks originate, you can take steps to prevent data disasters and be prepared to repair the damage they cause.

A simple way to lose the data in a file is to copy over it with another file. This human error is especially common while saving multiple versions of files or maintaining backups. Also, CDs, DVDs, and USB flash drives are surprisingly easy to lose, and they can become unusable if you damage them. If you misplace or damage removable media that contains the sole copy of an important file, your only recourse is to try reconstructing its content from memory.

Computer files can become corrupted when they are not closed properly and for other, sometimes unknown reasons. A **corrupted file** is damaged and either won't open, doesn't work properly, or interferes with other software. Corrupted operating system files are especially notorious for disrupting computer operations, sometimes denying access to your files or preventing your computer from booting.

Malicious software, such as computer viruses and worms, can alter the data on your computer. Some infections are limited to one or two files that can be disinfected, but a stubborn virus might not be dislodged without abandoning many of your files and essentially rebuilding your hard disk drive's data from scratch.

One of the most disastrous events that can strike a computer is a **head crash**. During normal operation, the read-write head of your hard drive hovers just above the disk surface, but does not touch it. If a drive malfunctions or gets knocked about, however, its read-write head might literally crash into the disk surface and damage the sectors that hold your data. Click the Play It! button in Figure 6-1 to see what happens when your computer's hard drive crashes.

PLAY**IT!**

Figure
6-1

Source: Western Digital

In the worst case, sectors damaged during a head crash are part of the Windows Registry that keeps track of file locations on your hard disk. If the Registry is corrupted, you might not be able to access any of the data or executable files on the damaged disk.

Even if you take preventive measures, your computer can lose data at any time. Therefore, you should become familiar with the tools that exist for protecting your data against events such as head crashes, viruses, and corrupted files.

FAQ How can I protect my files from malicious software?

The term **malicious software** refers to any program or set of program instructions designed to surreptitiously enter a computer, disrupt its normal operations, or gather sensitive data. Malicious software includes viruses and other exploits, which you'll read about in the Technology section of this chapter.

A common characteristic of malware is that it is unwanted. Disinfecting a computer that has been infected with a virus is much more difficult than blocking viruses and other malware. To completely eradicate a virus after it has infected your computer, you commonly have to delete some files, and the data they contain might not be retrievable. Also, malware can be persistent. Even when you think you've successfully eradicated an exploit, it may remain in stealth mode for weeks or months before resurfacing.

To protect your computer from malicious attacks, experts recommend that you practice "safe computing" and install antivirus software. Safe computing means avoiding sources of malicious software, such as online distributors of pirated content and fly-by-night download sites.

Antivirus software works in the background whenever your computer is on. It scans for virus signatures in e-mail attachments, downloads, and files that you access from USB flash drives, CDs, DVDs, or the Web. A **virus signature** is a series of unique bytes that, like a fingerprint, uniquely identifies a malicious computer program and distinguishes it from legitimate files on your PC.

Virus signatures are stored in a database that may be referred to as "virus definitions." Because new versions of malicious software continue to emerge, antivirus software publishers offer free updates to subscribers. Be sure your antivirus software is configured to automatically download and install updates to virus definitions so that it blocks all the newest viruses.

Windows 8 includes antivirus software called Windows Defender. Popular third-party antivirus software products are available from McAfee, AVAST, Kaspersky, Trend Micro, and Symantec. Click the Try It! button to find out how to verify that Windows Defender is actively scanning for viruses.

TRYIT!

Figure
6-2

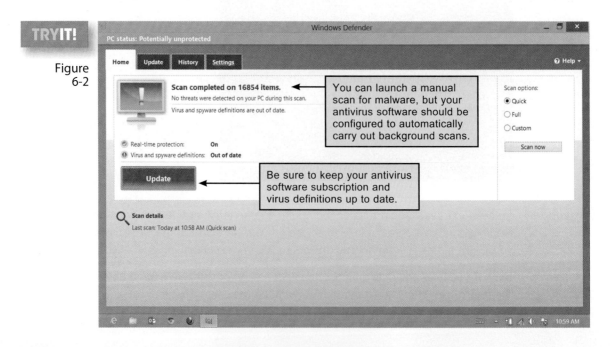

You can launch a manual scan for malware, but your antivirus software should be configured to automatically carry out background scans.

Be sure to keep your antivirus software subscription and virus definitions up to date.

FAQ How do I protect the files I'm working with?

A data file is most vulnerable while you are working with it. If an application hangs up and you have to use Task Manager to close a non-responding program, the file that you're working with might not close properly and could become corrupted. Hardware malfunctions and power problems can also corrupt open files.

Many applications offer an **AutoRecover** option (sometimes called autosave) that automatically makes copies of files as you are working with them. If available, make sure this feature is activated. You might have the option of specifying where and how frequently automatically saved data is stored.

Most applications that automatically save files can sense when a file has been corrupted, in which case they will revert to an autosaved copy. When using new software, check the way its AutoRecover feature works. Take note of the location of autosaved files in case you are required to access them manually. Figure 6-3 illustrates AutoRecover options for Microsoft Word.

Figure
6-3

AutoRecover options allow you to specify how often to save a file and where to put it.

Another strategy for protecting important files you're working with is to manually copy them to a USB flash drive or external hard disk. To copy files to an external device, open File Explorer's Computer folder and use the copy procedure you learned in the previous chapter.

Retrieving files that you've copied to flash drives and external hard drives is easy. You simply copy files from these storage media back to your hard disk. For example, suppose you discover that you inadvertently deleted an important file, and you've just emptied your computer's Recycle Bin. If you have a copy of the file stored on a USB flash drive, you can open the Computer folder and copy the file back onto the hard disk.

Copying important files to a safe location is simple and it takes just a few moments. You have to remember to make copies, however, and you have to remember where you put them—a task that gets more difficult if you accumulate lots of files and store them haphazardly on various flash drives and other media. For more comprehensive file security, you need a different plan.

FAQ How do I use File History?

A **backup** is a copy of one or more files that is made in case the originals become damaged. A backup is usually stored on a different storage medium than the original files. For example, you could back up files from your hard disk to an external hard disk, a writable CD or DVD, a USB flash drive, or an Internet-based cloud storage site.

Backup utilities are designed to back up and restore files from a computer's primary storage device. There are several types of backup utilities, each designed for a specific task. Some backup utilities are designed to back up data files, whereas other backup utilities recover the operating system or customization settings.

Many of the most popular backup utilities make incremental copies of data files to ensure that you don't lose the data they contain. An **incremental backup** makes backup copies of files as they are added or changed. It preserves old versions of files in addition to the current version.

The advantage of incremental backups is having access to past versions in case you change your mind about deletions and changes that you saved in recent versions of the file. The disadvantage of incremental backups is that saving multiple versions requires lots of storage space. You might have to limit the length of time that copies of old files are retained on the backup.

The process of retrieving files and folders from a backup is called **restore**. Restore routines are included as part of every backup utility. You can restore a single file, folder, or library from an incremental backup.

Windows 8 offers an incremental backup utility called File History that you can use to back up and restore files in your libraries, contacts, and favorites folders. It can also back up copies of files stored on Microsoft SkyDrive cloud storage. To access File History, enter File History at the Start screen, then select it from the Settings list.

TRYIT!

Figure
6-4

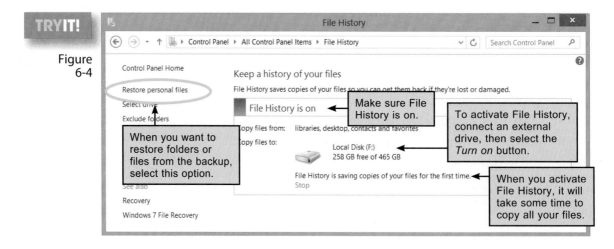

• How do I use File History? (continued)

You can initiate a restore from the File History window or while viewing a list of files in File Explorer. Using File Explorer is handy when you simply want to locate an old version of a file and retrieve it. Clicking the History button lists versions of the file that are available. After you select a version of the file from the History list, you can choose whether or not to replace the current file. Your options are:

Replace the file in the destination. The backup file will replace the current version of the file. Use this option only when you are certain that you don't want the current version.

Skip this file. This option is useful when restoring several files from a folder if you don't want one of the files to overwrite the current version.

Compare info for both files. Selecting this option gives you an opportunity to keep both the current version of a file and the backup. When restored, the file from the backup will be given a number to distinguish it from the current file. For example, if the current file is named Monthly Budget, the restored file will be named Monthly Budget1. Figure 6-5 illustrates the steps for restoring a single file.

Figure 6-5

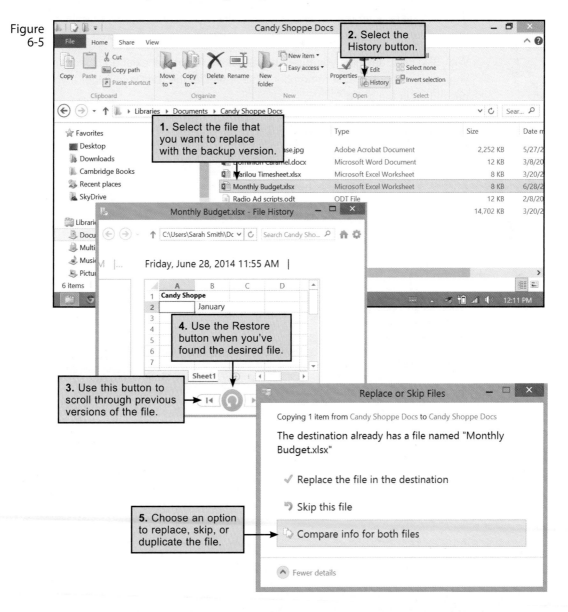

FAQ Can I back up to the cloud?

Cloud storage services such as Microsoft SkyDrive offer remote storage space on an Internet-based "cloud" server. Most of these services have a setting that synchronizes files on your local hard disk with your files stored in the cloud. With the files in two places, you essentially have a backup for both. If your hard disk fails, you can access files from the cloud. If the cloud becomes inaccessible, you can access files from your computer's local hard disk.

File synchronization (sometimes referred to as mirroring) ensures that files in two or more locations contain the same data. Synchronization software designed for file backup monitors the files on a hard disk, watches for changes, and automatically makes the same changes to files in a designated backup location.

Synchronization is ideal in situations when you want a copy of your most recent work stored in a location that you can access in the event that your main hard drive fails. Your synchronized drive contains only the most recent version of your files, however, which means that you cannot retrieve older versions. If you are interested in accessing old versions of your files, then incremental backups are a better choice. For added security, however, there is no reason why you can't use File History for incremental backups and use a cloud service such as SkyDrive for maintaining a synchronized set of files.

With SkyDrive, any files you put in the SkyDrive folder will exist on cloud storage and on your local computer. Just remember to save files in the SkyDrive folder if you want them backed up in the cloud.

Figure 6-6

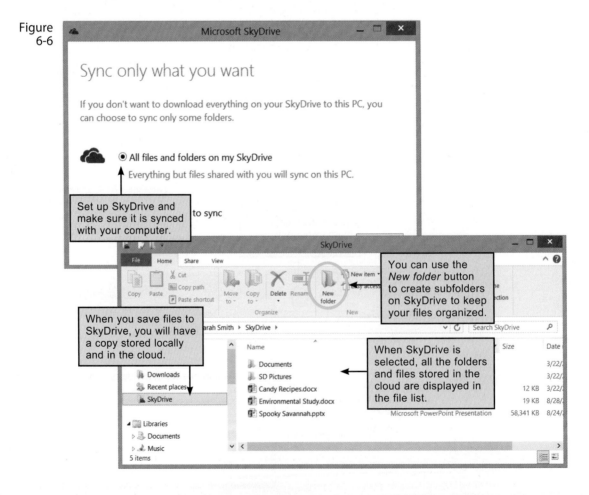

FAQ Can I back up settings and software?

File History and synchronization software are great for backing up your data files, but they are not optimized for backing up your settings or software. Two additional backup tools are restore points and system images.

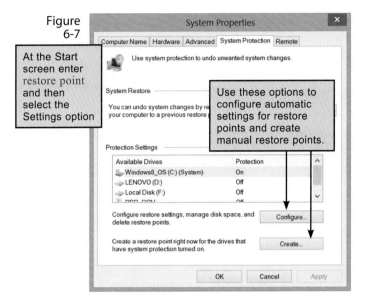

Figure 6-7

At the Start screen enter restore point and then select the Settings option

Use these options to configure automatic settings for restore points and create manual restore points.

Restore points. Windows offers a utility that creates restore points. A **restore point** is a snapshot of your computer settings, essentially a backup of the Windows Registry. If a hard disk problem causes system instability, you might be able to roll back to a restore point when your computer was operating smoothly.

Restore points are set automatically when you install new software. You can manually set restore points, too. For example, you might want to set a restore point before setting up a network or installing new hardware (Figure 6-7).

System images. If you'd like to have a complete copy of your hard disk that contains the operating system as well as all your programs and data files, you can create a system image. A **system image** is a bit-for-bit snapshot of the entire contents of a storage device.

A system image is the best insurance against a total hard disk failure because the image can be streamed onto a new hard disk, which restores your complete computing environment in one operation. A system image takes time to create; however, system images can be created while your computer is not in use. A system image is an all-or-nothing backup. The entire system image must be used; it cannot be used to restore individual files. It will overwrite all files created after the date of the system image.

The system image utility for Windows 8, called Windows 7 File Recovery, was supplied with previous versions of Windows. When using Windows 8, you can access the Windows 7 File Recovery utility from the Start screen by typing File Recovery, going to Settings, then selecting Windows 7 File Recovery.

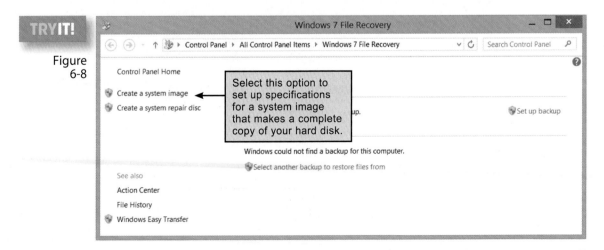

Figure 6-8

TRYIT!

Select this option to set up specifications for a system image that makes a complete copy of your hard disk.

FAQ When should I make a system recovery drive?

Let's suppose that your computer won't boot and you're afraid that your hard disk drive is no longer working. When your computer won't boot, it can't load Windows and you have no access to software or tools that reside on the hard disk.

The situation gets even more grim if your hard disk failed and must be replaced with a new, blank drive. Here's the catch: Your system image can't be restored unless you can run Windows. But you can't run Windows because the hard drive is blank. How can you get your computer started so that you can load Windows and then restore your programs and data?

When your computer's hard drive malfunctions, you need a **system recovery drive** that boots your computer from an external hard drive or USB flash drive, and helps you reinstall Windows along with the device drivers and utilities needed to get your computer up and running. You need to make this drive before your computer malfunctions.

The best time to make a system recovery drive is when you first set up your computer. At the Start screen, type recovery, then under Settings, choose *Create a recovery drive*. Connect an external hard drive or high-capacity USB flash drive. Depending on the brand and model of your computer, the recovery drive could require up to 8 GB of storage space. An 8 GB flash has only 7.45 GB of available space, however, so a 16 GB USB flash drive might be required. Be careful! The process of making a system repair drive erases all the content on the destination USB drive or external hard drive.

Label the drive and store it in a safe place. System recovery drives may contain settings specific to a particular computer, so be sure to have one for every computer you own.

To use a system recovery drive, connect the device on which it is stored. Turn on the computer power. Watch the screen and be prepared to press the BIOS key (F1, F2, or F12, depending on the model of your computer) to boot from an external drive. Recovery options are explained in Figure 6-9.

Figure 6-9

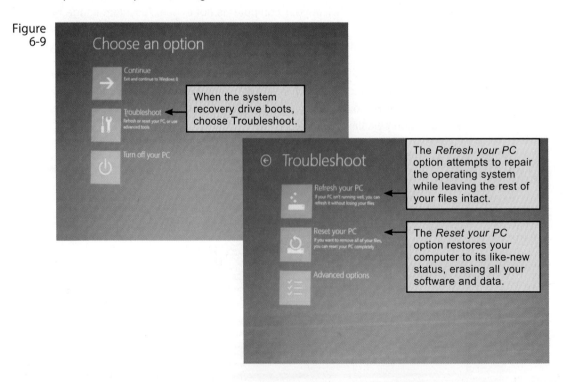

FAQ What's a simple and dependable backup plan?

A dependable basic backup plan should be easy to set up and as automated as possible. In this chapter, you were introduced to the backup tools included with Windows 8. Third-party tools are also available in stores and at download sites. Rather than getting embroiled in arcane backup options, you'll have a serviceable backup plan if you follow these five steps:

1. Make a system recovery drive. When you get a new computer, make a system recovery drive right away. Label the drive "System Recovery" and include the date as well as the computer brand and model. Keep the recovery drive in a safe place.

2. Create a system image. When you've installed most of your application software and have adjusted settings and preferences to your work style, make a system image. The system image is a snapshot of your computer, and is the best insurance for restoring your software, operating system, and settings along with your data files. Create additional system images on a regular schedule.

3. Activate File History. Set up File History to make weekly backups on an external hard disk. Remember that files from File History can be accessed and restored individually.

4. Activate autosave. Activate the AutoRecover feature of your software applications and be sure that you know where to find the autosaved files on your computer's hard disk.

5. Make copies of important files. When working on an important file, periodically copy it to a USB flash drive, an external hard drive, or a cloud storage service. Copying individual data files to an auxiliary storage device helps to ensure that you'll have a copy of important files in the event that your primary backup device is not maintaining backups as you intended.

From time to time, you might want to check the space available on your backup drive and verify that backups are proceeding on schedule. To do so, start File History. Information on available space and backup dates is displayed in the File History window as shown in Figure 6-10.

Figure 6-10

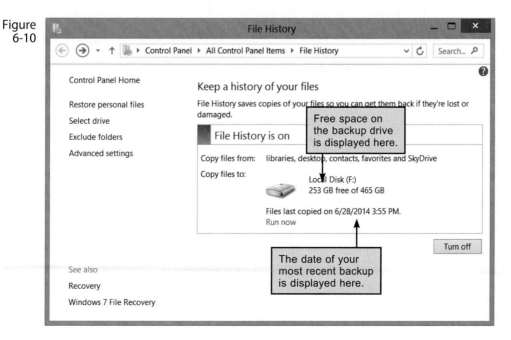

Technology

Malware

Malware is another term for malicious software and refers to any computer program designed to surreptitiously enter a computer, gain unauthorized access to data, or disrupt normal processing operations. Malware includes viruses, worms, Trojans, bots, and spyware.

Malware is created and unleashed by individuals referred to as hackers, crackers, black hats, or cybercriminals. Some malware is released as a prank. Other malware is created to distribute political messages or to disrupt operations at specific companies.

In an increasing number of cases, malware is unleashed for monetary gain. Malware designed for identity theft or extortion has become a very real threat to individuals and corporations. Once malware enters your computer, it can carry out a variety of unauthorized activities, such as those listed in Figure 6-11.

Figure
6-11

- Display irritating messages and pop-up ads
- Delete or modify your data
- Encrypt your data and demand ransom for the encryption key
- Upload or download unwanted files
- Log your keystrokes to steal your passwords and credit card numbers
- Propagate malware and spam to everyone in your e-mail address book or your instant messaging buddy list
- Disable your antivirus and firewall software
- Block access to specific Web sites and redirect your browser to infected Web sites
- Cause response time on your system to deteriorate
- Allow hackers to remotely access data on your computer
- Allow hackers to take remote control of your machine and turn it into a zombie
- Link your computer to others in a botnet that can send millions of spam e-mails or wage denial-of-service attacks against Web sites
- Cause network traffic jams

© MediaTechnics

Some malware does a good job of cloaking itself, so victims might not be aware of its presence. Cloaking techniques are great defense mechanisms because when victims aren't aware of malware, they won't take steps to eradicate it. Many victims whose computers are part of massive infections have no idea that their computers are compromised.

Hackers may cloak their work using rootkits. The term **rootkit** refers to software tools used to conceal malware and backdoors that have been installed on a victim's computer. Rootkits can hide all types of malware. With a rootkit in place, hackers can continue to exploit a victim's computer with little risk of discovery.

Technology
(continued)

Viruses. A **computer virus** is a set of program instructions that attaches itself to a file, reproduces itself, and spreads to other files. A common misconception is that viruses spread themselves from one computer to another. They don't. Viruses can replicate themselves only on files in the host computer and only when an infected file is run. Viruses are spread to other computers when people unknowingly download or share copies of infected files.

A key characteristic of viruses is their ability to lurk in a computer for days or months, quietly replicating themselves. While this replication takes place, you might not even know that your computer has contracted a virus; therefore, it is easy to inadvertently spread infected files to other people's computers.

In addition to replicating itself, a virus usually delivers a payload, which can be as harmless as displaying an annoying message or as devastating as trashing the data on your computer's storage device. It can corrupt files, destroy data, or otherwise disrupt computer operations. A trigger event, such as a specific date, can unleash some viruses.

Worms. A **computer worm** is a self-replicating program designed to carry out some unauthorized activity on a victim's computer. Worms can spread themselves from one computer to another without any assistance from victims.

Worms can enter a computer through security holes in browsers and operating systems, as e-mail attachments, and by victims clicking on infected pop-up ads or links contained in e-mails. For example, a mass-mailing worm called Ackantta is hidden in an attachment to an e-mail message that's a fake Twitter invitation. Clicking the attachment activates the worm.

A **mass-mailing worm** spreads by sending itself to every address in the address book of an infected computer. Your friends receive these messages and, thinking that they are from a trusted source, open the infected attachment, spreading the worm to their computers and on to their friends.

Although e-mail is currently the primary vehicle used to spread worms, hackers have also devised ways to spread worms over file sharing networks, instant messaging links, and mobile phones.

Trojans. A **Trojan horse** (sometimes simply called a Trojan) is a computer program that seems to perform one function while actually doing something else. Unlike a worm, a Trojan is not designed to spread itself to other computers. Also differing from viruses and worms, most Trojans are not designed to replicate themselves. Trojans are standalone programs that masquerade as useful utilities or applications, which victims download and install because they are unaware of the programs' destructive nature.

Trojans are notorious for stealing passwords using a keylogger that records keystrokes as you log in to your computer and various online accounts. Another type of Trojan called a **Remote Access Trojan** (RAT) has backdoor capabilities that allow remote hackers to transmit files to victims' computers, search for data, run programs, and use a victim's computer as a relay station for breaking into other computers.

Technology
(continued)

Bots. Any software that can automate a task or autonomously execute a task when commanded to do so is called an intelligent agent. Because an intelligent agent behaves somewhat like a robot, it is often called a **bot**.

Good bots perform a variety of helpful tasks such as scanning the Web to assemble data for search engines like Google. Some bots offer online help, while others monitor online discussions for prohibited behavior and language. Bad bots, on the other hand, are controlled by hackers and designed for unauthorized or destructive tasks. They can be spread by worms or Trojans. Most bad bots can initiate communications with a central server on the Internet to receive instructions. A computer under the control of a bad bot is sometimes referred to as a **zombie** because it carries out instructions from a malicious leader.

Like a spider in its web, the person who controls many bot-infested computers can link them together into a network called a **botnet**. Experts have discovered botnets encompassing more than one million computers. Botmasters who control botnets use the combined computing power of their zombie legions for many types of nefarious tasks such as breaking into encrypted data, carrying out denial-of-service attacks against other computers, and sending out massive amounts of spam.

Spyware. Spyware is a type of program that secretly gathers personal information without the victim's knowledge, usually for advertising and other commercial purposes. Once it is installed, spyware starts monitoring Web-surfing and purchasing behavior, and sends a summary back to one or more third parties. Just like Trojans, spyware can monitor keystrokes and relay passwords and credit card information to cybercriminals.

Spyware can get into a computer using exploits similar to those of Trojans. It can piggyback on seemingly legitimate freeware or shareware downloads. You can also inadvertently allow spyware into your computer by clicking innocuous but infected pop-up ads, or surfing through seemingly valid and secure Web sites that have been compromised by hackers.

Project

Explore file protection measures

This chapter introduced several ways you can lose your data and provided tips on how to protect and recover your files. Some file protection tools require an administrator password to keep unauthorized users from changing settings. Without an administrator account, however, you can use many backup utilities provided by Windows 8.

When you have completed this project, you should be able to:

- Check the status of your antivirus software.

- Determine the location of files automatically saved by your word processing software.

- Determine the status of File History.

- Locate and create restore points.

Requirements: This project requires Microsoft Windows 8. E-mail and word processing software are optional for submitting the deliverable.

The deliverable for this project is a document containing the following items:

1 The name of your antivirus software	4 The status of File History
2 The status of your antivirus software	5 The status of restore points on your computer
3 The status of your word processor's autosave feature	6 Information about a restore point that you create

1. Find out which antivirus software is protecting your computer. To complete this step:

   At the Start screen, type Action, then select Settings.

   Select Action Center from the list of matching utilities.

   Select the arrow in the Security section to display information about security software and settings.

   Make a note of the following:

   1a. What is the name of the software that provides spyware protection?

   1b. What is the name of the software that provides virus protection?

This button displays a list of security software and settings.

• Explore file protection measures (continued)

2. Check the status of your antivirus software. To complete this step:

   At the Start screen, type the name of your antivirus software.

   Select your antivirus software from the list of apps.

   Make a note of the following:

   2a. Is your antivirus software actively scanning (real-time protection)?

   2b. Are the virus and spyware definitions up to date?

   2c. What is the date of the most recent scan?

3. Find out if your word processing software is set to autosave documents in case of a power outage or software glitch. To complete this step:

   Start your word processing software. To start Microsoft Word, type Word at the Start screen.

   Find the link to Settings or Options. In Microsoft Word, you might have to start a blank document, then select the FILE tab where you'll find a link to Options.

   Find the link to the settings for saving documents. In Word, that is the Save link.

   Record the following information:

   3a. Is your word processor configured to automatically save documents?

   3b. How often is a document automatically saved?

   3c. What is the location of documents that are automatically saved?

4. Check the status of File History to see if it is making backups of your files. To complete this step:

   At the Start screen, type file history.

   Select Settings.

   Select File History from the list of programs.

   Record the following information:

   4a. Is File History on?

   4b. To which storage device are backups being copied?

   4c. How much free space is available in your backup location?

   4d. When was the last backup made?

• Explore file protection measures (continued)

5. Check the status of restore points on the computer you are using. To complete this step:

At the Start screen, type restore.

Select Settings, then select *Create a restore point* from the list of utilities.

Select the System Restore button.

Select the Next button.

Record the date and time of the most recent restore point.

Select the CANCEL button. You do not want to restore your computer to the state it was in when the restore point was made.

Leave the System Properties window open for the next step.

6. Suppose that the touchpad on your computer is not working. You are going to experiment with some settings; but if they don't fix the problem, you'd like to be able to revert back to the status before your changes. To do that, create a restore point by completing these steps:

With the System Properties window open from the previous step, select the Create button.

When asked for a description, type Before troubleshooting touchpad.

Select the Create button.

When the restore point has been created, return to the System Properties window.

Use the System Restore button to view your restore point.

Record the following information:

6a. The date and time the restore point was made

6b. The description

6c. The type

Select the CANCEL button. You do not need to use the restore point.

Close the System Properties window.

7. Consolidate the elements of the deliverable for Project 6 into printed format, a document file, or an e-mail message as specified by your instructor.

Issue

What about a "good" virus?

Like tagging subway cars with spray-painted graffiti, creating a virus or worm has some elements of artistry and risk. The artistry lies in the satisfaction of creating a really brilliant program that can elude detection from antivirus software and cause just the right amount of mischief on infected PCs. Some twisted person apparently took much delight in creating a virus that bellows in an Arnold Schwarzenegger–like voice, "Your files have just been TERMINATED!," as the file names disappear one-by-one from your personal folders.

Creating a virus or worm can be a risky business. Most states have laws that punish deliberate attacks on computer systems. Also, a surprisingly effective ad hoc group of virus watchdogs in the computer community seems to be able to track most malicious software to its source. The authors of several viruses and worms have been caught. Some boast about their exploits. A few innocently claim that their creations inadvertently "escaped" into the wild of public computing and mistakenly infected PCs in businesses, schools, and homes. Other malware authors claim that their work is a public service because it points out security holes and flaws in antivirus software.

According to a recent Microsoft Security Intelligence Report, worms have become more prevalent than viruses. They are increasingly more destructive and consequently more costly. Potential sources of infection are everywhere. Worms sneak into your computer from compromised Web sites, arrive as excess baggage in downloads, and land in your Inbox along with unwelcome spam. When they get past antivirus software, a frustrating amount of time can be spent trying to disinfect your files.

Could there be a "good" worm that can be used to eliminate bad worms? When the vicious Blaster worm wreaked havoc across the globe, a do-gooder released a worm called Nachi as a Blaster antidote. It erased copies of Blaster on infected PCs, then downloaded and installed a Windows update from Microsoft to protect the computer against further Blaster (and Nachi) attacks. However, just as Blaster caused major network traffic, so did Nachi. Still, some believe that the only way to stop major malware epidemics is to out-hack the hackers. Because it is impossible to anticipate interactions among all possible software programs, it is difficult to determine if the benefits of "good" worms might outweigh their risks.

What do you think?

1. Have you ever used a computer that had a virus or worm?   ◯ Yes ◯ No ◯ Not sure

2. Have you ever lost a file because of a virus or worm?   ◯ Yes ◯ No ◯ Not sure

3. Do you think the benefits of "good" viruses outweigh their risks?   ◯ Yes ◯ No ◯ Not sure

QuickCheck A

1. A(n) [_____] backup backs up files as they are added or changed. It preserves old versions of files in addition to the current version.

2. Antivirus software looks for a unique virus [_____] that identifies the virus and distinguishes it from the legitimate files on your PC.

3. Windows 8 includes a utility called File [_____] that creates a backup of personal folders and files.

4. When you get a new computer, make a system [_____] drive right away.

5. A(n) [_____] point is a snapshot of your computer settings that can be used to roll your computer back to a previous state.

CHECKIT!

QuickCheck B

Select the malware that best matches the following descriptions:

1. Disguises itself as a legitimate application [____]

2. Takes over control of a computer for unauthorized tasks [____]

3. Surreptitiously monitors purchasing behavior and sends information to third parties [____]

4. Self-replicating program that spreads from one computer to another [____]

5. Reproduces itself and delivers a payload when run [____]

A. **Virus**   B. **Trojan**

C. **Spyware**   D. **Bot**

E. **Worm**

CHECKIT!

 While using the digital textbook, click the Get It? button to see if you can answer ten randomly selected questions from Chapter 6.

CHAPTER 7

Connecting to the Internet

What's inside?

The Internet is in the news and on everyone's mind. Chapter 7 provides the information you need to get connected. In Chapter 8 you'll learn about the Web, and in Chapter 9 you'll learn about e-mail.

What's in the digital book?

Because the Internet has so much to offer, the pages in Chapter 7 can merely get you started on an exploration of the fascinating Internet world called cyberspace.

FAQ How does the Internet work?

The **Internet** is a global network connecting millions of smaller networks, computers, and other devices. The Internet is not owned or operated by any single corporation or government. Instead, it has grown over time in a somewhat haphazard configuration as networks connected to other networks and to the core Internet infrastructure.

The Internet is maintained by **network service providers** (NSPs) such as AT&T, British Telecom, Sprint, and Verizon. NSP equipment and links are tied together by **network access points** (NAPs), so that, for example, data can begin its journey on a Verizon link and then cross over to a Sprint link, if necessary, to reach its destination. NSPs supply Internet connections to large Internet service providers, such as EarthLink, AOL, and Comcast. An **Internet service provider** (ISP) is a company that offers Internet access to individuals, businesses, and smaller ISPs.

Devices connected to the Internet exchange data using a **communications protocol** (or simply a protocol) that sets standards and rules to help network devices transmit data in an efficient and orderly way. The Internet uses a protocol called **TCP/IP**. This protocol divides documents, e-mail messages, photos, and other digital files into standard-sized packets of data. A **packet** is simply a set of bits; it could be part of an e-mail message or part of a video download.

Packets are shuttled to their destinations by devices called routers. A **router** acts as an intermediary between network devices by reading the address on a packet and forwarding it to another router on the way to the packet's final destination.

Every device on the Internet has a unique **IP address** (also called an Internet address) that identifies it in the same way that a street address identifies the location of a house. When your computer is connected to any network that uses Internet protocols, it also has an IP address, which is attached to every packet of data you send or receive.

Although IP addresses work for communication between computers, people find it difficult to remember long strings of numbers. Therefore, many Internet servers also have an easy-to-remember name, such as *nike.com*. The official term for this name is fully qualified domain name (FQDN), but most people just refer to it as a **domain name**.

A domain name ends with an extension, such as .com, that indicates its classification. Some domain names include a country code, such as .ca (Canada), .uk (United Kingdom), or .au (Australia). Figure 7-1 lists the most prevalent domain extensions.

Figure 7-1

Domain	Description
biz	Unrestricted use; usually for commercial businesses
com	Unrestricted use; usually for commercial businesses
edu	Restricted to North American educational institutions
gov	Restricted to U.S. government agencies
info	Unrestricted use
int	Restricted to organizations established by international treaties
mil	Restricted to U.S. military agencies
net	Unrestricted use; traditionally for Internet administrative organizations
org	Unrestricted use; traditionally for professional and nonprofit organizations

FAQ What should I know about Internet service?

Computers can be connected to the Internet through telephone lines, cable television systems, satellites, cellular networks, wireless hotspots, and local area networks. An Internet connection may require a device called a **modem** to convert signals from your computer into signals that can travel over the Internet.

The capacity of an Internet connection is sometimes referred to as **bandwidth** and can be measured in bits per second. The slowest connections transmit a mere 56 Kbps (56,000 bits per second), whereas fast connections, called **broadband**, blaze away at 100 Mbps (100 *million* bits per second) or more.

Capacity is related to speed, and often the two are used interchangeably. Technically, however, connection speed indicates the rate at which data travels. Speed is measured in milliseconds (ms), rather than in megabits (Mbps). When it comes to speed, lower numbers are better. For example, 26 ms is faster than 51 ms. Higher capacity and faster speeds are desirable if you want to play online games, use voice over IP, participate in Web conferences, or watch online videos.

Some Internet services offer **symmetrical connections**, in which data travels **upstream** from your computer to the Internet at the same speed as data traveling **downstream** from the Internet to your computer. However, **asymmetrical connections** are more common, with data traveling faster downstream than upstream. When using an asymmetric connection, for example, uploading a video typically requires more time than downloading it.

Most people have lots more data coming to their computer than leaving it. Therefore, downstream speed is more important unless you are participating in a project that requires you to transfer lots of large files to other participants.

Internet service providers advertise various upstream and downstream speeds. More expensive service plans offer faster speeds. Consumers should be aware that advertised speeds are applicable under ideal conditions. You can use Web apps or local software, such as Ping, to compare the actual speed of your Internet connection to your service provider's advertised speed. Click the Try It! button in Figure 7-2 to find out how.

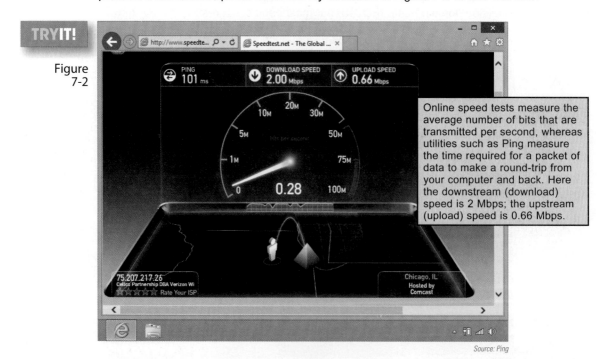

TRYIT!

Figure 7-2

Online speed tests measure the average number of bits that are transmitted per second, whereas utilities such as Ping measure the time required for a packet of data to make a round-trip from your computer and back. Here the downstream (download) speed is 2 Mbps; the upstream (upload) speed is 0.66 Mbps.

Source: Ping

FAQ What are my options for Internet service?

Cable Internet service distributes broadband Internet access over the same infrastructure that offers cable television service. Cable companies, such as Comcast and Charter Communications, offer cable Internet service for a monthly subscription. Of all Internet services, cable Internet currently offers the fastest access speeds. However, advertised speeds are usually for downstream data transfer. Upstream speeds might be much slower. Cable Internet service uses a cable modem to transfer data from your computer to your home cable connection and then to the Internet.

DSL (digital subscriber line) is a broadband, Internet access technology that works over standard phone lines. It offers fast, affordable connections. DSL is available from local telephone companies and third-party DSL providers. DSL services can be symmetrical or asymmetrical. If you need lots of upstream speed, a symmetrical DSL connection could be the best choice.

Dial-up Internet service uses a voiceband modem and telephone lines to transport data between your computer and your ISP. Many ISPs—including AT&T, AOL, and EarthLink—offer dial-up Internet access. The service typically costs less than $10 per month, but access speed is slow. Dial-up connections are not suitable for playing online games, teleconferencing, or watching videos that stream to your computer as they play. Even downloading software and essential operating system updates can take hours.

Satellite Internet service distributes broadband asymmetric Internet access by broadcasting signals to and from a personal satellite dish. In many rural areas, satellite Internet service is the only alternative to dial-up access. Susceptibility to bad weather makes satellite service less reliable than cable-based services. In addition, the time required for a signal to travel to a satellite and back—called **latency**—makes this type of connection too slow for online gaming.

An alternative wireless technology called **WiMAX** transmits data from your computer to a nearby communications tower, which then links to the Internet. WiMAX is one of the newest technologies for Internet access and is available in fewer locations than other Internet services.

Mobile broadband supplies access to the Internet through high-speed cellular technologies, popularly referred to as 3G and 4G. Offered by cell phone providers, mobile broadband is designed for handheld devices, such as smartphones, as well as laptop, tablet, and netbook computers. The key feature of this technology is that you can use it on the go. Like a cell phone, your Internet connection is handed off from one communications tower to the next as you travel within the coverage area.

Mobile broadband data transfer rates can be slower, however, than other broadband services like cable and DSL. Connections are sometimes dropped or blocked by buildings, so mobile broadband is one of the least reliable services. Most subscribers use it as a supplement to cable or DSL service, though it can be an expensive addition to monthly cell phone bills.

FAQ How do local area networks offer Internet access?

You can connect to the Internet from a **local area network** (LAN). A LAN connects personal computers within a very limited geographical area—usually within a single building. Home networks and computer labs are classified as LANs.

Typically, the LAN's router is connected to a cable Internet or DSL service and can pass Internet access along to any computers connected to the LAN. Devices can connect to the LAN's router using Ethernet or Wi-Fi technology.

- **Ethernet** is a popular network standard for businesses, school computer labs, and home networks. Ethernet is a fast and secure wired network technology, requiring a cable to connect network devices.

- **Wi-Fi** (or WiFi) is a popular wireless network technology. Pronounced "Why Fhy," this technology transmits data using radio waves (also called RF signals). It is slower and less secure than Ethernet, but eliminates the need to run cables through walls and ceilings. Wi-Fi and Ethernet can coexist, so some networks include devices connected wirelessly and others connected with wires.

Coffee shops, airports, hotels, libraries, school campuses, and many other locations offer public access to the Internet through Wi-Fi hotspots. A **Wi-Fi hotspot** is basically a wireless local area network that provides access to guests using laptop computers or mobile devices.

Some hotspots are free, whereas others require guests to register, pay a fee, and obtain a user ID and password to log in. Many hotspots are unsecured, so legitimate users should be cautious about sending and receiving sensitive data while connected to hotspots.

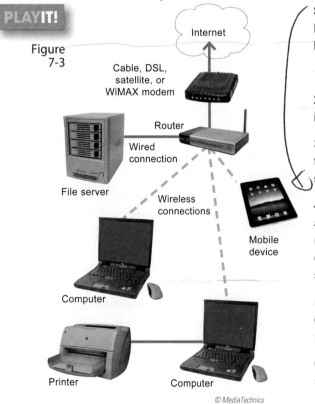

PLAYIT!

Figure 7-3

Internet

Cable, DSL, satellite, or WiMAX modem

Router

Wired connection

File server

Wireless connections

Mobile device

Computer

Printer

Computer

© MediaTechnics

Setting up a local area network to access the Internet is not difficult. The Play It! button in Figure 7-3 shows you how:

1. Purchase a router, unpack it, and plug it in.

2. Follow the router manufacturer's instructions to access the router setup utility.

3. In setup, create a new router password that will be required to change network settings.

4. Enter an **SSID** (service set identifier) as the public name for your network. It is useful for a network to have a unique name, especially in neighborhoods where there are several overlapping networks.

5. Activate wireless encryption and select an encryption key that serves as the password required to connect to the network.

6. Connect the router to a cable, DSL, satellite, or WiMAX modem.

FAQ How do I connect to the Internet from a local area network?

To take advantage of a LAN's Internet access, you simply have to connect to the LAN. Windows automatically senses nearby networks and displays their SSIDs. To see a list of available networks when using Windows 8, click the network icon, which is located in the notification area of the desktop. With a touchscreen, you can swipe from the right side of the screen and choose the network icon from there.

Some networks are secured, while others are open to the public. As shown in Figure 7-4, the icon that shows network strength also indicates if a network is secured.

Figure
7-4

Secured network icons

Unsecured network icons

The first time you want to connect to a secured network, you are required to enter the correct encryption key. When using a network that you did not set up, you can obtain the encryption key from the network administrator.

Figure
7-5

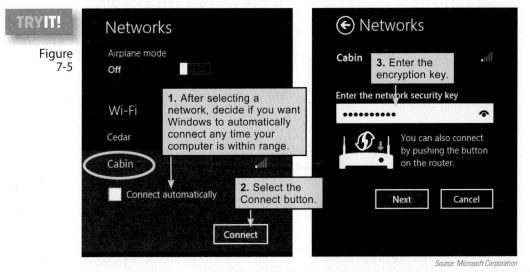

Source: Microsoft Corporation

Devices configured with the iOS and Android operating systems can connect to LANs if they have Wi-Fi capability. The connection procedure is similar to the one you use with Windows. First, make sure that Wi-Fi is enabled, then wait for the device to sense the network. When asked, enter the encryption key as shown in Figure 7-6.

Figure
7-6

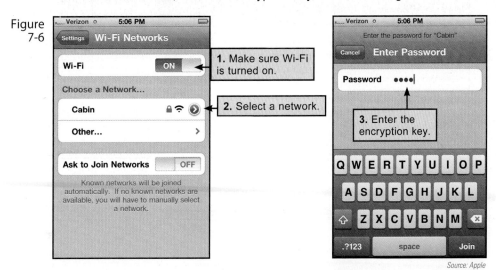

Source: Apple

FAQ How does firewall software protect my computer from intrusions?

In the context of computers, an **intrusion** is any access to data or programs by hackers or other unauthorized persons. As the result of an intrusion, data can be stolen or altered, system configurations can be changed to allow even more intrusions, and software can be surreptitiously installed and operated under the remote control of a hacker.

One of the most common ways of gaining unauthorized access to a network-based computer is by looking for open ports. The term **port** refers to any pathway that can be used to transfer data into or out from a computer. Ports can be physical, as in the case of USB ports, or they can be virtual ports created by software.

Hackers look for virtual ports used for transmitting and sharing data over networks. Open ports are like unlocked doors. Hackers are continuously canvassing the Internet and probing ports to find their next victims.

Firewall software (sometimes referred to as a personal firewall) is designed to analyze the flow of traffic entering your computer from a network. It makes sure that incoming information was actually requested and is not an unauthorized intrusion. It blocks activity from suspicious Internet addresses, and it reports intrusion attempts so that you know when hackers are trying to break into your computer.

Firewall software is essential for computers that are connected directly to the Internet. If you don't have a router, then make sure firewall software is installed and running at all times. The Windows operating system includes a utility called Windows Firewall that you can use to block intrusion attempts. Your computer should have only one firewall active at any given time. If your antivirus software or security suite includes a firewall, then Windows Firewall can be deactivated.

To access Windows Firewall, type Firewall in the Windows Search box, select Settings, then select the Windows Firewall option. Using the window shown in Figure 7-7, you can turn the firewall on or off, and you can adjust settings to allow or block specific programs and services.

TRYIT!

Figure 7-7

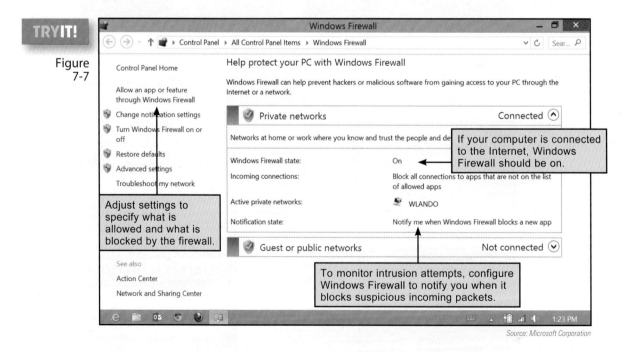

Source: Microsoft Corporation

FAQ How does encryption protect my network from intrusions?

Wireless networks broadcast signals that can be picked up by any device within the network coverage area. Airborne transmissions are easily captured by hackers or by innocent neighbors who just happen to be within the range of your wireless network. The data carried by Wi-Fi signals can be encrypted with WEP, WPA, or PSK.

The original wireless encryption was called **WEP** (Wired Equivalent Privacy) because it was designed to provide a level of confidentiality similar to that of a wired network. WEP is very easy to bypass. It does, however, protect a wireless network from casual hacks and inadvertent crosstalk from nearby networks.

WPA (Wi-Fi Protected Access) and its follow-up version, WPA2, offer stronger protection by making sure that packets have not been intercepted or tampered with in any way. **PSK** (pre-shared key), also referred to as personal mode, is a type of WPA used on many home networks.

When setting up wireless encryption, you create an **encryption key**, which works like a password. When a computer tries to join the network, the encryption key is required. To activate encryption for your wireless network, open the router's configuration software as explained in Figure 7-8.

Figure 7-8

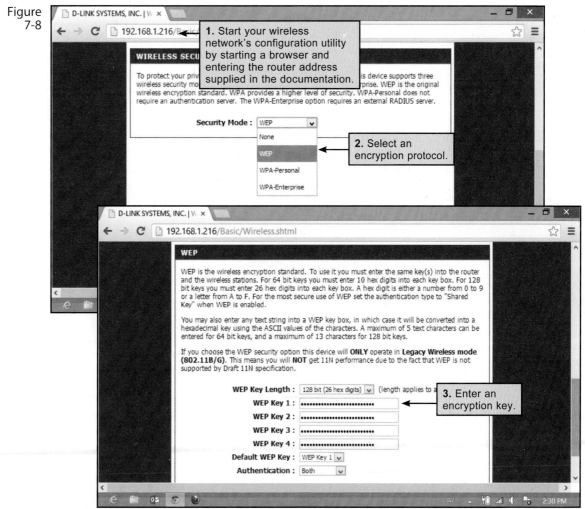

Source: D-Link Corporation

Technology

TCP/IP

TCP/IP is the primary protocol suite responsible for message transmission on the Internet. A **protocol suite** is a combination of protocols that work together. TCP (Transmission Control Protocol) breaks a message or file into packets. IP (Internet Protocol) is responsible for addressing packets so that they can be routed to their destination. TCP/IP provides a protocol standard for the Internet that is public, free, extensible, and easy to implement.

Early communications networks used a technology called **circuit switching** to establish dedicated links between two communicating parties. For example, the telephone system used circuit switching technology to establish a private link between one telephone and another for the duration of a call. In practice, circuit switching is rather inefficient. For example, when a phone call is on hold, no communication is taking place, yet the circuit is reserved and cannot be used for other communications.

A more efficient alternative to circuit switching is **packet switching** technology, which divides messages into several packets that can be routed independently to their destination, where they are reassembled into the original message.

Packets from many different sources can share a single communications channel or circuit. Packets are shipped over the circuit on a first-come, first-served basis. If some packets from an e-mail message, for example, are not quite ready to send, the system does not wait for them. Instead, the system moves on to send packets from other sources. The end result is a steady stream of packets that take optimal advantage of the carrying capacity of a communications channel. Figure 7-9 illustrates how packets of data produced by TCP travel over a packet switched network.

PLAYIT!

Figure 7-9

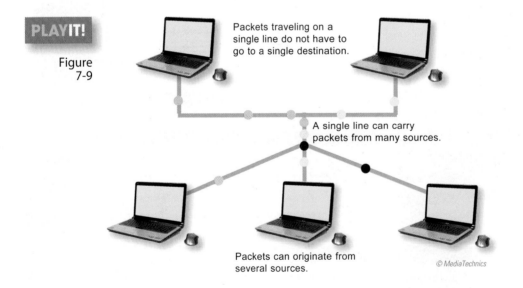

Packets traveling on a single line do not have to go to a single destination.

A single line can carry packets from many sources.

Packets can originate from several sources.

© MediaTechnics

Technology
(continued)

IP addresses originated on the Internet as part of the TCP/IP protocol. IP addresses are used to uniquely identify computers on the Internet as well as on LANs. In the context of the Internet, IP addresses are sometimes referred to as TCP/IP addresses or Internet addresses.

There are two kinds of IP addresses: IPv4 and IPv6. **IPv4** (Internet Protocol version 4) addresses, such as 204.127.129.1, are divided by periods into four segments. Longer **IPv6** addresses, such as FE80:0000:0000:0000:0202:B3FF:FE1E:8329, are divided by colons into eight segments.

IPv4 provides about 4.3 billion unique IP addresses, but most have been allocated. IPv6 supports far more addresses and can better accommodate the growing number of Internet users. Mobile broadband providers, such as Verizon and T-Mobile, already use IPv6, but other service providers may take several years to discontinue IPv4.

Devices connected to a network can have a permanently assigned **static IP address** or a temporarily assigned **dynamic IP address**. Typically ISPs, Web sites, Web hosting services, and e-mail servers that always need to be at the same address require static IP addresses. Most other network users have dynamic IP addresses.

Devices that connect to the Internet can be assigned an IP address by a network administrator or an ISP. IP addresses can also be assigned by **DHCP** (Dynamic Host Configuration Protocol) servers. Figure 7-10 shows you how to find the IP address of your Internet connection.

Figure 7-10

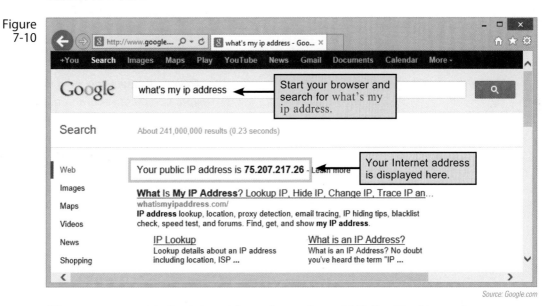

Source: Google.com

When you connect to the Internet through a router or LAN, the IP address of your computer can be different from the address used for your Internet connection. That difference might seem odd, but it can work to your advantage by shielding your computer from intrusion attempts. Let's see how that works.

In a LAN, your router is the point of contact with the Internet and it uses the IP address assigned to it by your Internet service provider. That IP address is the one shown when you use a browser to search for what's my ip address. Routers are assigned routable IP addresses. A **routable IP address** is one that can be used to transport data on the Internet.

Technology
(continued)

Computers within a LAN are assigned IP addresses by the router, not by an ISP. The router assigns addresses that are selected from a group of private IP addresses. A **private IP address** is not routable, which means that it cannot be used to send packets of data over the Internet. Three ranges of IP addresses are reserved for private use: 10.0.0.0 to 10.255.255.255, 172.16.0.0 to 172.31.255.255, and 192.168.0.0 to 192.168.255.255. Figure 7-11 explains how to check your computer to see if it is using a private IP address.

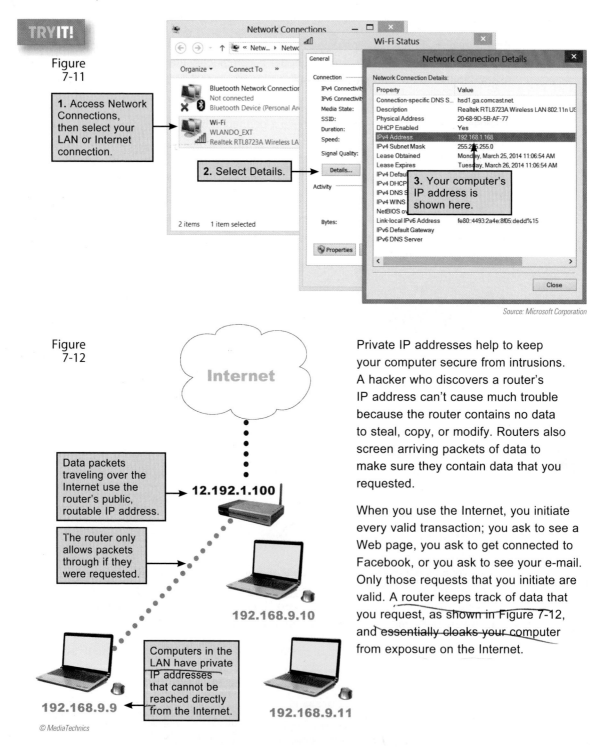

TRYIT!

Figure 7-11

1. Access Network Connections, then select your LAN or Internet connection.

2. Select Details.

3. Your computer's IP address is shown here.

Source: Microsoft Corporation

Figure 7-12

Data packets traveling over the Internet use the router's public, routable IP address.

The router only allows packets through if they were requested.

12.192.1.100

192.168.9.10

Computers in the LAN have private IP addresses that cannot be reached directly from the Internet.

192.168.9.9

192.168.9.11

© MediaTechnics

Private IP addresses help to keep your computer secure from intrusions. A hacker who discovers a router's IP address can't cause much trouble because the router contains no data to steal, copy, or modify. Routers also screen arriving packets of data to make sure they contain data that you requested.

When you use the Internet, you initiate every valid transaction; you ask to see a Web page, you ask to get connected to Facebook, or you ask to see your e-mail. Only those requests that you initiate are valid. A router keeps track of data that you request, as shown in Figure 7-12, and essentially cloaks your computer from exposure on the Internet.

Project

Explore your Internet connection

This chapter introduced you to basic concepts associated with the Internet. You were shown the types of Internet service available, some tools that can be used to check your computer's Internet connection speed, and vulnerabilities that can arise from being connected to the Internet.

When you have completed this project, you should be able to:

- Test your Internet connection speed using Ping and Traceroute.

- View Internet connection speeds worldwide.

- Test your computer's ports using the ShieldsUP!! utility.

- Find your routable and private IP addresses.

Requirements: This project requires Microsoft Windows, Paint, and browser software, such as Internet Explorer, Safari, Chrome, or Firefox. E-mail and word processing software are optional for submitting deliverables electronically.

Deliverables:

1 A screenshot of the Ping report for www.yahoo.com, along with minimum, maximum, and average times labeled and circled

2 A screenshot of the Traceroute report for www.yahoo.com, with your IP address, the total number of hops, and potential problems labeled and circled

3 A document listing the results from the Speedtest Web app

4 A screenshot of an Internet traffic report, plus a comparison of your average response time to that of the rest of your country

5 A screenshot of the ShieldsUP!! report

6 A comparison of your IP addresses from a Web report and from Windows

1. Check your Internet connection speed by pinging www.yahoo.com.

   Enter Command Prompt in the Start menu's Search box. A window displaying a command line prompt, such as in the example below, should appear.

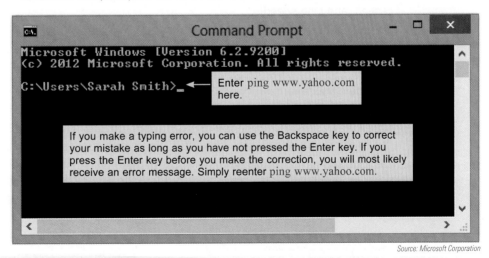

Source: Microsoft Corporation

Using the Print Screen key and the Paint program, take a screenshot of the Ping report. Use tools on Paint's toolbar to circle and label the minimum, maximum, and average times. Save the screenshot as Project 7A [Your Name] and close Paint.

• Explore your Internet connection (continued)

2. Gather more information about your Internet connection using Traceroute.

    At the next command prompt, type tracert www.yahoo.com and press the Enter key.

    Take a screenshot of the Traceroute results, which should look similar to the example below.

© MediaTechnics

3. Analyze the Traceroute results by doing the following:

    Circle and label the total number of hops.

    Circle any asterisks in your report.

    Save your screenshot as Project 7B [Your Name] and close Paint.

    Close the command prompt window by typing exit at the next command prompt.

4. Use a Web app to check the speed of your Internet connection by completing the following steps:

    Open your browser and connect to www.speedtest.net.

    Click the Begin Test button.

    When the test is complete, write down your connection's download speed, upload speed, and ping speed.

    In a sentence or two, describe how this speed compares to the speed advertised by your ISP.

5. Compare your Internet connection speed to that of the rest of the country using the Internet Traffic Report.

    Open your browser and connect to www.internettrafficreport.com. You should see a world map and statistics for connections in various regions.

    Select your region and look at the average response time. Compare it to the response time in ms that was produced by the Ping report in step 1.

    Take a screenshot of the report and save it as Project 7C [Your Name].

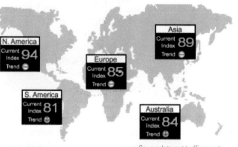

Source: Internet traffic report

• Explore your Internet connection (continued)

6. Run the ShieldsUP!! utility to check your computer for open ports by doing the following:

   Open your browser software.

   In the address bar, type www.grc.com and press the Enter key.

   Select the Services button, then select ShieldsUP!.

   Select the Common Ports test.

   When the TruStealth Analysis is displayed, scroll down to the bottom of the page and click the Text Summary button. The results should be similar to the example below.

   Take a screenshot of your summary and save it as Project 7D [Your Name]. If you are running the test on your computer, you might consider following the instructions to beef up security.

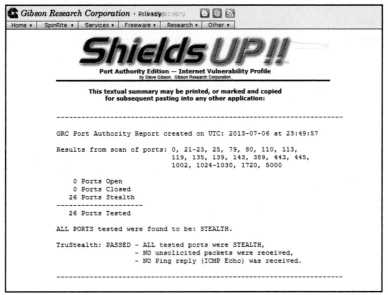

Source: Gibson Research Corporation

7. Compare your computer's IP address to your router's IP address by completing the following steps:

   Open your browser and google what's my ip address.

   Write down the address that is displayed.

   Close the browser.

   From the Start screen, type ip address, select Settings, then select *View network connections*.

   Double-click your local network.

   From the Wi-Fi status window, select Details.

   Record your IP address and note whether it is a private IP address or a routable one. (See page 118 for a list of private IP addresses.)

8. Consolidate the deliverables for Project 7 into printed format, a document file, or an e-mail message as specified by your instructor.

Issue

Do we need anonymous digital cash?

The Internet is increasingly used for **e-commerce** activities, such as shopping online, paying utility bills, and subscribing to various online services. E-commerce typically requires e-payment. Today's consumer usually pays for online transactions using a credit card. But many people wonder whether it is safe to transmit their credit card information over the Internet. Could their credit card numbers be intercepted and then used by crooks?

Although it is possible to intercept data flowing over the Internet, it is not so easy to filter out credit card numbers from the rest of the data. Your credit card number is more likely to be stolen by someone who finds a receipt in your trash or by a dishonest restaurant employee who jots down your card number while processing your dinner payment.

Online security at most e-commerce sites protects your credit card transactions by providing a special connection that encrypts your card number as it travels over the Internet. Although it is fairly safe to use your credit card on the Internet, the process has what many people view as a major disadvantage—it leaves a trail of what you buy and who you pay. Many consumers would prefer to use an anonymous form of payment.

Digital cash is an electronic replacement for cash that can be stored by your PC and spent on the Internet—without leaving a trail to its source. Bitcoin, introduced in 2008, was one of the first digital cash systems to gain acceptance. Bitcoins can be used to purchase all kinds of goods online—from yoga clothing to jewelry, candy, and cosmetics. They are accepted for donations by several nonprofit organizations such as WikiLeaks and the Electronic Frontier Foundation. Bitcoins are also used on black-market Web sites, such as Silk Road, and at porn sites.

Currently, governments issue cash because controlling the money supply plays an important role in maintaining a stable economy. Tracking purchases and other transactions has become a national security tool, and in many countries it is also a way of monitoring citizens' behaviors and beliefs. In 2013, the U.S. government took steps to regulate digital cash and other virtual currencies in an attempt to gain access to transactions and remove the cloak of anonymity associated with digital cash technologies.

Is it really a good idea to have anonymous transactions? Many honest consumers think so, but so do many criminals. With digital cash, consumers enjoy privacy with regard to their purchases, but governments lose the ability to uncover illegal transactions, identify money laundering operations, and keep close tabs on taxable income.

What do you think?

1. Have you ever felt uncomfortable providing your credit card number at an e-commerce site?   ◯ Yes ◯ No ◯ Not sure

2. Do you think that most people believe that using a credit card in a restaurant is safer than using a credit card on the Internet?   ◯ Yes ◯ No ◯ Not sure

3. Do you think that anonymous digital cash is a good idea?   ◯ Yes ◯ No ◯ Not sure

QuickCheck A

1. In addition to acting as a central point of connection for computers and other network devices, a(n) [＿＿＿＿＿＿＿＿] is also an important security device.

2. True or false? 192.168.1.1 is a private IP address, which is likely to be assigned to a router by DHCP. [＿＿＿＿＿]

3. The Internet uses a communications protocol called [＿＿＿＿＿＿＿＿] to divide messages in to packets and assign addresses to them.

4. WEP, WPA, and PSK protect wireless networks by [＿＿＿＿＿＿＿＿] data.

5. True or false? Most Internet connections are symmetrical. [＿＿＿＿＿]

CHECKIT!

QuickCheck B

Fill in the letter from the diagram that correctly matches each description.

1. An ISP router [＿＿＿]

2. A LAN router [＿＿＿]

3. An NSP router [＿＿＿]

4. A modem [＿＿＿]

5. A networked computer [＿＿＿]

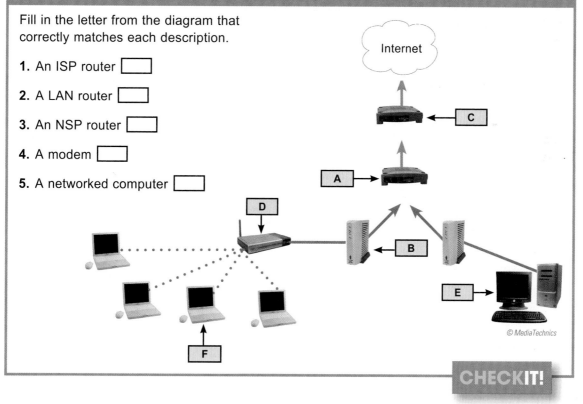

© MediaTechnics

CHECKIT!

GETIT?   While using the digital textbook, click the Get It? button to see if you can answer ten randomly selected questions from Chapter 7.

Browsing and Searching the Web

What's inside?

The Web is the most precious jewel in the crown of the Internet. On the Web you can find information, order products, interact with other people, and more! Chapter 8 highlights the Web's key features and provides tips for surfing the Web like a pro.

What's in the digital book?

In Chapter 8, you'll find out how to efficiently use a Web browser and a search engine—the two required software tools in the Web surfer's toolkit. You'll also see what goes on behind the scenes of a Web page and a browser.

FAQ What should I know about Web pages?

A **Web page** is the product or output of one or more Web-based files, which are displayed on your computer in a format similar to a page in a book. Unlike book pages, however, Web pages can dynamically incorporate pictures, videos, sounds, and interactive elements. Millions of Web pages are interlinked and available on an Internet service called the **Web** (short for the "World Wide Web").

The computers that store Web pages are known as **Web servers**. Each Web server hosts one or more **Web sites** that contain information about a specific topic, company, organization, person, event, or place. The main page for a Web site is sometimes referred to as a **home page**.

Every Web page has a unique URL that functions as its address. A **URL** (uniform resource locator) specifies the Web server that stores the page, the folder (or folders) that hold the page, and the name of the page. For example, the Wikipedia page about love has the following URL: http://en.wikipedia.org/wiki/Love.

You can navigate to a Web page by using its URL or clicking links. Clickable links between Web pages, sometimes called **hypertext links**, allow you to follow a thread of information from one Web page to another within a site or across to other sites. **Text links** usually appear as underlined words in colors such as blue, green, or orange. Some Web pages also have **graphics links** that appear as pictures, rather than as underlined text. When you point to a text or graphics link, the arrow-shaped pointer changes to a hand-shaped **link pointer**.

By clicking a link, you are requesting the Web page indicated by the link. To fulfill your request, a Web server sends data for the Web page to your PC's memory. Your PC can then display the Web page on the screen.

Figure
8-1

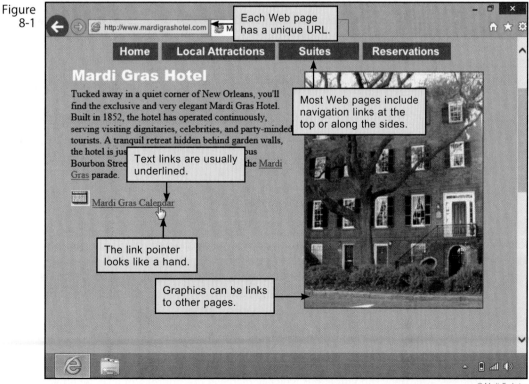

FAQ How do I access the Web?

The Web is one of the Internet's most popular services, so access requires an Internet connection. You'll also need software called a **browser** that displays Web pages and helps you navigate from one page to another. Windows includes a browser called Internet Explorer (IE). Other popular browsers include Google Chrome and Mozilla Firefox.

You can start Internet Explorer by selecting its tile on the Windows Start screen or by selecting the 🅔 icon from the desktop. Select the Try It! button for a tour of Internet Explorer's key features.

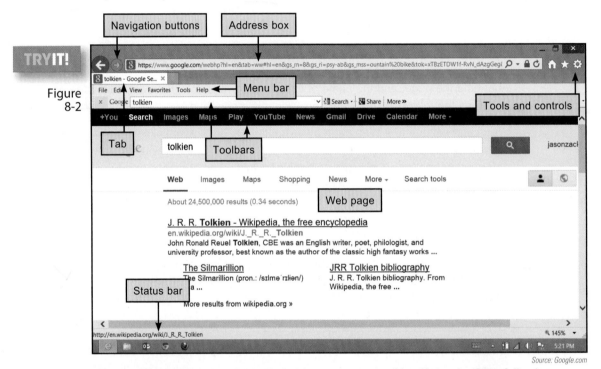

Figure
8-2

Source: Google.com

When working with a new browser, make sure you can identify each of the following elements:

- **Web page window.** The Web page appears in the main panel of the browser window.

- **Navigation buttons.** Forward and back buttons navigate from one page to another.

- **Address bar.** The address bar displays the address of the current Web page and can be used to enter the address of pages you would like to view.

- **Tools and controls.** Browsers provide icons for quick access to security settings and personal preferences.

- **Tabs.** Each tab provides access to a Web page when you have multiple pages open at the same time.

- **Menu bar.** The menu of browser commands may be presented on a toolbar or menu bar. In some browsers these options are hidden unless you turn them on in settings or display them using a shortcut key such as Alt.

- **Toolbars.** Browsers can display various toolbars. For example, the Google toolbar provides a Search box so you can search the Web from any page.

 - **Status bar.** The status bar typically displays the address of links when you hover the pointer over them.

FAQ How do I locate information on the Web?

The most popular way to find information on the Web is by using a **search engine**, such as Google, Ask.com, Yahoo! Search, or Bing. Depending on the search engine, you can look for information by entering keywords, filling out a form, or clicking a series of links to drill down through a list of topics and subtopics.

TRYIT!

Figure
8-3

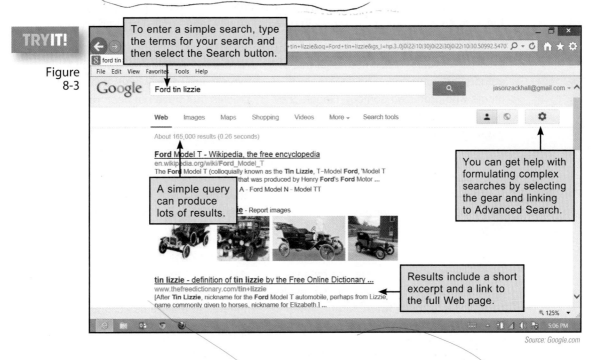

To enter a simple search, type the terms for your search and then select the Search button.

A simple query can produce lots of results.

You can get help with formulating complex searches by selecting the gear and linking to Advanced Search.

Results include a short excerpt and a link to the full Web page.

Source: Google.com

- When entering keywords, be as specific as possible. A keyword search for "Ford" produces millions of links to pages about Ford automobiles, as well as pages about former president Gerald Ford and actor Harrison Ford. "Ford tin lizzie" formulates a much more targeted search and returns a more manageable number of results.

- As a general rule, the more keywords you use, the more targeted your search becomes. You can often refine your search by looking at the short descriptions presented by the search results and using keywords from those results that seem most pertinent to your search.

- Search engines provide tools for advanced searches. These tools vary somewhat, depending on which search engine you're using, but are explained in detail somewhere on the search engine Web site. In general, advanced search tools help you formulate searches based on exact phrases, Boolean operators, dates, and file types.

- An exact-phrase search requires the search engine to find pages that include a particular phrase with the words occurring in a specified order. To specify an exact-phrase search, surround the phrase with quotation marks.

- A Boolean search uses the operators (or symbols) AND (+), OR, and NOT (-) to specify how your keywords are to be combined. For example, if a search for Model T automobile turns up a lot of pages about car clubs that don't interest you, refine your search by entering Model T automobile -club. Using the minus sign before the word "club" indicates you don't want to see links to any pages containing that word.

FAQ How do I separate online facts from fiction?

The quality of information available online varies. Some is accurate and complete, whereas other information is erroneous, deliberately misleading, or false. You may find articles that are well researched, factual, and meticulously documented. Other articles may be based entirely on opinion, rumors, or made-up statistics. The following tips should prove useful for evaluating the quality of information at a Web site. Try applying them to the Web page shown in Figure 8-4 to give it a quality rating of 1 (low) to 5 (high).

Who produced the content and what are their credentials? Look for the names of authors, photographers, designers, and others who produced content. Google their names to link to their biographies, social pages, or other work.

What is the top-level domain? Recognizing .edu, .com, .org, and other top-level domains helps to classify the person, organization, or business that is responsible for the site.

What else can the URL tell you? The Web page title or site name can help you identify whether the information is provided by a Web site, blog, tweet, forum, news aggregator, or social network post.

Who sponsors the site? Check the site copyright or About page to determine who or what is the site sponsor.

Is the material date-appropriate? Check the date when the material was created or posted.

Has the information been peer reviewed? Articles reviewed by topic experts are usually more accurate than articles that have not been reviewed. If an article includes public comments, those comments may provide insight into the accuracy or bias of the author.

Are there ads on the page? Sites with advertising might not publish content that is unfavorable to its advertisers.

Did the material originate at the site, or was it re-posted, republished, or retweeted? Redistributed material might be altered; you can refer to the original material to ensure its accuracy.

Is the material a mashup or derivative work? Stay alert for doctored photos and parodies.

What is the site's access policy? Sites that require a subscription or registration may have higher quality information, or information that is tailored to a specific clientele.

Figure 8-4

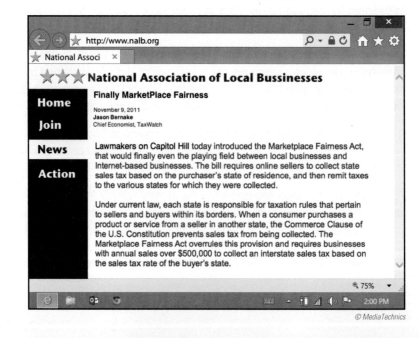

© MediaTechnics

FAQ Can I save text and graphics that I find on the Web?

If you come across an interesting article or graphic on the Web, you might want to save it on your PC. You can save a copy of an entire Web page, or just save selected paragraphs. You can also save copies of Web page graphics, including photos and borders.

Save the entire Web page. Click or touch File. (If the menu is not displayed, press the Alt key.) Select Save As, then specify a file name and location.

Save text from a page. Highlight the text, then right-click the highlighted passage. Select Copy or press Ctrl C. Switch to your word processor software, then select Paste.

Save a graphic. Right-click the graphic, then select *Save picture as*. Specify a file name and location.

When using material from the Web, be sure to respect the author's intellectual property rights. Assume that everything you see on the Web is copyrighted. If you would like to use a graphic that you've downloaded, you should obtain permission by e-mailing the copyright holder. Look for the copyright holder's e-mail address at the bottom of the Web page that contains the graphic, or check the main page of the site.

When incorporating Web page text excerpts into your own documents, you must include a citation that follows a standard style, such as MLA or APA. The citation should contain the author's name, the title of the Web page, the title of the site, the date of publication, the date when you accessed the page, and the URL for the page, as in the example below:

Canine, Claire. "No One Knows You're a Dog." <u>Dogs on the Net</u>. 2009. 11 Nov. 2011 <http://www.dogsonthenet.org/main.html>.

Click the Try It! button to find out how to save a copy of text and graphics that you find on Web pages.

Figure 8-5

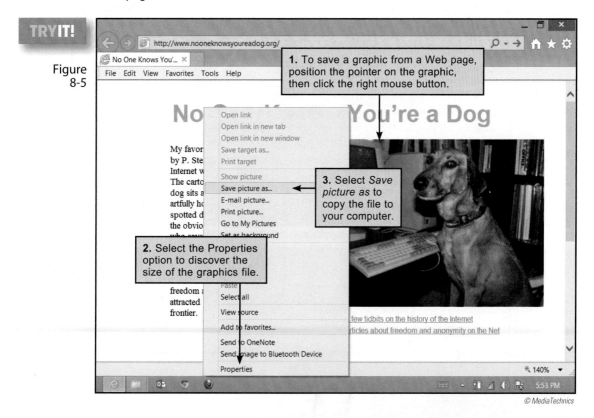

FAQ Is the Web safe?

Among the millions of businesses and individuals that offer products, services, and information on the Web, some are unscrupulous and try to take advantage of unwary shoppers, chat group participants, and researchers. Internet-borne viruses and online credit card fraud are regularly featured on news reports. However, security tools and some common sense can make using the Web as safe as, or safer than, paying with a credit card at your local mall.

Use a secure connection for sensitive data. Most commercial Web sites encrypt sensitive information sent to and from the site during the payment phase of an e-commerce purchase. URLs for secure Web connections begin with *https* instead of *http*. Before submitting credit card numbers, Social Security numbers, or other sensitive data, look for https in the URL and a padlock icon in the browser window.

Figure
8-6

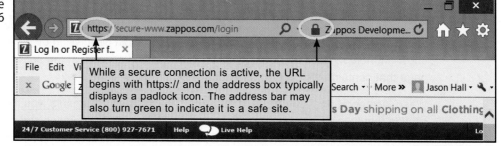

Source: Microsoft Corporation

Block third-party cookies. A Web site might store a cookie on your computer's hard disk. A **cookie** is a small chunk of data generated by a Web server and stored in a text file on your computer's hard disk. Cookies can be used to keep track of the pages you view at a site, the merchandise you select, and other profile information. Legitimate cookies are necessary for key Web operations.

Some Web sites, however, feature banner ads supplied by third-party marketing firms. If you click the ad, this third party can create a **third-party cookie** and use it to track your activities at any site containing banner ads from that third party. You can block third-party cookies, as shown in Figure 8-7.

Figure
8-7

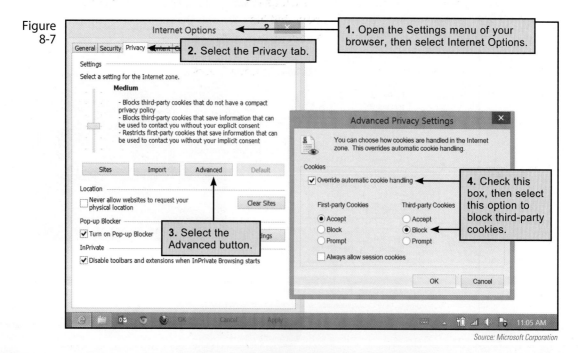

Source: Microsoft Corporation

Is the Web safe? (continued)

Erase your tracks on public computers. A **browser cache** is a temporary local storage area for Web page elements. As you jump back to previously viewed pages, the text and graphics for those pages can be retrieved from the browser cache in your computer's memory or on the hard disk, rather than being downloaded again from a Web server.

Web pages in the cache are a sort of record of your activities on the Web. Like cookies, a cache is relatively safe; but you might want to clear it if you use a public computer, if you're concerned that people with access to your computer might be curious about your Web activities, or if you're short on hard disk space. You can delete the browser history manually by following the steps in Figure 8-8.

Figure
8-8

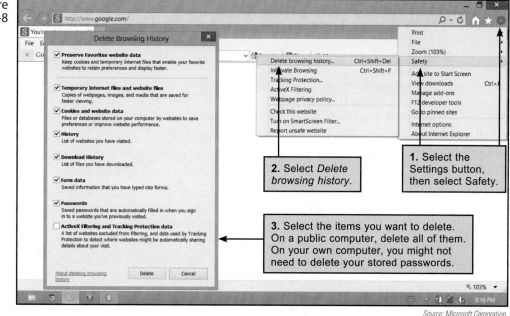

Source: Microsoft Corporation

Rather than manually deleting the browser cache, you can take advantage of **private browsing** offered by browsers such as Internet Explorer. When private browsing is turned on, cookies are stored in memory, but they are cleared when you close the browser. Temporary Internet files are stored on disk, but they are deleted when the browser is closed. Web page history, form data, and passwords are not stored. Figure 8-9 explains how to turn on InPrivate browsing for Internet Explorer.

Figure
8-9

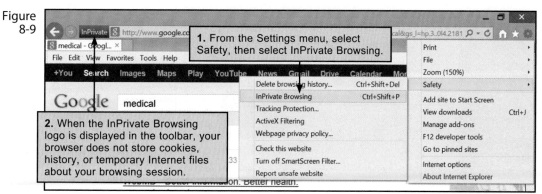

Source: Microsoft Corporation

Technology

HTML, URLs, and HTTP

 The Web is based on a trilogy of foundational technologies: HTML, URLs, and HTTP. Understanding these technologies makes it easier to understand what makes the Web work and why it entails some security risks.

HTML. Most Web pages are stored as HTML documents. **HTML** (Hypertext Markup Language) is a set of instructions that can be embedded into a document to produce specific effects, such as bold text, colored backgrounds, and underlined links.

Embedded instructions are called **HTML tags** and they are encased in angle brackets. For example, when creating a title in an HTML document, you can specify that it will be displayed in bold by using the <b> HTML tag. The <imagedata src> tag is used to insert an image; the <a href> tag is used to create a hypertext link.

An HTML document is like a screenplay, and your browser is like a director who makes a screenplay come to life by assembling cast members and making sure they deliver their lines correctly. As the HTML "screenplay" unfolds, your browser follows the instructions in an HTML document to display lines of text on your computer screen in the right color, size, and position.

If the screenplay calls for a graphic, your browser collects it from the Web server and displays it. Although the HTML screenplay exists as a permanent file, the Web page you see on your computer screen exists only for the duration of the "performance."

Technically speaking, you can distinguish HTML documents (the screenplay) from Web pages (the performance). However, in everyday conversation, the term "Web page" is often used for the HTML document as well as the Web page displayed on the screen.

An HTML document is sometimes referred to as a **source document** because it is the source of the instructions used to construct a Web page. You can view the HTML source documents for most Web pages if you are curious about how they were constructed. When using Internet Explorer, select Source from the View menu. (If menus are hidden, use the Alt key to display them.)

Figure 8-10 illustrates the difference between an HTML source document and the Web page it produces. The Try It! shows you even more.

TRYIT!

Figure 8-10

The HTML document for the Healthy Cooking Web page contains no graphics, but an <imagedata src> tag produces one when the Web page is displayed.

`<v: imagedata src="index_files/veggies.jpg">`

This graphic is displayed by an HTML tag.

Source document

Web page displayed by browser

© MediaTechnics

Technology
(continued)

The framework for an HTML document consists of two sections: the head and the body. The head section begins with <!DOCTYPE html> and <head> tags. It may also include information that defines global properties, including the Web page title that appears in the browser tabs and information about the page that can be used by search engines.

The body section of an HTML document begins with the <body> HTML tag. This section of the document contains text, HTML tags that format the text, plus a variety of links to graphics, sounds, and videos. Figure 8-11 contains basic HTML for a Web page. You can use it as a template for creating your own pages.

Figure 8-11

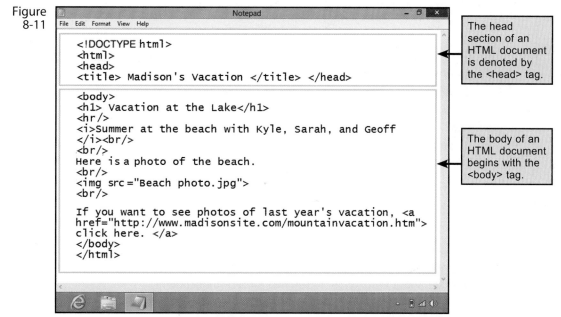

The head section of an HTML document is denoted by the <head> tag.

The body of an HTML document begins with the <body> tag.

Source: Microsoft Corporation

URLs. Most Web sites have a main page that acts as a doorway to the rest of the pages at the site. The URL for a Web site's main page is normally short and to the point, like www.cnn.com. The inclusion of www is a convention that indicates a Web server.

Web pages are stored as files on a Web server. Files can be grouped into folders, similar to the way in which files and folders are stored on your personal computer. The URL for a Web page includes the server name and the name of any folders and subfolders that hold the file. For example, the CNN Web server might store files for weather information at www.cnn.com/weather/ and files for entertainment information at www.cnn.com/showbiz/.

The file name of a specific Web page always appears last in the URL. Web page file names usually have an .htm or .html extension, indicating that the page was created with Hypertext Markup Language. Figure 8-12 helps you identify the parts of a URL.

Figure 8-12

http://www.cnn.com/showbiz/movies.htm

Web protocol standard   Web server name   Folder name   File name and file extension

© MediaTechnics

Technology
(continued)

HTTP. **HTTP** (Hypertext Transfer Protocol) is a protocol that works with TCP/IP to get Web resources to your desktop. A Web resource can be defined as any chunk of data that has a URL, such as an HTML document, a graphic, or a sound file.

Understanding how HTTP works explains why your browser cache grows so large, why connecting to the Web opens a potentially unsecure port on your computer, and why cookies are necessary.

An HTTP exchange takes place over a pair of sockets. A **socket** is an abstract concept that represents a port at one end of a connection. For HTTP, sockets routinely are associated with port 80 on the client and server. Port 80 is open whenever you access the Web. Like any open port, it is a potential security weakness that a hacker could exploit.

In an HTTP exchange, your browser opens a socket on your PC, connects to a similar open socket at the Web server, and issues a command, such as "send me an HTML document." The server receives the command, executes it, and sends a response back through the socket. The sockets are then closed until the browser is ready to issue another command. The Web page you see in your browser might consist of many text and graphic elements, each requiring a separate transfer. These are the files that build up in your browser cache.

Each HTTP exchange transmits one element of a Web page. When the sockets are closed, the server essentially forgets your previous requests. A cookie is a mechanism that helps a Web server remember your activities at the site. Cookies provide information about the pages that you've visited and items that you've loaded into your shopping cart.

Figure 8-13 demonstrates how HTTP handles the messages that flow between your browser and a Web server to retrieve an HTML document.

Figure 8-13

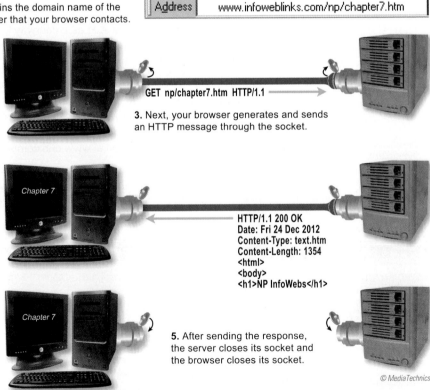

1. The URL in the browser's Address box contains the domain name of the Web server that your browser contacts.

Address www.infoweblinks.com/np/chapter7.htm

2. Your browser opens a socket and connects to a similar open socket at the Web server.

GET np/chapter7.htm HTTP/1.1

3. Next, your browser generates and sends an HTTP message through the socket.

4. The server sends back the requested HTML document through the open sockets.

Chapter 7

HTTP/1.1 200 OK
Date: Fri 24 Dec 2012
Content-Type: text.htm
Content-Length: 1354
<html>
<body>
<h1>NP InfoWebs</h1>

Chapter 7

5. After sending the response, the server closes its socket and the browser closes its socket.

© MediaTechnics

Project

Explore browser security

The Web has made the world a much smaller place, allowing people of all cultures and languages to have a wealth of information at their fingertips. To enable you to comfortably surf the Web for documents, videos, music, photos, and all sorts of products, you were introduced to two of the Web's most significant tools (browsers and search engines) along with the trilogy of Web technologies (HTML, URLs, and HTTP).

When you have completed the project, you should be able to:

- Identify the elements used by your browser to indicate that a Web site is secure and legitimate.

- Find out if your browser is set to block third-party cookies.

- Turn location services on and off.

- Take steps to erase your browser cache.

Requirements: This project requires Microsoft Windows and a browser. Internet Explorer is recommended.

Deliverables:

1   A screenshot of your browser displaying the Bank of America home page with three security items circled

2   The answer to the question in Step 9

1.   Open a browser, such as Internet Explorer, and navigate to the Bank of America Web site at www.bankofamerica.com.

Source: Microsoft Corporation

2.   When the Bank of America Web site is displayed, the address bar includes three elements that indicate this is a secure and legitimate site. Take a screenshot and use Paint to add callouts identifying those three elements. Save your screenshot as Project 8 [Your Name].

• Explore browser security (continued)

3. Cookies can be used to track your browsing habits, and third-party cookies are frequently used to compile your shopping profile and display targeted advertising. Check your browser settings to make sure it is blocking third-party cookies. To complete this step using Internet Explorer:

    Select the ⚙ Settings icon.

    Select Internet Options.

    Select the Privacy tab.

    Select the Advanced button.

    Make sure that first-party cookies are marked Accept.

    Make sure that third-party cookies are marked Block.

    Click the OK button, then close the Internet Options window.

4. You can keep your location private, whether you are using a desktop computer or a mobile device, by turning your browser's location services off. To complete this step using Windows Explorer:

    Select the ⚙ Settings icon.

    Select Internet Options.

    Select the Privacy tab.

    Select the option *Never allow websites to request your physical location*.

    Click the OK button, then close the Internet Options window.

Source: Microsoft Corporation

5. Browsers store information about the sites you've visited in the History list and browser cache. Make sure that you know how to delete the browser history. To delete the browser history in Internet Explorer:

    Select the ⚙ Settings icon.

    Select Safety.

    Select *Delete browsing history*.

    When using a public computer, you should check all the boxes so that your browsing history is completely deleted.

    At home, you may choose not to delete some of the history data. For example, you might want to retain the saved passwords that you use for sites such as Facebook and Gmail.

    Clear any history items if you would like to do so.

    Close the Delete Browsing History window.

• Explore browser security (continued)

6. Suppose that you are using a public computer, and you would like your browser to automatically delete the history information when you close it. To do so, you can activate private browsing. To start Internet Explorer's InPrivate Browsing feature:

   Select the ⚙ Settings icon.

   Select Safety.

   Select InPrivate Browsing.

InPrivate is turned on

When InPrivate Browsing is turned on, you will see this indicator

| InPrivate | 🌐 about:InPrivate | ▼ ↻ ✕ |

InPrivate Browsing helps prevent Internet Explorer from storing data about your browsing session. This includes cookies, temporary Internet files, history, and other data. Toolbars and extensions are disabled by default. See Help for more information.

To turn off InPrivate Browsing, close this browser window.

Source: Microsoft Corporation

Read the information supplied on the screen so that you know how InPrivate Browsing works.

7. Test the InPrivate Browsing feature to make sure it works. To complete this step using Internet Explorer:

   Navigate to www.oldtowncanoe.com and make sure that InPrivate Browsing is still active.

   Navigate to your home page.

   Look at your History list for today.

   Make sure that Old Town Canoe is not listed.

   Close your browser window.

   Reopen your browser window. Because you have started a new browser session, InPrivate Browsing should no longer be active.

   Look at your History list. As before, Old Town Canoe should not be included.

8. Close your browser.

9. Thinking back over the activities in this lab, how do you expect each of these settings to be configured when you start your browser again?

   First-party cookies

   Third-party cookies

   Location Services

   InPrivate Browsing

10. Submit your screenshot from Step 2 and your answer for the question in Step 9 as an e-mail message, as an e-mail attachment, as a printout, on a USB flash drive, or in any other format specified by your instructor.

Issue

Is it filtering or censorship?

Democracies have a rich tradition of free speech and a free press that stands watch against censorship. Developments on the Internet have brought new attention to the tug-of-war between free speech and public decency. Without too much effort, anyone surfing the Internet can find some very unsavory material, including child pornography, hate group rhetoric, terrorist handbooks, graphic violence, and sexually explicit Web pages.

Many parents are concerned about what their children might encounter while surfing the Web. Even an innocent search for "Valentine" might lead to Web sites where sex is for sale. **Filtering software** makes it possible to block access to certain Web sites. Most operating systems include basic filtering software, and more sophisticated products can be purchased from third-party developers. Parents can activate this software on their home PCs, select the sites that they want to block, and use a password to prevent anyone else from removing the blocks.

In many communities, children also have access to the Internet from computers at school and the public library. Although filtering software makes it possible to block access to sites on these PCs, some librarians are reluctant to use it. They fear that it would be impossible to reach a consensus on the sites that should be filtered.

Even more controversial is the use of broad-scale filtering by government censors. Many dictatorial regimes do not want their citizens to have access to political and cultural ideas that conflict with official government ideology. More than 20 countries use sophisticated tools to block Web sites, filter e-mail, and censor discussion groups. Technology giants, such as Microsoft, Yahoo!, and Cisco Systems, have been criticized for providing foreign governments with tools for blocking culturally objectionable sites. Critics question whether companies in a free society should aid foreign governments' attempts to censor cyberspace.

What do you think?

1. If you had children, would you use filtering software on your home PC to block access to certain Web sites?   ○ Yes   ○ No   ○ Not sure

2. Do you think schools and public libraries that provide Internet access to children should use filtering software?   ○ Yes   ○ No   ○ Not sure

3. Should a government prevent its citizens from accessing Web-based material that does not conform with its political and cultural agenda?   ○ Yes   ○ No   ○ Not sure

QuickCheck A

1. Now that you understand how URLs are constructed, you could guess that the URL for Microsoft's home page is http:// [_____] .

2. Your PC is able to display a Web page correctly because your browser can interpret [_____] tags. (Hint: Use the acronym.)

3. When you shop at an e-commerce site, the site's Web server will probably create a(n) [_____] and store it on your PC.

4. True or false? HTTP tags such as <b> are inserted in Web pages and interpreted by your browser. [_____]

5. Yahoo! and Google are popular [_____] engines.

CHECKIT!

QuickCheck B

Fill in the letter from the diagram that correctly matches each description below.

1. A text link [____]

2. A URL [____]

3. The link pointer [____]

4. Tabs [____]

5. Settings [____]

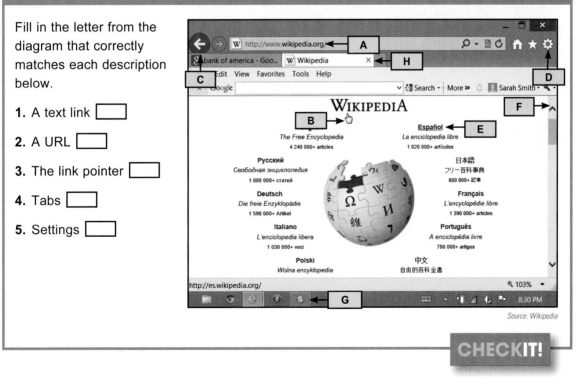

Source: Wikipedia

CHECKIT!

GETIT? While using the digital textbook, click the Get It? button to see if you can answer ten randomly selected questions from Chapter 8.

CHAPTER

9 Sending E-mail and Attachments

What's inside?

Chapter 9 takes you from e-mail basics to more advanced topics such as attachments and file compression. You'll get some tips on avoiding spam so you can protect your identity and keep your data secure.

What's in the digital book?

In addition to the basics of creating, reading, replying to, and forwarding e-mail, you'll learn how to use both Webmail and local e-mail, how to send attachments, and how to compress those attachments for more efficient transmission.

FAQ How does e-mail work?

E-mail (also called email or electronic mail) is an electronic version of the postal system. An **e-mail message** is a digital document that can be transmitted from one computer to another, usually over the Internet. E-mail is easy to use, delivers mail in a matter of minutes, and lets you broadcast a message simultaneously to more than one person.

The computers and software that provide e-mail services form an **e-mail system**. At the heart of a typical e-mail system is an **e-mail server**—a computer that essentially acts as a central post office serving a group of people. It runs special **e-mail server software** that provides an electronic mailbox for each person, sorts incoming messages into these mailboxes, and routes outgoing mail over the Internet to other e-mail servers. Many ISPs maintain an e-mail server to handle electronic mail for their subscribers. To access an e-mail system, you must have an account on an e-mail server and your PC must have software that helps you read, compose, and send messages.

Two types of e-mail systems are commonly used: Webmail and local mail. With **Webmail**, you connect to the Web to read and compose e-mail messages using Web browser software, such as Internet Explorer, Chrome, or Firefox. Your incoming mail remains on the Web server, rather than your own computer. The advantage of Webmail is that you can easily access it from any computer that has an Internet connection.

Local e-mail allows you to compose and read your mail while you are offline. It is called local e-mail because you run e-mail software that's installed on your local hard disk or USB drive, and because you store your incoming mail there, too. "Local" doesn't mean that your mail is limited to a local area network; you can use local e-mail to send messages anywhere on the Internet.

Local e-mail is based on **store-and-forward technology**, which means that an e-mail server stores incoming messages until your client computer connects and requests them. The server then forwards this mail to your computer when you're ready to read it.

Local e-mail is sometimes called **POP mail**, a name derived from the Post Office Protocol software used on the e-mail server that holds mail until your computer retrieves it.

Figure 9-1 illustrates the differences between Webmail and local e-mail. Remember, you don't have to limit yourself to one type of e-mail account; you can have a Webmail account and a local account.

Figure
9-1

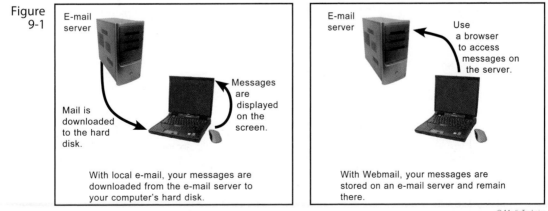

With local e-mail, your messages are downloaded from the e-mail server to your computer's hard disk.

With Webmail, your messages are stored on an e-mail server and remain there.

© *MediaTechnics*

FAQ How do I set up local e-mail?

Before you can work with a local e-mail system, you need an e-mail account, an e-mail address, and a password on a POP server. Most ISPs offer e-mail accounts and instructions on how to set one up on your computer. As part of the setup process, you must have local **e-mail client software**, such as Microsoft Outlook or Mozilla Thunderbird.

When you want to compose or read e-mail messages, your first step is to start your e-mail client. To get your mail, connect to the mail server and download new messages to your **Inbox**, a folder on your PC's hard disk that holds incoming e-mail. Selecting a button labeled Send/Receive usually initiates the download process.

To compose a new message, simply fill in the e-mail header and then type the text of your message. With a broadband Internet connection, you can send each message as it is completed. With a dial-up connection, you can compose your messages offline and queue them in your Outbox. The **Outbox** is a folder on your PC's hard disk that temporarily stores outgoing e-mail messages. When you're ready to send the messages, use the Send/Receive button to connect to the mail server. Your e-mail client software then transmits the message files from your Outbox to the mail server.

Because local e-mail is stored on your computer's hard disk, you control messages once they have been downloaded. But even after you download messages, copies of them remain on backups of the e-mail server, which are not necessarily secure or private. If your computer hard disk crashes, you can't access those backups. Therefore, it is your responsibility to back up your mail. Consult the Help file for your e-mail client software to find out how to archive your e-mail to protect it in case of a hardware failure.

Click the Try It! button for an overview of local e-mail using Microsoft Outlook; you'll see how to use basic features as well as how to set up an account.

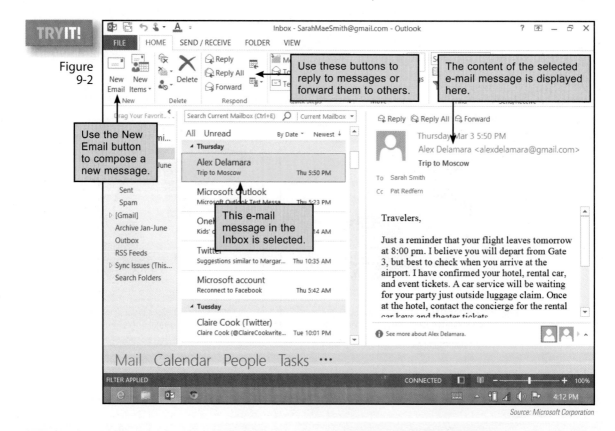

Figure 9-2

FAQ What should I know about Webmail?

The most popular free Webmail services are Google Gmail, Outlook.com, and Yahoo! Mail. To obtain a Webmail account, connect to the provider's Web site and enter the information required to obtain an e-mail address, a user ID, and a password.

Armed with these identifiers, use a browser on any computer to connect to the Webmail site where you can write, read, reply to, and delete e-mail messages. In addition to basic e-mail activities, your Webmail service might provide tools for automatically filtering and organizing messages based on the subject of the message or the person who sent it.

Most Webmail services also provide subscribers with tools to block unwanted messages, report nuisance e-mail, and deal with malicious exploits that could result in identity theft. Be sure to check Help for your Webmail to become familiar with all the tools that are available to you.

One of the advantages of Webmail is its availability from any computer that's connected to the Internet. Accessibility is a great feature when you're traveling or on the go and don't have your own computer with you. You can get your mail from a computer in a school lab, at work, in a coffee shop, or in an airport. When using a public computer to access your e-mail account, it is important to log off when you are done to make sure that unauthorized persons do not use your account.

Disadvantages of Webmail include not being able to access mail during an Internet outage, and the potential privacy risk of storing your e-mail on a remote server where your messages could be accessed without your knowledge or approval. Figure 9-3 contains an overview of the main elements of Gmail.

Figure 9-3

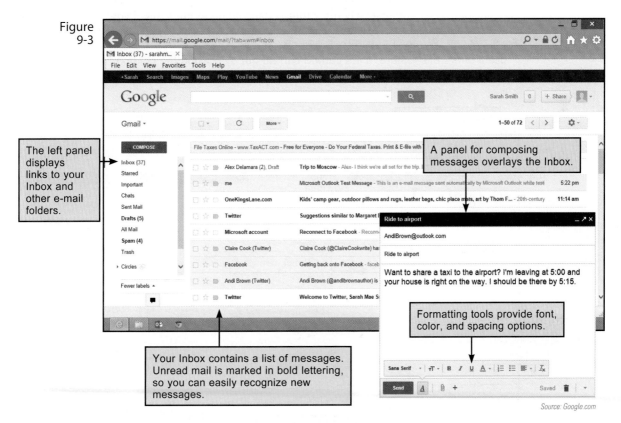

The left panel displays links to your Inbox and other e-mail folders.

A panel for composing messages overlays the Inbox.

Your Inbox contains a list of messages. Unread mail is marked in bold lettering, so you can easily recognize new messages.

Formatting tools provide font, color, and spacing options.

Source: Google.com

FAQ How can I organize messages and contacts?

Sifting through thousands of messages in an unorganized Inbox is inefficient, so it pays to learn how to use the organizational tools your e-mail client offers. E-mail clients differ, but most offer tools for the following organizational activities:

- **Mark as read or unread.** Unread mail is usually displayed in bold, and that feature helps to ensure that you've not missed an important message. Once you open a message, the bold font is removed and the message status becomes "read." You can manually change the read/unread status of a message. The most typical use of this feature would be when you've read a message but want to respond to it later. Using the Unread/Read option reinstates the bold font, putting the message visually in a category with unread messages.

- **Prioritize.** Your e-mail client might provide a way to prioritize messages, allowing you to deal with the most urgent correspondence first. For example, in Gmail, you can select the star icon or the important icon. Then you can group messages using those categories.

- **Group.** You can group e-mail messages that pertain to a specific subject in a folder. You can also create folders to hold old messages so that they don't clog up your inbox.

- **Label.** Mail clients, such as Gmail, allow you to add grouping labels to messages, then use search filters to display all messages with matching labels.

- **Work with threads.** An **e-mail thread** (sometimes referred to as a conversation) consists of an original message and all of the replies and forwards that stem from it. The ability to pull up all the messages that pertain to a thread can be useful. Some e-mail packages automatically track threads according to the subject line.

- **Sort.** It can be handy to sort messages by sender, rather than by date. If your e-mail client offers this feature, sorts can be carried out by clicking the column headings in the Inbox listing.

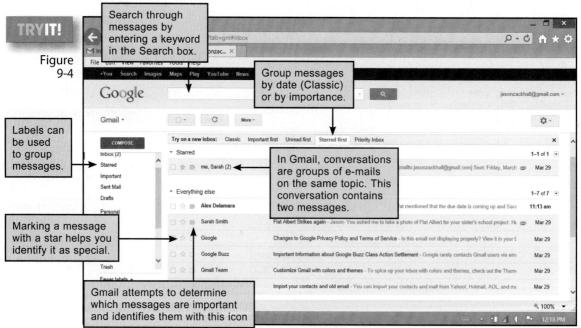

TRY IT!

Figure 9-4

Search through messages by entering a keyword in the Search box.

Group messages by date (Classic) or by importance.

Labels can be used to group messages.

In Gmail, conversations are groups of e-mails on the same topic. This conversation contains two messages.

Marking a message with a star helps you identify it as special.

Gmail attempts to determine which messages are important and identifies them with this icon

Source: Google.com

FAQ What should I know about sending e-mail attachments?

E-mail systems were originally designed for sending short, text-only messages. If you want to send graphics, video, music, software, or large document files, you can use e-mail attachments. An **e-mail attachment** is a file that travels along with an e-mail message.

You can attach files that are in virtually any format, including DOCX documents, PDF documents, MP3 music, and JPEG images. Although you can technically send any type of file as an attachment, in practice, some types of files are blocked by various e-mail systems because they tend to harbor viruses. Files with executable extensions, such as .exe, .com, .bat, and .app, are blocked by most e-mail servers. If you have reason to send these types of files, zip them first. You'll learn more about zipping files in the Technology section of this chapter.

Most people are on alert for e-mail scams and understand the potential danger of attachments that could contain malware. To help assure recipients that your attachments are legitimate, refer to them in the body of your message.

You can also help recipients by indicating which software you used to create the attachment. You might say, for example, "This e-mail includes a DOCX attachment created with Microsoft Word 2013." That information will give recipients a clue about the software they can use to open and view the attachments you've sent.

Figure 9-5 explains more about e-mail attachments. Click the Try It! button to learn how to send them.

TRYIT!

Figure 9-5

1. When using Outlook to send an attachment, first create a reply or create a new message and address it as usual.

3. Click the Attach File button, then select a file from the Insert File list.

4. The name of the file you've selected for the attachment is listed in the header.

2. The text of your message should contain a brief explanation about the attachment.

Jason-
You asked me to take a photo of Flat Albert for your sister's school project. Here it is.

Source: Microsoft Corporation

FAQ What should I know about receiving attachments?

Most e-mail software indicates the existence of an attachment with an icon, such as a paper clip. Some attachments harbor viruses, so you should exercise caution when opening them—especially those with an .exe extension. Never open an e-mail attachment from an unknown sender. Most antivirus software automatically scans attachments as they are delivered to your Inbox. Check your antivirus software to make sure this feature is turned on.

Typically, you can double-click the paperclip icon to open the attachment. Attachments open, however, only if your PC has software that can work with files stored in the format of the attachment. For example, if you receive an e-mail message with a DOCX attachment, you can open it only if your PC has word processing software, such as Microsoft Word, that can work with DOCX files.

Various e-mail clients work with attachments in different ways. Gmail automatically displays attachments containing photos, whereas Outlook does not. Neither e-mail client automatically displays attachments containing documents, PDFs, and other types of files. To display the contents of these types of attachments, look for a Preview button or View link. If a preview is not available, save the attachment and then open it with a software application.

The steps for saving an attachment depend on the e-mail client you're using. In general, Webmail attachments are downloaded from the mail server if and when you save them. Attachments to local mail are stored in a temporary folder on your computer's hard disk; the process of saving an attachment moves it to one of your personal folders. Select the Try It! button for Figure 9-6 to work with Outlook to save an attachment.

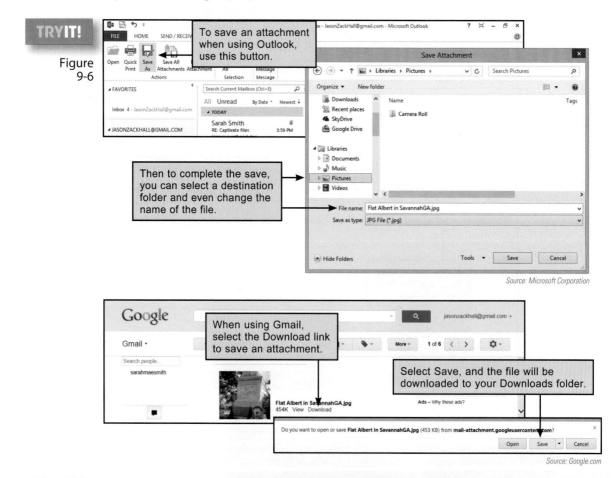

Figure
9-6

Source: Microsoft Corporation

Source: Google.com

FAQ How should I deal with spam?

One of e-mail's main disadvantages is **spam**—unwanted electronic junk messages about medical products, low-cost loans, and fake software upgrades that arrive in your online mailbox. Today's proliferation of spam is generated by marketing firms that harvest e-mail addresses from mailing lists, membership applications, and Web sites.

In the past, spam flooding your Inbox with unsolicited and often pornographic messages was merely an annoyance. These days, however, spam has turned into another major hacking tool for cybercriminals. Spam sometimes contains viruses, worms, and other malicious software that can wreak havoc on your computer or steal personal information such as passwords. Spam can also be used for phishing scams. **Phishing** is an e-mail–based scam that's designed to persuade you to reveal confidential information, such as your bank account number or Social Security number.

A potentially damaging spam scam starts with an e-mail message that appears to come from a legitimate organization such as a bank, an online payment service, an online store, or even your ISP. The message directs you to click a link to verify confidential data. The link connects you to a bogus site cleverly disguised to look very much like a legitimate Web site. There you are urged to enter your bank account number, PIN, password, credit card number, or other data.

You can reduce the amount of spam that shows up in your Inbox by using spam filters. A **spam filter** is a type of utility software that captures unsolicited e-mail messages before they reach your Inbox. It works by checking the text of e-mail headers and messages based on a series of rules. For example, a rule such as "Message header contains viagra, v1agra, or vi@gra" would help identify spam that's trying to hawk cheap pharmaceuticals. Spam filters are included in most security software.

Another way to reduce spam is to use a disposable e-mail address when you have to register at Web sites that are primarily interested in beefing up their mass mailing databases. A **disposable e-mail address** is simply a Webmail account that you can discontinue if your account begins to accumulate lots of spam. Figure 9-7 lists steps that can help to reduce the amount of spam you receive.

Figure
9-7

- Never reply to spam when you receive it.

- Don't click links in e-mail messages, even if it's an opt-out link.

- Give your e-mail address only to people from whom you want to receive e-mail. Be wary of providing your e-mail address at Web sites, entering it on application forms, or posting it in public places such as online discussion groups.

- Use a disposable e-mail address when you register for online sites. You can use this disposable address to get your confirmation number for online registrations, but don't use it for regular e-mail correspondence.

- If your e-mail provider offers a way to report spam, use it.

- When spam gets out of hand, consider changing your e-mail account so that you have a different e-mail address.

Technology
Compression

Compression refers to any technique that recodes the data in a file so that it contains fewer bits. Smaller files produced as a result of compression require less storage space and can be transmitted more rapidly than the larger, original files. Compression is routinely used to shrink file size before sending images and other large files as attachments. Files can be compressed using lossy or lossless compression.

Lossy compression. **Lossy compression** throws away some of the original data during the compression process. Lossy compression can be used for image, video, and music files. With a moderate level of compression, the human eye or ear won't miss the information lost during the compression process. Applying too much compression, however, can produce fuzzy images and low-quality audio.

Most lossy compression techniques have adjustable compression levels so that you can decide how much data you can afford to lose.

Lossless compression. **Lossless compression** is a technique for compressing a file and then reconstituting all its data into its original state. This type of compression is used for files containing text and numeric data. It can also be used for images, videos, and music.

Various techniques exist for lossless compression. As a simple example, consider a type of lossless compression called run-length encoding. **Run-length encoding** (RLE) replaces a series of similarly colored pixels with a binary code that indicates the number of pixels and their colors.

Figure 9-8   Suppose that a section of a picture has 167 consecutive white pixels, and each pixel is described by one byte of data, as in a 256-color bitmap image. RLE compresses this series of 167 bytes into as few as two bytes, as shown in Figure 9-8.

1. The data for the first 167 white pixels can be compressed as 10100111 11111111. The first byte is the binary representation of 167. The second byte is the code for white.

2. The next five pixels are coded 00000101 00000000. The first byte is the binary representation of the number 5. The second byte is the code for black.

3. With compression, the first nine rows of the graphic require only 30 bytes—the binary numbers in columns 2 and 4 of this table. The uncompressed graphic requires 288 bytes.

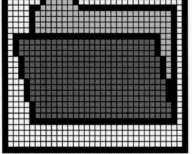

© MediaTechnics

Number of Repetitions (Decimal)	Number of Repetitions (Binary)	Pixel Color	Pixel Color (Binary)
167	10100111	White	11111111
5	00000101	Black	00000000
26	00011010	White	11111111
1	00000001	Black	00000000
5	00000101	Yellow	10100000
1	00000001	Black	00000000
23	00010111	White	11111111
2	00000010	Black	00000000
7	00000111	Yellow	10100000
18	00010010	Black	00000000
5	00000101	White	11111111
1	00000001	Black	00000000
25	00011001	Yellow	10100000
1	00000001	White	11111111
1	00000001	Black	00000000

© MediaTechnics

Technology
(continued)

There are two ways to compress files. You can use the compression routines built into software applications, or you can use a general purpose compression utility.

Software compression. Suppose you take a photo, and the software built into your camera stores it in RAW format. The file is very large and retains its high-quality resolution. If your camera stores the same photo in JPEG format, the file would be much smaller than the RAW file and the image quality would be slightly reduced.

Software designed for creating images, videos, and music usually offers ways to save your work in compressed file formats. When you use such software to save a file, the data is automatically compressed. You do not have to take additional steps to compress these files before sending them as e-mail attachments, posting them, or handling them in any way that calls for small rather than large files. The table in Figure 9-9 lists common file formats that are compressed and those that are not.

Figure 9-9

	Compressed	Not Compressed
Image	GIF PNG TIF JPEG	RAW Windows Bitmap (BMP)
Music	MP3 M4A OGG WMA	WAV AIFF
Video	H.264 Ogg-Theora MPEG4 WebM MOV	

© MediaTechnics

Compression utilities. When working with file types that do not offer built-in compression, you can use a standalone compression utility to shrink the size of a file that you have saved in a non-compressed format. File compression utilities apply lossless compression to shrink file size. Use these utilities to shrink files containing text and numbers as well as image and music files stored in RAW, WAV, and other non-compressed formats.

Compressing files is sometimes called zipping, and the process is said to produce zipped files or folders. Many compression utilities can be used to zip multiple files into one package. Windows supplies a compression utility that produces compressed folders. These folders can contain a single file or a combination of several files and folders, which is handy for packaging a group of files related to a project. In one unit, you have more assurance that all files will reach their destination.

Technology (continued)

Suppose you want to send two files and a folder to your rowing team coach. The original files are called Rowing Book DTP.indd and Rowing Book.pdf. The folder is called Rowing Photos. You can use the compression utility supplied by Windows to zip the folder and files into a single compressed folder, as shown in Figure 9-10.

TRY IT!

Figure 9-10

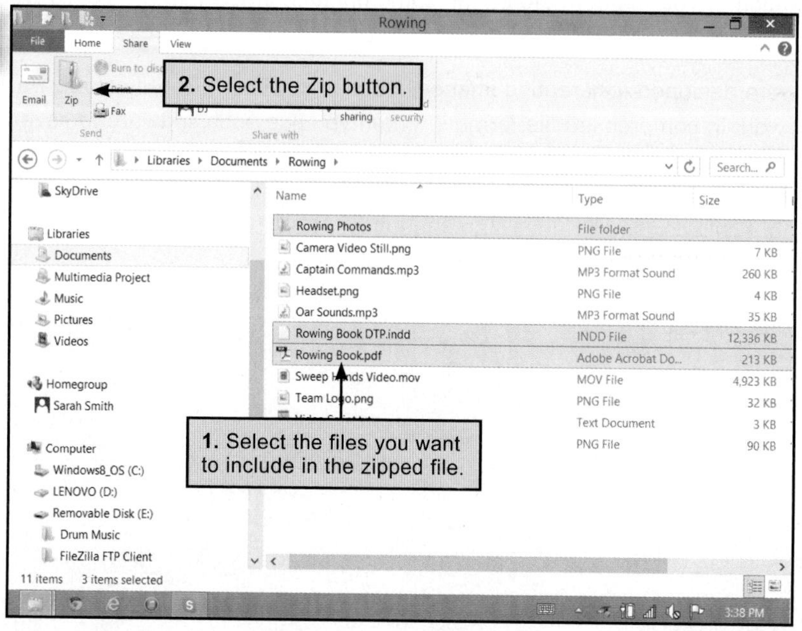

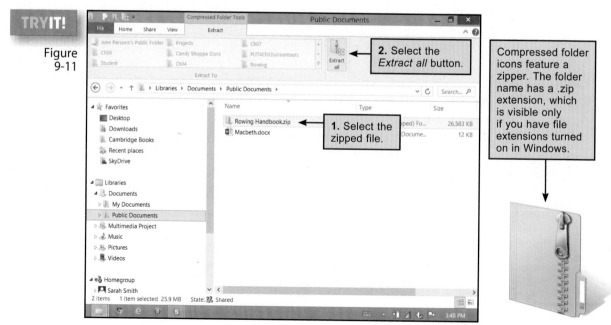

Source: Microsoft Corporation

When you receive a zipped folder, you have to unzip it to extract the files and folders it contains, reconstituting them to their original state. Folders that display a zipper contain compressed files. Work with Figure 9-11 to walk through the process of unzipping a compressed folder.

TRY IT!

Figure 9-11

Compressed folder icons feature a zipper. The folder name has a .zip extension, which is visible only if you have file extensions turned on in Windows.

Source: Microsoft Corporation

Project

Explore e-mail

In this fast-paced world, e-mail has proven to be such a vital means of communication that one can hardly survive without it. A missed e-mail message can result in losing a prospective job or missing an important meeting. This chapter covered the essentials of e-mail, such as how to use local and Webmail, organize e-mail folders, and include attachments in your messages. You also learned about the dangers that can lurk inside e-mail messages and how to protect yourself from them.

When you have completed the project, you should be able to:

- Create a label to group messages on a specific topic.

- Compress an image file.

- Create a group of contacts in the address book.

- Send a message to a contact group.

- Send messages with attachments.

- Follow netiquette guidelines for e-mail.

- Find the privacy policy for your e-mail service.

Requirements: This project requires Microsoft Windows, a browser, and Paint.

The deliverable for Project 9 is a group e-mail message containing the following:

1. The original file size of your Project 9 screenshot

2. The compressed file size of your Project 9 screenshot

3. A list of five netiquette guidelines that you've researched

4. An attachment containing a screenshot of your Gmail window

1. The process of signing up for a Webmail account is fairly straightforward. In this exercise, you will work with Google Gmail. Open your browser. In the browser's address bar, type mail.google.com, then press the Enter key. If you already have a Gmail account and don't want to create a disposable account to use for unimportant mail, sign in.

   If you do not have a Gmail account, create one by doing the following:

   Select the CREATE AN ACCOUNT button.

   Fill in the online registration form.

Source: Google.com

• Explore e-mail (continued)

2. When Gmail opens, it displays your Inbox. Create a label called Order Confirmation by completing the following steps:

Look at the labels list on the left side of the Gmail window.

If there is a link to *More labels*, select it to expand the list.

Scroll down, if necessary, to select *Create new label*.

Enter Order Confirmation as the new label name, then select the Create button. (Hint: If you make a mistake, scroll down the Labels list and select *Manage labels*, where you can edit or delete labels.)

Select the checkbox for an e-mail message that confirms an online order that you've placed. If you have no messages of this sort, select any message.

Select the Labels icon from the Gmail toolbar.

Select the Order Confirmation label to apply it to the selected message.

Source: Google.com

3. Take a screenshot of the Gmail window showing the message you labeled as an order confirmation. Save the screenshot as a 24-bit bitmap in the Pictures library with the file name Project 9 [Your Name].bmp. Close the Paint window.

4. Later in the project, you'll send this image to your instructor. Because it is a fairly large file, you should compress it. To do so, follow these steps:

Select the ⬚ File Explorer icon on the toolbar.

Open the Pictures folder.

Select, but don't open, the Project 9 file, then write down the size that's displayed.

Select the Share tab, then select the Zip button.

Your compressed file is stored in a zipped folder named Project 9 [Your Name].

Write down the size of the compressed folder. Close File Explorer.

• Explore e-mail (continued)

5. Create a contact group by completing the following steps:

   Click the Gmail link on the left side of the screen, then select Contacts.

   Select *More labels* on the left side of the screen, if necessary, to display all the Contact options.

   Scroll down, if necessary, and select *New group*.

   Enter Study Group, then select the OK button.

   Check the boxes for your instructor and three of your contacts.

   Select the 👥▾ Group icon.

   Select Study Group to add the four contacts.

6. Compose a message to the study group by following these steps:

   Select the Contacts link on the left side of the screen, then select Gmail from the list.

   Select the Compose button.

   Start typing Study Group in the To: box.

   A list of addresses for your study group should appear. Press the Enter key.

   Enter Netiquette Assignment [Your Name] in the subject line, then proceed to the next step.

7. Use a search engine to research the meaning of "netiquette." Locate at least five netiquette guidelines that pertain to e-mail and add them to your e-mail message.

8. At the end of your message, add a paragraph that describes your attachment, including its uncompressed and compressed sizes. Don't send the message yet.

9. Before sending the message, check the message for any misspelled words.

10. Attach the Project 9 zipped folder and send the message by completing the following steps:

    Click the *Attach files* icon.

    Select your Project 9 zipped folder, then click the Open button.

    Click the Send button.

11. When you use an online service, you should understand how it could affect your privacy. Click the Privacy Policy link at the bottom of the Gmail window to locate Google's Gmail Privacy Notice. Read the policy to discover how much information Gmail stores about your account, use and how it determines what targeted advertising to display in your e-mail window. Close the Gmail Privacy window.

12. For security, you should log out of e-mail when you are not using it. Click the *Sign out* button near the top of the Gmail window. Close your browser to complete the project.

Issue

Just how private is e-mail?

Most people assume that e-mail has similar privacy protections as telephone conversations and as letters that are carried by the postal service. However, that is not necessarily the case. The electronic technology that makes e-mail so popular also tends to make it less private than a phone call or a letter.

It is easy for the recipient of an e-mail message to forward copies of it to other people. The contents of an e-mail message might appear on a technician's screen in the course of system maintenance or repairs. Also, your e-mail messages—including those that you have deleted from your own PC—might be stored on backups and archives of an e-mail server where you cannot control access to them.

When a Caltech student was accused of sexually harassing a female student by sending lewd e-mail to her and to her boyfriend, investigators retrieved all of the student's e-mail from archives of the e-mail server. The student was expelled from the university even though he claimed that the e-mail had been "spoofed" to make it look as though he had sent it, when it had actually been sent by someone else.

Various government agencies can access e-mail messages, either by requesting them from an ISP or by intercepting them from various devices on the Internet. Theoretically, intercepting e-mail requires a warrant or court order, but legislation aimed at combating terrorism has loosened restrictions. A whistleblower revealed in 2013 that the U.S. National Security Agency has been collecting and storing all domestic communications, including e-mail messages.

Employee use of company-supplied e-mail accounts is the subject of continuing controversy because employers often monitor e-mail exchanges that take place on company e-mail systems. Your employer should keep you informed of company e-mail privacy policies. Use that information to determine which messages you'll send on the company e-mail system and which you'll send on your personal Webmail or local e-mail account.

Until the legal system resolves the many issues surrounding e-mail, you should think of your e-mail messages as postcards, rather than as letters. Assume that your e-mail message might be read by people other than the person to whom it was sent, and save your controversial comments for face-to-face conversations.

What do you think?

1. Do you think most people believe that their e-mail is private?   ⬤ Yes ◯ No ◯ Not sure

2. Do you agree with Caltech's decision to expel the student who was accused of sending harassing e-mail to another student?   ◯ Yes ◯ No ◯ Not sure

3. Do you think that your government is justified in collecting and storing all e-mail and similar correspondence that travels over the Internet?   ◯ Yes ◯ No ◯ Not sure

QuickCheck A

1. True or false? Local e-mail is limited to computers within a business, school, or home LAN. [_____]

2. Webmail is accessed using a(n) [_____] .

3. An e-mail [_____] consists of an original message and all of the replies and forwards that stem from it.

4. [_____] refers to an e-mail–based scam designed to fool users into disclosing confidential information.

5. Compressed attachments typically have a(n) [_____] file extension.

CHECKIT!

QuickCheck B

Indicate the letter of the screen element that best matches the following:

1. A message with an attachment [____]

2. The folder that holds a copy of all mail you've sent out [____]

3. A subject line [____]

4. An unread e-mail message [____]

5. The control you'd use to send the current message to another person [____]

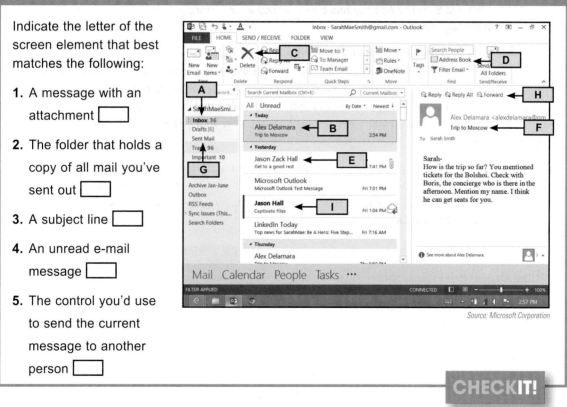

Source: Microsoft Corporation

CHECKIT!

GETIT? While using the digital textbook, click the Get It? button to see if you can answer ten randomly selected questions from Chapter 9.

Working with Documents

What's inside?

Computers were originally designed to work with numbers and make calculations. Ever since Apple Writer 1.0 arrived in 1979, however, most of our interaction with computers has dealt with words rather than numbers. Chapter 10 focuses on word processing software.

What's in the digital book?

The Try It! features in Chapter 10 show you how to improve your writing with word processing software. This chapter's video feature looks at laser printers.

FAQ Can word processing software improve my writing?

Word processing software provides tools for entering and revising text, adding graphical elements, specifying formats, and printing documents. Popular word processing software includes Microsoft Word, Google Docs, and LibreOffice Writer.

Good writing requires a coherent progression of ideas expressed in grammatically correct sentences. Before focusing on how your document looks, pay attention to how it reads by using your word processing software to organize your ideas and clarify your wording. Entering text on the screen gives you flexibility to sketch out your main points, then move them around to improve the progression of your ideas.

When you first type the raw text for a document, don't press the Enter key at the end of each line—just keep typing. Your word processing software will automatically **word wrap** to the next line. You should, however, press the Enter key at the end of a title, paragraph, or bullet point. Work with the Try It! in Figure 10-1 if you need a quick overview of word processing basics.

Figure 10-1

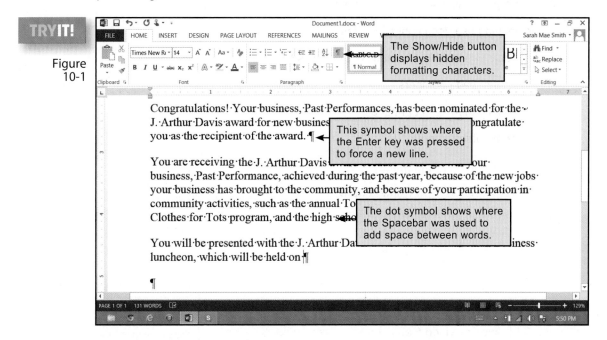

When you are satisfied with the flow of ideas in your document, you can drill down to the sentence level and do a bit of wordsmithing using features such as the thesaurus, Search and Replace, grammar checker, readability statistics, and spelling checker.

Thesaurus. Your word processing software might provide a thesaurus that you can use to find synonyms for trite and overused words.

Search and replace. You can also use your word processor's Search and Replace feature to hunt down words that you tend to overuse. For example, if you habitually overuse the word "typically," you can use Search and Replace to find each occurrence of "typically," and then decide whether you should substitute a different word, such as "usually" or "ordinarily."

Can word processing software improve my writing? (continued)

You can also use Search and Replace to make global changes, for example, if you want to change the name of the villain throughout a story you've written, or if you've used the wrong city throughout a research report. Search and Replace also comes in handy for adjusting spacing, such as when you want to change a space into a tab. Search and Replace options such as those in Figure 10-2 are explained in the Try It! below.

TRYIT!

Figure 10-2

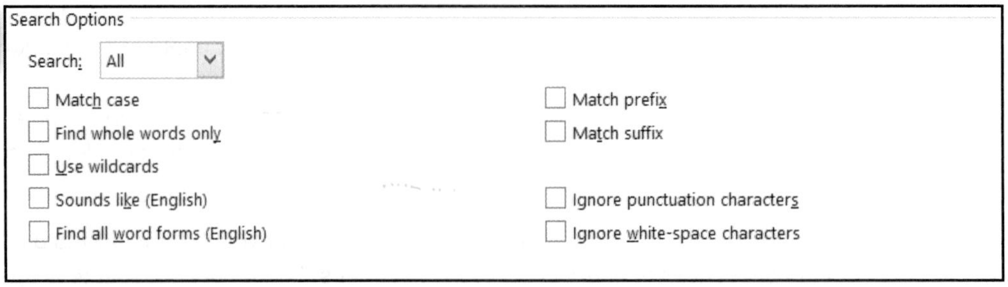

Grammar checker. A **grammar checker** reads through your document and points out potential grammatical trouble spots, such as incomplete sentences, misused words, incorrect punctuation, and verbs that don't agree with nouns.

Readability statistics. To find out if your writing style is suitable for your target audience, your word processing software might be able to analyze the reading level of your document based on the document's average number of syllables per word and words per sentence. For most documents, you can target average readers. Readability statistics are summarized as a score between 1 and 100 (aim for a score of 60–70) or a grade level (aim for 7th or 8th grade).

Spelling checker. Word processing software can also help you find and fix spelling errors. A **spelling checker** compares each word in your document to an electronic dictionary. For words not found in the dictionary, the spelling checker displays a list of possible corrections. Work with the Try It! below for an overview of spelling, grammar, and readability features.

TRYIT!

Figure 10-3

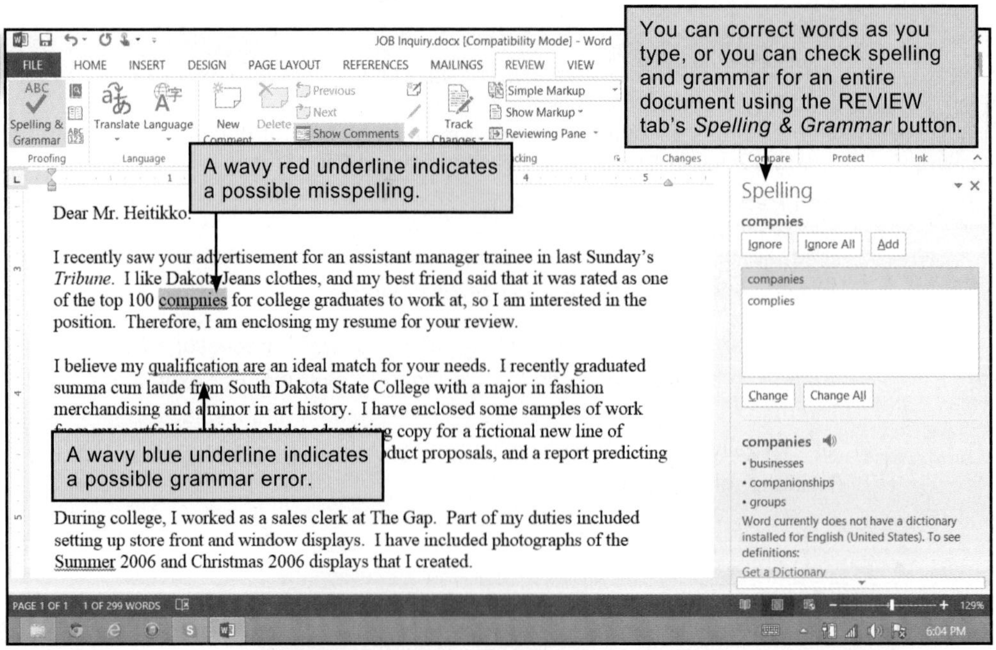

FAQ When should I use document templates?

You can create a document from scratch by entering text in the blank, new document workspace. As an alternative, you can use a **document template**, which is a preformatted document that can be used as the foundation for creating a new document. Most word processing software supplies templates for many basic documents, such as letterheads, fax cover sheets, memos, posters, resumes, greeting cards, calendars, and reports.

Templates are useful if you are unsure of the proper format for a document, such as a business letter or resume. Templates provide the basic format for a document, including line spacing, margin settings, paragraph spacing, and headings. In addition, templates include placeholders into which you enter text that personalizes the document. Common placeholders provide entry areas for the date, your name, a report title, or the text for a poster. To use a placeholder, select it and then type your text.

If you work in a large business or organization, you might be required to use templates created by managers, supervisors, or designers. Using these official templates helps businesses maintain professional standards.

For academic writing, look for templates that conform to APA (American Psychological Association), MLA (Modern Language Association), or CMS (Chicago Manual of Style) guidelines. If not supplied with your word processing software, you can find templates for these styles online. Using document templates is easy. Figure 10-4 steps through the basics.

Figure 10-4

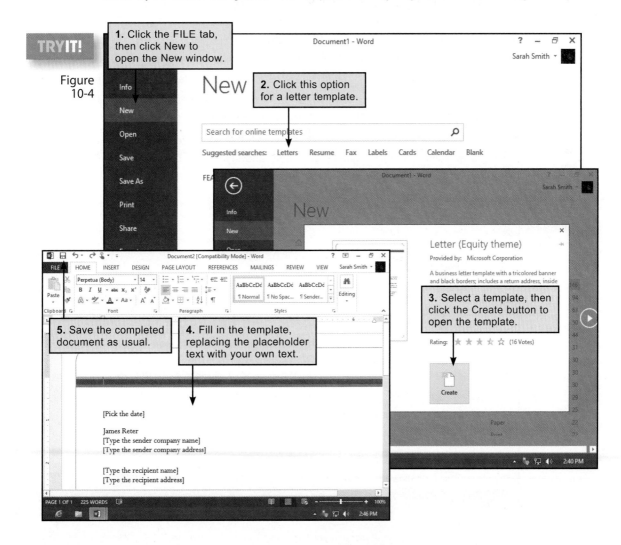

1. Click the FILE tab, then click New to open the New window.

2. Click this option for a letter template.

3. Select a template, then click the Create button to open the template.

4. Fill in the template, replacing the placeholder text with your own text.

5. Save the completed document as usual.

FAQ What should I know about formatting and styles?

You can use your word processing software to **format** a document, changing its appearance to create a professional, high-impact, or casual look. Formatting can be applied to single characters, words, sentences, or paragraphs, or to an entire page.

You can format one or more characters in a document to change text colors, fonts, and sizes. The term **font** refers to the design or typeface of each text character. Font size is measured in points (pt), with 10 pt being a typical size for text in the body of a document. You can apply additional character formats, such as bold, italic, and underlining. To apply character formats, select the text to be formatted, then use a toolbar button, ribbon tool, or menu option to indicate the format you want.

Paragraph format options include margin settings, line spacing, bulleted and numbered lists, columns, centering, left and right alignment, and "justification" that creates blocks of text evenly aligned on both the right and left sides. To apply paragraph formats, select the paragraph, then use a menu option to select a format.

Figure 10-5

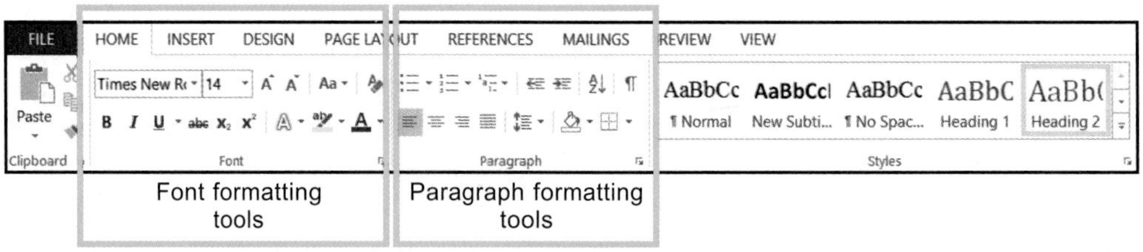

Font formatting tools   Paragraph formatting tools

A **style** is a set of character and paragraph attributes. For example, the Heading 2 style might be defined as 18-point, bold, green, Cambria font that is single-spaced and left-aligned. Your word processing software may provide predefined styles, and you also can create your own styles. Available styles are displayed in a list, making it easy to choose the one you want to apply.

Once you have defined a style, you can apply all of its attributes in one operation by making a selection from the style list. Formats and styles can be applied to selected characters or to entire paragraphs. Use the Try It! button to learn more about styles.

TRY**IT!**

Figure 10-6

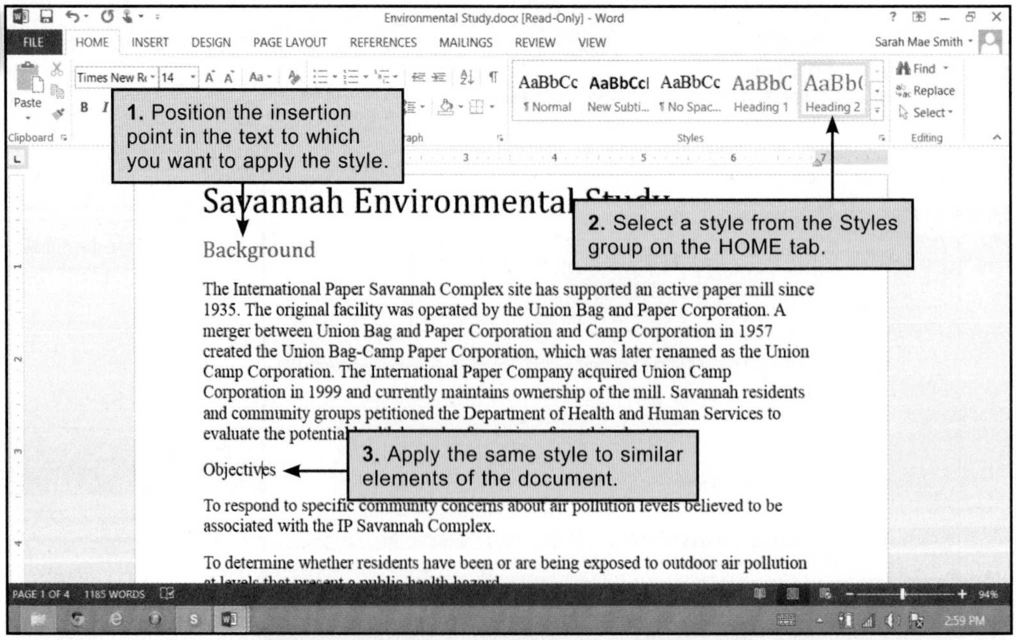

1. Position the insertion point in the text to which you want to apply the style.

2. Select a style from the Styles group on the HOME tab.

3. Apply the same style to similar elements of the document.

FAQ How do I print page numbers?

Page numbers usually appear in the **header** located within the top margin of a document or in a **footer** within the bottom margin. Headers and footers often contain additional information such as the document's title, the date, and the author's name. Headers and footers are useful for keeping printed documents intact, for example, when a document is dropped or a part of it is misfiled.

When creating a document in APA style, the header should contain the text "Running head:" followed by a short title of your paper in all caps, aligned with the left margin. The page number should be aligned with the right margin. Popular styles, such as APA, MLA, and CMS, differ on header formats. If you are not using a template for one of these styles, check an online style guide to ensure that your header format is correct.

Figure 10-7

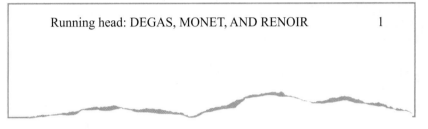

Running head: DEGAS, MONET, AND RENOIR   1

Rather than manually typing page numbers on each page, you can use the page number feature to automatically number pages. Most word processors also offer buttons that add the date, time, author name, document title, or file path to a header or footer. Figure 10-8 explains how to work with headers in Microsoft Word.

TRYIT!

Figure 10-8

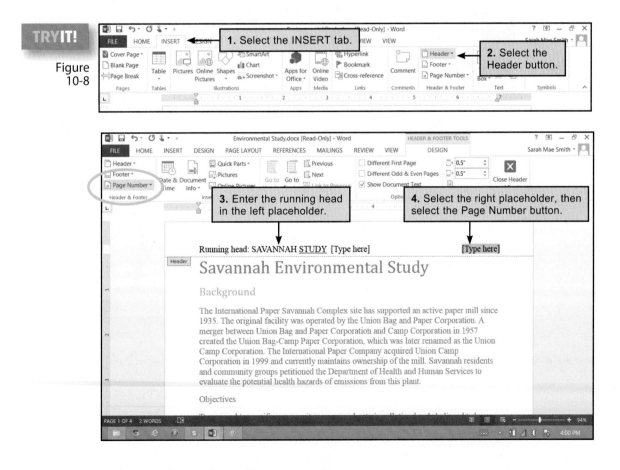

1. Select the INSERT tab.

2. Select the Header button.

3. Enter the running head in the left placeholder.

4. Select the right placeholder, then select the Page Number button.

Running head: SAVANNAH STUDY [Type here]   [Type here]

Savannah Environmental Study

Background

The International Paper Savannah Complex site has supported an active paper mill since 1935. The original facility was operated by the Union Bag and Paper Corporation. A merger between Union Bag and Paper Corporation and Camp Corporation in 1957 created the Union Bag-Camp Paper Corporation, which was later renamed as the Union Camp Corporation. The International Paper Company acquired Union Camp Corporation in 1999 and currently maintains ownership of the mill. Savannah residents and community groups petitioned the Department of Health and Human Services to evaluate the potential health hazards of emissions from this plant.

Objectives

FAQ What should I know about printing?

Printed documents are becoming less common. Many documents are now transmitted digitally as e-mail attachments. Yet there are still situations in which a printed document is useful. A printed business letter is a formal form of communication used to apply for employment, request information, or register a complaint. Contracts and other legal documents are commonly printed so that they can be signed by the contracting parties. Flyers and posters are printed so that they can be distributed and displayed.

When necessary, you can easily print one or more copies of a document. To access print settings using Microsoft Word, select the FILE tab, then select Print. Word displays a preview of your printout. Take the time to look at the preview so that you don't waste paper printing a document that is not formatted to your satisfaction.

Figure
10-9

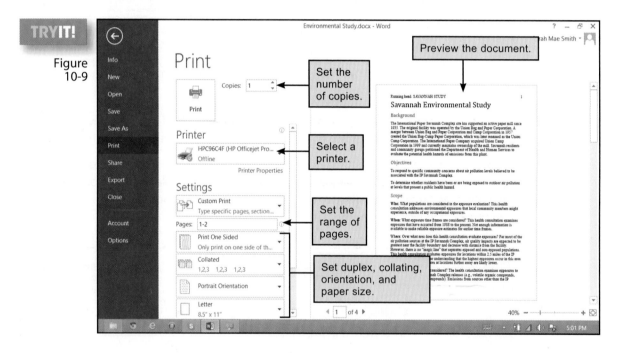

- You can select a printer by clicking the Printer button, then selecting the printer you want to use.

- To print a range of pages, enter the first page, a hyphen, then the last page in the range. To print specific pages that are not in a sequence, enter the page numbers in the Pages text box, separated by commas (such as 3, 7, 12).

- To print more than one copy of a document, use the Copies spin box.

- You can print on one side of the paper, or set a duplex printer to print on both sides of the paper. You can simulate duplex printing using the *Manually Print on Both Sides* option and turning the paper when prompted to do so.

- When the Collated option is selected, each copy of a multipage document prints in sequential page order so you don't have to collate it manually.

- The preview provides options for adjusting magnification when you want a closer look at a section of text. If the print preview is acceptable, select the Print button to print the document. To return to the document without printing, select the arrow in the upper-left corner of the Print window.

FAQ What are my other output options?

Word processing software outputs documents in its native file format. For Microsoft Word, that format is DOCX. There are times when distributing a document in a word processor's native file format is not the most desirable course of action. When that is the case, you might use PDF or HTML formats.

PDF. **PDF** (Portable Document Format) was created by Adobe Systems and has become a universal standard for exchanging documents, spreadsheets, and other types of data files. Converting a file into a PDF ensures that when the file is viewed or printed, it cannot be altered. PDFs retain the original layout of text and graphics, so PDF is sometimes referred to as a fixed-layout format.

Another reason for converting documents into PDFs is to distribute them to recipients who might not have software that opens your word processing files. Software for viewing PDFs is free and therefore most computers have the ability to display PDF files.

HTML. You can also output HTML documents that can be posted on the Internet as a Web page and viewed with Web browsers, such as Internet Explorer, Google Chrome, or Mozilla Firefox.

To convert a Microsoft Word document into a PDF or an HTML file, save it first as a normal Word document. Then save it again using the Save As command and selecting either the PDF or HTML type from the *Save as type* list.

TRY IT!

Figure
10-10

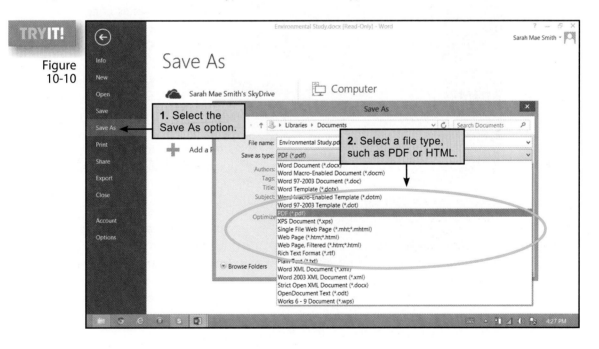

Technology

Printers

A **printer** is a device that converts computer output into images on sheets of paper or other media, such as labels, envelopes, and iron-on transfers. Most of today's printers use ink-jet or laser technology, and many popular models are multifunction printers that incorporate copy, scanning, faxing, and printing functions into a single unit.

Printer technologies produce characters and graphics as a series of small dots. The quality of a printout depends on its **print resolution**—the density of the gridwork of dots that form the image. Print resolution is measured by the number of dots printed per linear inch, abbreviated as dpi. At normal reading distance, a resolution of about 900 dots per inch appears solid to the human eye, but a close examination of color sections on a page will reveal the dot pattern. Although 900 dpi might be considered sufficient for magazines, expensive coffee-table books are typically produced on printers with 2,400 dpi or higher resolution.

An **ink jet printer** has a nozzle-like print head that sprays ink onto paper to form characters and graphics. Considered today's most popular printer technology, ink jets produce low-cost, black-and-white or color printouts. These printers also work well for outputting digital photos onto photo-quality paper that you can purchase at most office stores.

Figure 10-11

Black ink cartridge   Color ink cartridge

© MediaTechnics

The print head in a color ink jet printer consists of a series of nozzles—one for each print color. Most ink jet printers use **CMYK color**, which requires only **c**yan (blue), **m**agenta (pink), **y**ellow, and blac**k** inks to create a printout that appears to have thousands of colors. Alternatively, some printers use six ink colors to print additional midtone shades that create slightly more realistic photographic images.

Operating costs for an ink jet printer are reasonable, though the ink cartridges periodically need to be refilled or replaced. You can reduce costs somewhat and help the environment by refilling your empty ink cartridges rather than throwing them away. Your local office or electronics store is likely to have an ink refill station, or you can send your empty cartridges to a mail-order refill depot.

Today's ink jet printers have excellent resolution; depending on the model, resolution can range from 600 dpi to 5760 dpi. You can expect to pay more for a printer with a higher resolution in order to get better quality when printing photographic images. Some ink jet printers achieve their ultra-high resolution by making multiple passes over the paper.

You can purchase a good-quality ink jet printer for less than $100 that produces a respectable 9 pages per minute when printing in color, and 16 pages per minute when printing in black and white. A high-resolution photo may take up to 17 seconds to print. Manufacturers include Hewlett-Packard, Epson, Lexmark, Dell, Canon, and Brother.

Technology
(continued)

A **laser printer** uses the same technology as a photocopier to "paint" dots of light on a light-sensitive drum. Electrostatically charged ink is applied to the drum and then transferred to paper. For less than $200, you can purchase a laser printer that produces 24 pages per minute for black and white or color output. More expensive professional laser printers with faster print speeds and extended-run capacity begin at $500 and can exceed $10,000.

The **duty cycle** of a printer is specified in pages per month and indicates how many pages you can expect your printer to produce without breaking down. A personal laser printer has a duty cycle of about 2,500 pages per month—that means about 100 pages a day. You won't want to use it to produce 5,000 campaign brochures for next Monday, but would find it quite suitable for printing ten copies of a five-page outline for a meeting tomorrow.

Some people are surprised to discover that laser printers are less expensive to operate than ink jet printers. On average, you can expect to pay about three cents per page for black-and-white laser printing. This per-page cost includes periodically replacing the toner cartridge and drum. A toner cartridge and a drum unit each cost about $70, though prices vary by manufacturer and model.

Laser printers accept print commands from a PC, but use their own printer language to construct a page before printing it. **Printer Control Language** (PCL) is the most widely used printer language, but some printers also use the **PostScript** language, which is preferred by many publishing professionals.

Printer languages require memory, and most lasers have between 2 and 32 MB of RAM. A large memory capacity is required to print color images and graphics-intensive documents. A laser printer comes equipped with enough memory for typical print jobs. If you find that you need more memory, check the printer documentation for information. Click the Play It! button to take a tour of a laser printer and see how it works.

PLAYIT!

Figure
10-12

© MediaTechnics

Technology
(continued)

Impact

When PCs first began to appear in the late 1970s, dot matrix printers were the technology of choice. Still in use today, a **dot matrix printer** produces characters and graphics by using a matrix of fine wires. As the print head noisily clatters across the paper, the wires strike the ribbon and paper in a pattern prescribed by your PC. With a resolution of 360 dpi, a dot matrix printer produces low-quality output with clearly discernible dots forming letters and graphics. Dot matrix speed is typically measured in characters per second (cps). A fast dot matrix device can print at speeds up to 600 cps—about six pages per minute.

Unlike many newer printer technologies, a dot matrix printer actually strikes the paper and therefore can print multipart carbon forms. Today, dot matrix printers, which are sometimes referred to as impact printers, are used primarily for back-office applications that demand low operating cost and dependability but not high print quality.

Regardless of the type of printer you use, it must be properly installed so that it operates correctly. The first step of the installation process is easy. Simply plug the power cord into a wall outlet and plug the USB cable into your computer. Most printers can also be installed on network servers, and some printers can be directly connected to network routers to provide printing services to multiple computers.

Windows includes device drivers for many printers. Most printers are shipped with a CD containing driver software, and drivers can be downloaded from the manufacturer's Web site. It is possible to have access to more than one printer, in which case you must designate one printer as the default. The **default printer** will be used for day-to-day print jobs. You can use the *Devices and Printers* utility to change the default printer and check the status of print jobs. Click the Try It! button to learn how.

TRY IT!

Figure 10-13

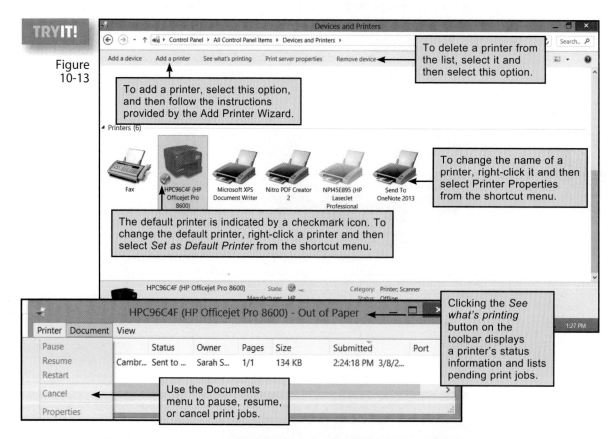

To delete a printer from the list, select it and then select this option.

To add a printer, select this option, and then follow the instructions provided by the Add Printer Wizard.

To change the name of a printer, right-click it and then select Printer Properties from the shortcut menu.

The default printer is indicated by a checkmark icon. To change the default printer, right-click a printer and then select *Set as Default Printer* from the shortcut menu.

Clicking the *See what's printing* button on the toolbar displays a printer's status information and lists pending print jobs.

Use the Documents menu to pause, resume, or cancel print jobs.

Project

Explore word processing software

Word processing software has proven invaluable in creating all types of documents. This chapter showed you that not only is word processing software useful for formatting your documents, but its special tools can actually help enhance your writing.

When you have completed the project, you should be able to:

- Use templates to create documents.
- Apply formatting options to your documents.
- Add images to documents.
- Use a spelling checker.

Requirements: This project requires Microsoft Windows, a browser, and word processing software. Detailed instructions are provided for Microsoft Word 2013.

The deliverable for this project is a fax document containing the following:

1. A completed fax cover sheet
2. A note to your guest speaker providing location details
3. A map to the seminar location

1. Imagine that a field expert has agreed to be the guest speaker at a university seminar that you are organizing. This person has requested a fax containing details about the seminar date, time, and location. To begin, select the Fax link from Microsoft Word's preliminary screen.

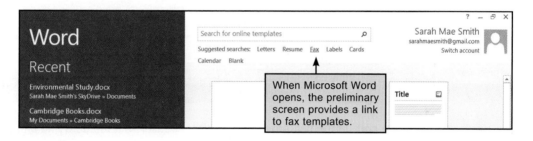

2. Select one of the fax templates.

• Explore word processing software (continued)

3. Enter the following data in the placeholders provided by the fax template:

   To: Andrew Schell

   From: [Your Name]

   Re: Technology Seminar

   Fax number: 904-992-1773

   Date: [Enter today's date]

   Pages: 1 including cover sheet

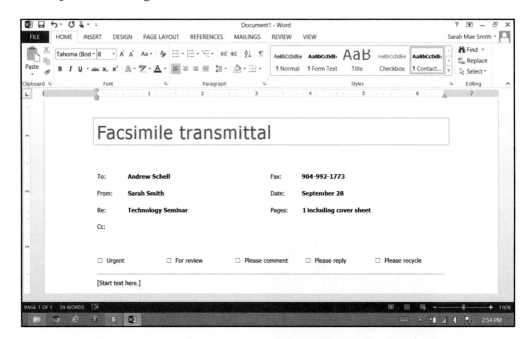

4. In the body of the fax, provide your guest speaker with the date and time of the seminar. Indicate that a map is included.

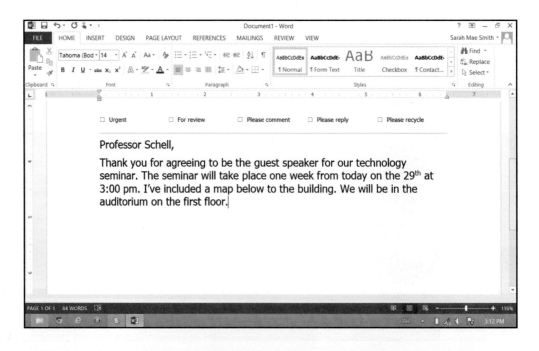

• Explore word processing software (continued)

5. Produce a map of the seminar location by completing the following steps:

   Open your browser and navigate to www.openstreetmap.org.

   Use OpenStreetMap to locate your school.

   Select the Export button.

   Export the map to a file.

Source: OpenStreetMap.com

6. Insert the map into your fax document by following these steps:

   Switch to your word processing program.

   Position the insertion point below the previous text in your fax.

   Select the INSERT tab, then select the Pictures button.

   Locate the file Map.png, which is probably in your Downloads folder.

   Select the map to insert it into the fax.

7. At the end of your fax, use the Times New Roman font for your signature. Click the Italic button to italicize your name.

8. Check spelling, then use the File menu or FILE tab to save the document in your My Documents folder as Project 10 [Your Name]. Close the word processor window.

9. Submit your document as a file, an e-mail attachment, or a printout according to your instructor's preference.

Issue

Who needs literary gatekeepers?

Amazon released the Kindle e-book reader in 2007. Barnes & Noble released the NOOK two years later. Before the brave new world of digital books, publishers worked with a tried and true model for producing, marketing, and selling literature.

In the traditional publishing model, authors submitted manuscripts, which were read and evaluated by skilled editors. Books that showed promise were reworked and refined through a collaborative process between authors and editors.

The final manuscript was sent to a copy editor, then to the typesetter, and finally to a printer. The hardcover edition of a book was the first to hit store shelves, priced at a premium for readers anxious to dig in to the words of their favorite authors. Paperback books followed, priced for mass consumption.

The price of printed books took into account not just the cost of printing, shipping, and warehousing, but also the cost of editorial services: the book editor, copy editor, and proofreader, plus royalties to the author, and profit margins required by retailers.

Digital books have challenged the traditional publishing model by eliminating printing, shipping, and warehousing costs. But although that might seem like a big savings, which can be passed on to customers, digital products incur other costs, such as the cost of uploading them to servers, the equipment required to store them, the e-commerce software needed to sell them, and the security software needed to protect them from piracy.

Digital books further eroded the traditional publishing model by giving opportunities to authors who might otherwise be rejected by traditional publishers. Self-publishing is much easier in the digital world, where anyone can write a novel and then post it on a Web site, upload it to Amazon, or submit it to iTunes. This opportunity to bypass the gatekeepers is sometimes referred to as the democratization of literature.

But the idea of a hoard of new Hemingways being discovered by vast new audiences is not necessarily a reality, even in a world where billions of people have access to the Internet. Every day, thousands of hopeful authors upload their work. Some of it is good, but most of it needs more work. Readers get discouraged after slogging through books with grammar errors, missing chapters, and unfathomable plots. Whereas literary gatekeepers used to reject manuscripts, digital manuscripts are now languishing in exabytes of data in which finding a literary gem is as rare as finding a needle in a haystack.

What do you think?

1. Do you know the price of your favorite novel in paperback and digital formats?   ○ Yes ○ No ○ Not sure

2. Have you purchased a $1 digital novel written by an aspiring author?   ○ Yes ○ No ○ Not sure

3. Do you think that literary gatekeepers play a valuable role in maintaining the quality of literature that is published?   ○ Yes ○ No ○ Not sure

QuickCheck A

1. When word processing software automatically begins a new line as you reach the right margin, it is called word [＿＿＿＿＿＿] .

2. [＿＿＿＿＿＿] provide the basic formatting for a document and are useful if you are unsure of the proper format for a document.

3. Page numbers are usually inserted in the [＿＿＿＿＿＿] at the top of a document.

4. Converting a file into a(n) [＿＿＿＿＿＿] ensures that when the file is viewed or printed, it retains the original layout. (Hint: Use the acronym.)

5. The Control Panel indicates the [＿＿＿＿＿＿] printer with a checkmark.

CHECKIT!

QuickCheck B

In the right column of the table, indicate which type of printer would **best** fit the job in the left column. Abbreviate your answers, using **D** for dot matrix, **J** for ink jet, and **L** for laser.

1. An individual wants to print color photographic images of family and friends.	
2. A school secretary wants to print 300 copies of the black-and-white program for tomorrow's school play.	
3. A salesperson needs to print out a multipart carbon invoice form.	
4. A publisher wants to specialize in full-color brochures.	
5. A student wants a dependable and low-cost color printer.	

CHECKIT!

 **GETIT?**   While using the digital textbook, click the Get It? button to see if you can answer ten randomly selected questions from Chapter 10.

Working with Spreadsheets

What's inside?

Chapter 11 begins with a whirlwind tour of spreadsheet software used for number crunching applications, such as balancing checkbooks, estimating construction costs, recording student grades, and creating graphs. The technology topic for this chapter focuses on computer display devices and setting up an ergonomic work area to prevent physical stresses and strains from computer use.

What's in the digital book?

Chapter 11 animates spreadsheet software to show you how to create worksheets and graphs. In addition, you'll find out how to change your computer's screen resolution and configure your computer for two displays.

FAQ What should I know about spreadsheets?

A **spreadsheet** is a tool for working with numbers. It is arranged in a grid of columns and rows forming cells that hold labels, numbers, and formulas. You can use spreadsheets for simple or complex calculations, such as computing loan payments, figuring out your taxes, or dividing expenses with your roommates.

Spreadsheet software, such as Microsoft Excel, LibreOffice Calc, and Google Sheets, allows you to create electronic spreadsheets that you can easily edit, print, save, post on the Web, or transmit via e-mail. An electronic spreadsheet is often referred to as a **worksheet**.

A worksheet functions much like a visual calculator. You place each number needed for a calculation in a **cell** of the grid. You can then enter formulas to add, subtract, or otherwise manipulate these numbers. Your worksheet automatically calculates the formulas and displays results. As an added bonus, you can create graphs based on the data in a worksheet.

Using spreadsheet software helps ensure the accuracy of your calculations by displaying all of your data and formulas on the screen. It can also help you to create numeric models of real-world entities.

As an example, you could create a numeric model of a new business, then examine projected income and expenses to determine whether the business will make you rich beyond your wildest dreams. You can even use your model to examine several alternative **"what-if" scenarios**, such as "What if sales are double what I projected?" or "What if sales are only half of what I projected?" Click the Try It! button to take a tour of basic spreadsheet features.

Figure 11-1

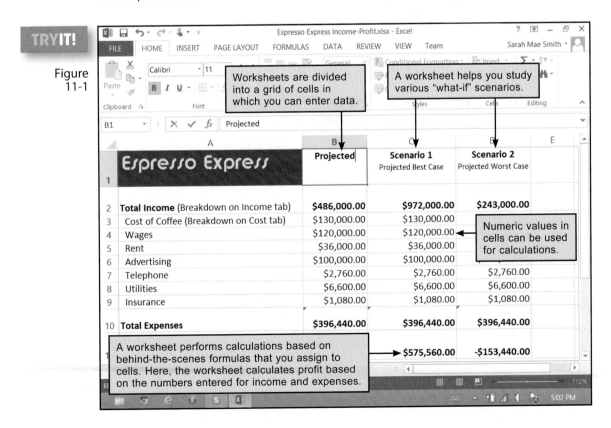

FAQ How do I create a worksheet?

When you have a clear idea of the purpose of your worksheet, you can begin by entering a title and **labels** that will identify your data. Next, you can enter the numbers, or **values**, that will be incorporated in calculations. Finally, you can enter formulas in any cells where you want the result of a calculation to appear.

A **formula** specifies how to add, subtract, multiply, or divide the numbers in worksheet cells. Typically, a formula begins with an equal sign (=) and contains cell references instead of the raw numbers for a calculation.

A **cell reference** is the column and row location of a cell. In Figure 11-2, the projected income of $486,000.00 is in column B and row 2, so its cell reference is B2. To create the formula that calculates profit (=B2-B10), you should use cell references instead of the actual numbers. Then, if the projected income changes, you can simply enter the new number in cell B2, but you won't have to change the formula. Spreadsheet software will recalculate the profit based on the new number you've entered.

After you've entered labels, numbers, and formulas, you can format your worksheet to make it more attractive and easier to understand. Formatting options include font treatments, cell colors, and data alignment within the cells. An additional set of formatting options helps you control the way your numbers are displayed, such as whether to include dollar signs, decimal places, and commas.

Learn more about entering formulas by selecting the Try It! button in Figure 11-2.

TRY IT!

Figure 11-2

The formula for the selected cell (B11) is displayed here. Excel formulas begin with an equal sign and can contain mathematical operators, such as + (add), - (subtract), * (multiply), and / (divide).

You can use fonts, graphics, and color to jazz up the appearance of your worksheet.

Enter a formula in the cell where you want the results to appear. The formula in this cell adds up all the expenses.

When referring to a number in a formula, use its cell reference. The formula for this cell, =B2-B10, calculates profit by subtracting the number in cell B10 from the number in cell B2.

	Projected	Scenario 1 Projected Best Case	Scenario 2 Projected Worst Case
Espresso Express			
2 **Total Income** (Breakdown on Income tab)	$486,000.00	$972,000.00	$243,000.00
3 Cost of Coffee (Breakdown on Cost tab)	$130,000.00	$130,000.00	$130,000.00
	$120,000.00	$120,000.00	$120,000.00
	$36,000.00	$36,000.00	$36,000.00
	$100,000.00		,000.00
7 Telephone	$2,760.00		,760.00
8 Utilities	$6,600.00		,600.00
9 Insurance	$1,080.00		,080.00
10 **Total Expenses**	$396,440.00		,440.00
11 **Profit**	$89,560.00	$575,560.00	-$153,440.00

FAQ What if I don't know the right formula?

Some formulas are easy to figure out. If you follow baseball, you know that a player's batting average is the number of hits divided by the number of times at bat. Easy. But suppose that you want to buy an amazing vintage Volkswagen Beetle. You'll have to get a loan, so you want to calculate the monthly payments. The calculation must somehow factor in interest rates, the number of payments, and the cost of the car.

Spreadsheet software includes built-in functions. A **function** is a predefined formula that performs simple or complex calculations. Handy functions include AVERAGE, SUM, PMT (calculate monthly payments), STDEV (calculate a standard deviation), and ROUND (round off a decimal number).

To use a function, simply select it from the function list, then follow the on-screen instructions to select the cells that contain arguments for the calculation. An **argument**, sometimes called a parameter, is a value or cell reference that a function uses as the basis for a calculation. When you use the PMT function to calculate monthly car payments, the arguments include the interest rate, number of payments, and cost of the car.

The arguments for a function are generally separated by commas and enclosed in parentheses. Use the Try It! button to explore worksheet functions and learn how to incorporate them into your worksheets.

$$=PMT(B8/12,B9,B7)$$

Function name   Arguments

Figure 11-3

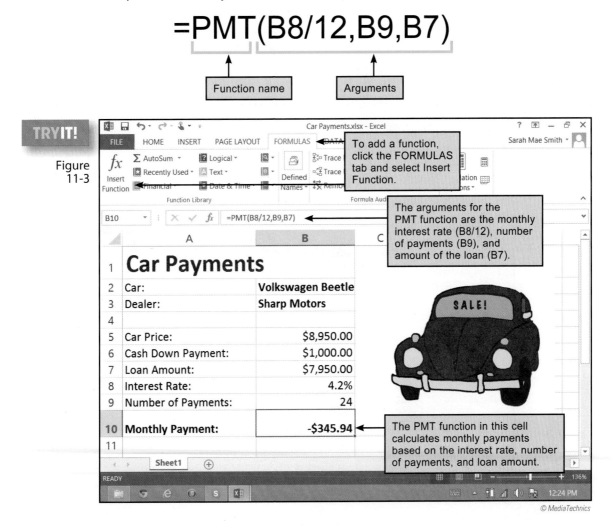

© MediaTechnics

FAQ How do I know whether worksheet results are accurate?

The person who creates a worksheet is responsible for its accuracy. Therefore, before you use or distribute a worksheet, you should test it to verify that it produces the correct results. Most spreadsheet software includes sophisticated tools for testing worksheets. If possible, however, you should first simply check the results using a handheld calculator on data that is known to be correct. Worksheet errors typically result from one of the following factors:

- A value that you entered in a cell is incorrect due to a typographical error.

- A formula contains a mathematical operator that is not correct, includes an incorrect cell reference, or is simply wrong.

- A formula produces the wrong results because the order for the calculations is not correct. Spreadsheet software first performs any operations in parentheses, then performs multiplication and division, and finally performs addition and subtraction. For example, the result of the formula =2+10/5 is 4, whereas the result of =(2+10)/5 is 2.4.

- A specified series of cells does not encompass all the values needed for a calculation. For example, you may have intended to add the values in cells C5 through H5, but specified cells C5 through G5.

- The worksheet was created using a built-in function, but the wrong cells were selected as the arguments. For example, in the PMT function, the first argument is supposed to be the interest rate. However, if the first argument has been assigned to the cell that contains the loan amount, the PMT function will produce the wrong result.

Click the Try It! button for tips on how to check the accuracy of your worksheets.

TRY IT!

Figure 11-4

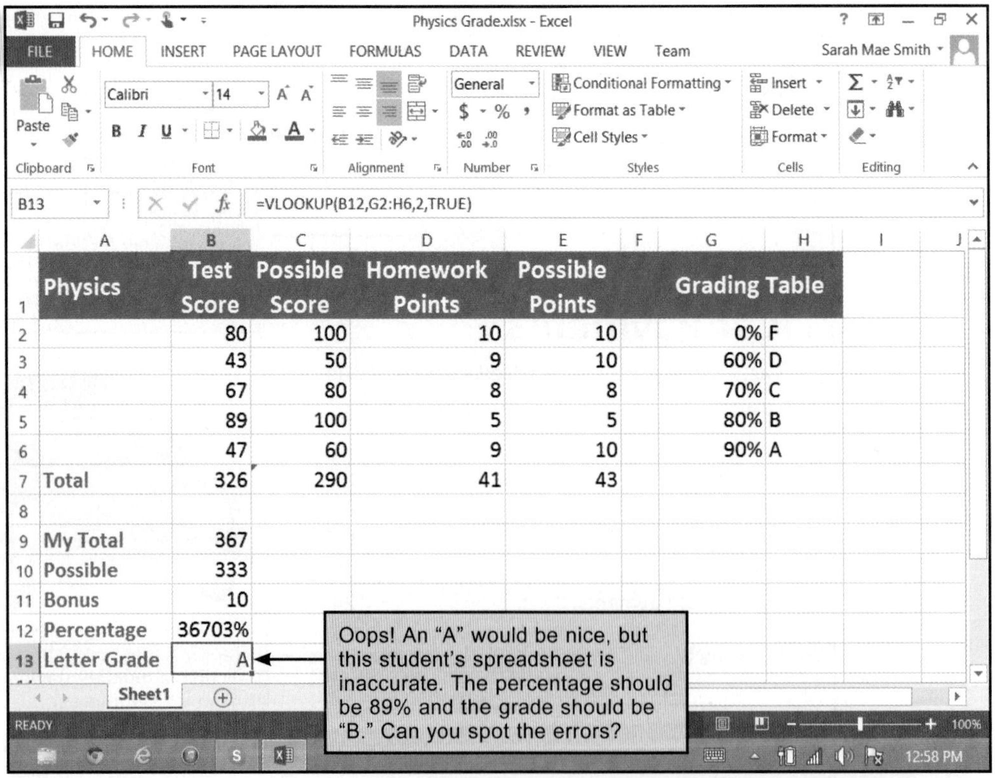

FAQ How do I create graphs?

Most spreadsheet software includes features that create graphs—sometimes called charts in spreadsheet terminology. A graph is based on the data in a worksheet. When you alter worksheet data, the graph automatically reflects the change.

Typically, you'll want to graph the data contained in one or more ranges. A **range** is a series of cells. For example, the range B3:B6 includes cells B3, B4, B5, and B6. The range for a graph is also referred to as a data set or data series. Your spreadsheet software allows you to create many types of graphs, such as bar, line, pie, column, scatter, area, doughnut, and high-low-close graphs. The process of creating a graph consists of a few easy steps:

- Plan your chart by deciding which worksheet data you want to chart, then select it.

- Select the chart type.

- Use the CHART TOOLS tabs menu options to change the appearance of the chart labels, data markers, and dimensions.

Click Try It! to see how easily you can create graphs using Microsoft Excel.

TRY IT!

Figure 11-5

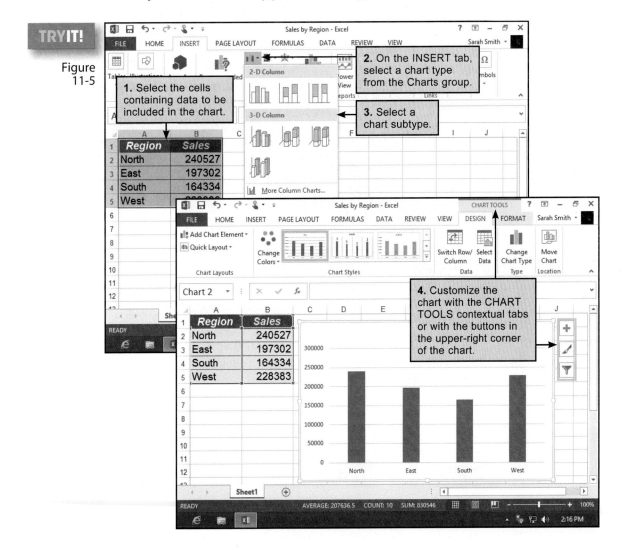

Technology

Display devices

A computer display device is usually classified as an output device because it shows the results of processing tasks. Touch-sensitive screens, however, can be classified as both input and output devices because they accept input and display output. Computer display devices can be standalone units, sometimes called monitors, or they can be integrated into the system unit of laptops, tablets, and smartphones.

Figure
11-6

© MediaTechnics

Most computer displays use **LCD** (liquid crystal display) technology that produces on-screen images by manipulating light within a layer of liquid crystal cells. Modern LCD technology is compact in size and lightweight, and provides an easy-to-read display. LCDs are standard equipment on laptop computers. Additional advantages of LCD technology include low-radiation emission and energy efficiency.

A computer display system requires graphics circuitry that generates signals for displaying images on the screen. One type of graphics circuitry, referred to as **integrated graphics**, is built into a computer's system board. Graphics circuitry can also be supplied by a small circuit board called a graphics card. A **graphics card** (also called a graphics board or video card) typically contains a graphics processing unit and special video memory. The graphics card in Figure 11-7 can be plugged into the system unit of a desktop computer.

Figure
11-7

© MediaTechnics

Graphics card

A **graphics processing unit** (GPU) executes graphics commands, leaving the main processor free for other tasks. **Video memory** stores screen images as they are processed but before they are displayed. A fast GPU and lots of video memory are the keys to lightning-fast screen updating for fast action games, 3D modeling, and graphics-intensive desktop publishing.

Monitors connect to computers using VGA, HDMI, DVI, or Mini DisplayPort ports. You can use these ports to connect a monitor to your laptop or desktop computer.

Figure
11-8

VGA port   HDMI port   DVI port   Mini
                                                            DisplayPort

All © MediaTechnics

Technology
(continued)

Each dot of light on a computer screen is called a **pixel**, short for "picture element." The number of horizontal and vertical pixels that a device displays on the screen is referred to as **screen resolution**. Today's 1080i and 1080p display devices typically have 1920 x 1080 resolution, which makes them compatible with HDTV standards, including the widescreen 16:9 aspect ratio.

At higher screen resolutions, text and other objects appear small, but the computer can display a large work area. At lower screen resolutions, text and objects appear larger, but the apparent work area is smaller. Figure 11-9 illustrates this difference.

Figure 11-9

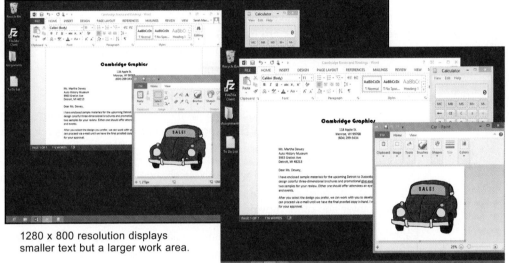

1280 x 800 resolution displays smaller text but a larger work area.

800 x 600 resolution displays larger text but a smaller work area.

© MediaTechnics

As shown in Figure 11-10, you can change the resolution displayed on your computer screen up to the maximum resolution of your display device. Most displays have a recommended resolution at which images are clearest and text is crispest.

TRYIT!

Figure 11-10

Right-click the desktop and select Screen resolution to view and adjust display settings.

When more than one display is connected to your computer, it is shown here.

Select a resolution here.

Technology
(continued)

Display devices are a key computer system component; their selection and placement affect the ergonomics of your work environment. **Ergonomics** is the science of configuring tasks, equipment, and workplaces with regard to worker health and safety. You can use ergonomic principles to set up your own work areas to minimize repetitive stress injuries, eye strain, and back pain.

When evaluating standalone monitors or laptop computer displays, you might want to check the following factors that contribute to ergonomic viewing:

Brightness and contrast. Brighter monitors that offer higher contrast give you more options for adjustments that can help you avoid eye strain. Measured in candelas per square meter (cd/m^2), devices with 200 to 250 cd/m^2 are fine for most productivity tasks, whereas brighter devices are more desirable for movies and gaming. Glossy screens can seem to increase brightness and contrast, but might not be optimal in an environment where there is glare from windows or bright lights.

Viewing angle. The best displays can be viewed from the front or sides without drastic changes in brightness or shifting colors. Some vendors provide a measurement of viewing angle; higher numbers correspond to wider viewing angles and better quality devices.

Response time. The speed at which pixels change color is referred to as response time. Display devices with poor response rate can appear blurry and leave "ghost" trails of the mouse pointer and other moving objects.

Laptop computers present an ergonomic challenge because the screen and keyboard are attached to each other. Placement becomes a compromise between the best viewing angle and the best typing height. Figure 11-11 illustrates optimal equipment placement; consider how you can adjust your computer, monitor, keyboards, desk, and chair for a more ergonomic work area.

Figure 11-11

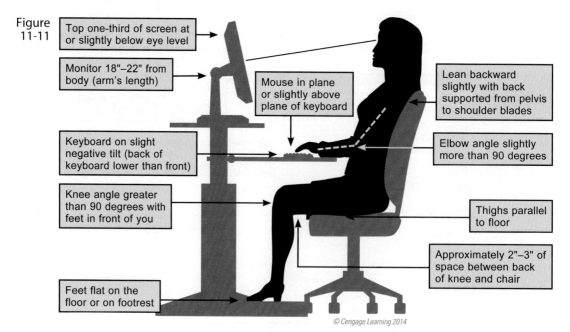

© Cengage Learning 2014

Project

Explore spreadsheet software

With its many useful features, spreadsheet software has proven to be a major timesaver in accomplishing personal tasks, such as managing household budgets, tracking grades, analyzing "what-if" scenarios for future expenses, and balancing checkbooks.

When you have completed the project, you should be able to:

- Create worksheets using handy features, such as drag-and-fill.

- Apply formatting options to worksheets.

- Create formulas and use built-in functions.

- Build charts based on worksheet data.

Requirements: This project requires Microsoft Windows and spreadsheet software, such as Microsoft Office Excel or LibreOffice Calc. Detailed instructions are provided for Microsoft Excel.

Deliverables:

1. A worksheet containing donation data for a nonprofit organization

2. A 3D bar chart comparing quarterly donation amounts

1. Open your spreadsheet software. If necessary, select a blank workbook template.

2. A blank worksheet should appear on the screen. Enter the labels and values for the worksheet shown below.

   (Hint: If you notice an error after pressing Enter, click the cell containing the error to display the text in the Formula Bar. Click the text in the Formula bar, correct it, then press the Enter key.)

Increase the size of any column by positioning the pointer on the column border line and dragging the double-arrow pointer to the right.

	A	B	C	D	E	F
1	Nonprofit Fund-raiser					
2		First Quarter	Second Quarter	Third Quarter	Fourth Quarter	Annual Total
3	Donations by Mail	8560	9200	4500	8800	
4	Online Donations	10800	7200	3340	7700	
5	Matching Funds Donations	2500	3650	5400	5555	
6	Matching Funds					
7	Total					

• Explore spreadsheet software (continued)

3. Matching fund donations are supplemented by a sponsoring corporation that pays an additional $0.25 for every dollar donated by individual donors. To find the amount of matching donations, do the following:

Select cell B6.

Type the formula =B5*.25 and then press the Enter key.

You've entered the formula correctly if cell B6 displays 625.

4. Copy the formula from cell B6 to cells C6, D6, E6, and F6 by completing the following steps:

Click cell B6.

Point to the small box located in the lower-right corner of the cell.

When the pointer changes to a skinny plus sign, hold down the mouse button and drag to cell F6.

Matching Fund Donations	2500	36!
Matching Funds	625	
Total		

If you copied correctly, row 6 should look like this:

6	Matching Funds	625	912.5	1350	1388.75	0

5. Now, use the SUM function to calculate totals:

Select cell B7.

Click the Σ SUM button.

Be sure the selected range is B3:B6.

Press the Enter key.

First Quarter
8560
10800
2500
625
=SUM(B3:B6)

Use the copy procedure you learned in Step 4 to copy the formula from B7 to cells C7, D7, E7, and F7.

6. Use the SUM function to calculate totals for the Annual Totals in cells F3, F4, and F5.

7. Format all the numbers as currency by completing the following steps:

Drag the fat plus-shaped pointer over cells B3 through F7 to select them.

On the HOME tab, click the down-arrow to change General to Currency.

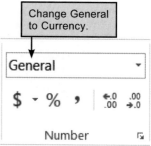

Change General to Currency.

8. Format important labels by completing the following steps:

Select cell A1 and change the font size to 20 pt; make the text blue and bold.

Select cells B2 through F2 and apply bold to the font.

Select cells A7 through F7 and apply bold to the font.

• Explore spreadsheet software (continued)

9. Compare your worksheet to the following, and make corrections if necessary.

10. Create a stacked bar chart comparing donations for each quarter by completing the following steps:

Select the INSERT tab.

Select cells A2 through E6 by dragging the fat plus-shaped pointer over them.

From the Charts area of the INSERT tab, select the Insert Column Chart button.

Select 3-D Stacked Column for the chart type.

Move the chart under the worksheet data.

Move the chart borders until the chart is the same width as the data table.

11. Save your worksheet and chart as Project 11 [Your Name]. Submit it in the format requested by your instructor.

Issue

Who's to blame for faulty software?

Back in the days when spreadsheets first captured the attention of corporate bean counters, a Florida contractor created a worksheet to itemize the costs of a large construction project. Somehow, $254,000 of expenses were not incorporated in the final total. The company lost money on the project and sued the software publisher, who countered that it was not responsible for user errors, and pointed to a disclaimer in the end-user license agreement (EULA) limiting liability to the cost of the software.

Since the first salvo over software product liability, several cases have been settled in court, usually in favor of the software publisher. Consumer advocates have expressed dismay over the liability chasm that exists between software and other products. Lawsuits against manufacturers that produce malfunctioning physical products are often successful. Car manufacturers, toymakers, and pharmaceutical companies have all felt the legal bite of angry consumers.

What makes software different from other products when it comes to liability? Software publishers claim that their products are so complex that perfection is impossible. They point to the fact that patches designed to fix bugs are available free of charge—the software industry's version of a product recall. Publishers also reiterate that license agreements clearly state the terms and conditions of software use; anyone who is not comfortable with those terms can simply choose not to use the software.

After a spate of lawsuits in which the courts sided with software publishers, consumers seemed resigned to software being marketed "as is" with flaws, bugs, and limited liability. However, the issue resurfaced in the context of security. A class action suit in California took Microsoft to task for selling software riddled with security flaws. Consumers were unhappy that various parts of the Windows operating system, e-mail client, and Web browser could be exploited by hackers to spread viruses and gain unauthorized access to personal computers. Microsoft responded to the accusation by blaming hackers: "The problems caused by viruses and other security attacks are the result of criminal acts by the people who write viruses."

Today's software contains flaws and users can make mistakes, especially when it comes to number-crunching. The moral of this story: Don't trust your results until you've verified them.

What do you think?

1. Do you usually read the EULA that's supplied with your software?　　　　○ Yes ○ No ○ Not sure

2. Should software publishers be held responsible for errors that result from errors, or bugs, in the software code?　　　　○ Yes ○ No ○ Not sure

3. Should software publishers be held responsible if user errors result in business or personal losses?　　　　○ Yes ○ No ○ Not sure

QuickCheck A

1. You can design a worksheet to be a numeric [_____] that you can use to examine "what-if" scenarios.

2. D9, A6, and Q8 are examples of cell [_____] .

3. SUM, PMT, and AVERAGE are spreadsheet [_____] .

4. True or false? If you create a graph showing baseball players' home runs, you can change the number of runs for a player on the worksheet and the graph will automatically reflect the change. [_____]

5. True or false? VGA, HDMI, and DVI are examples of numeric formats available for formatting worksheet cells. [_____]

CHECKIT!

QuickCheck B

Indicate the letter that correctly matches each description.

1. The SUM button [____]

2. A cell containing a value [____]

3. A cell containing a formula [____]

4. The formula for cell B4 [____]

5. A "what-if" analysis [____]

CHECKIT!

 GETIT? While using the digital textbook, click the Get It? button to see if you can answer ten randomly selected questions from Chapter 11.

What's inside?

In Chapter 12, you'll find out how to decide whether you need database software. You'll learn how to create your own databases, and you'll discover some of the privacy issues associated with databases that contain information about you. The Technology section examines tracking devices; you'll see how they relate to databases and privacy issues.

What's on the CD?

The Try It! features in Chapter 12 show you the inner workings of databases and tracking technologies.

FAQ What should I know about databases?

In popular usage, the term "database" simply means a collection of data. Some databases are structured, whereas others are free-form. Examples of structured databases include phone books, flight schedules, and a store's inventory list. A CD containing back issues of *TIME* magazine would be an example of a free-form database. You could consider the documents stored on your computer to be a free-form database. You could also regard the Web, with its millions of documents, as a free-form database.

A **structured database** contains information that is organized as fields, records, and files. A **field** contains a single piece of information, such as a name, birth date, or zip code. A **record** contains fields of information about a single entity in the database—a person, place, event, or thing. A group of similarly structured records can be stored in a file.

A structured database makes it easy to locate records using a query. A **query** is a search specification, usually consisting of one or more keywords. When you search for music on iTunes, for example, the musicians' names and song titles you enter into the search box are a query.

A **relational database** allows you to store information in two or more different types of records and form a link between them. Each type of record is stored in a **table**. For example, a video store database might include a table of movies and a table of customers. Suppose that a customer rents the movie, *The Hobbit: There and Back Again*. The clerk simply enters the customer number on the record for that movie. If the movie is never returned, the customer number acts as a link to the customer table that displays the customer's address, phone number, and credit card billing information. Figure 12-1 illustrates how two tables can be joined together based on data in the Customer # field.

Figure
12-1

Video Store Database

A table contains a series of records.

Movie Table

Each record contains data for a single entity—in this case, for the movie, *The Hobbit: There and Back Again.*

A field contains the smallest unit of meaningful data. In today's databases, a field can contain text, numbers, graphics, sound, or video clips.

DVD #: 20000001
Title: *The Hobbit: There and Back Again*
Director: Peter Jackson
Studio: Columbia Pictures
Release date: December 17, 2014
Stars: Cate Blanchett, Orlando Bloom, Luke Evans, Martin Freeman
Checkout date: 4-15-2
Customer #: 356778

Tables can be linked to automatically show related information. Here, the tables are related using the Customer # field so that the video store clerk can view contact and billing information for the person who rented the movie.

Customer Table

Customer #: 356778
Last name: Gannett
First name: Bill
Address: 4566 JR Ave.
City: Lakewood State:
Phone #: 732-905-8876
Credit card: Visa
Card number: 6785 3342 5678 211
Expiration date: 12-12-15

© *MediaTechnics*

FAQ Do I need database software?

Database software, sometimes referred to as a database management system (DBMS), provides a set of tools to enter and update information in fields, delete records, sort records, search for records that meet specified criteria, and create reports. Most people use databases with surprising frequency, but might not need database software. Why?

Consider the databases that you typically access. You might access a database to register online for a class at a college or university. You might search a product database at a Web site, such as Amazon.com. You might access your bank's database at an ATM to check your account balance. When you access such databases, the database software runs on a computer at the host site—not on your own PC. Therefore, you do not need database software to interact with the databases at school, on the Web, or at your bank. Having database software is useful primarily to create and maintain your own databases.

If you have a use for database software, a variety of options are available. For example, Microsoft Access and MySQL provide a wealth of data management capabilities, but using them to create production-quality databases requires a substantial learning commitment. MyDatabase, FileMaker Pro, and LibreOffice Base can be easier to learn and they include the basic features needed to manage typical files and databases.

Web apps, such as Zoho Creator, are available for creating online databases. You can also use spreadsheet software for simple databases. You'll learn more about this option in a later FAQ.

Click the Try It! button for a tour of database software. You'll learn how to work with tables, searches, queries, forms, and reports. You'll also see how relational databases link multiple tables to provide flexible access to data.

Figure 12-2

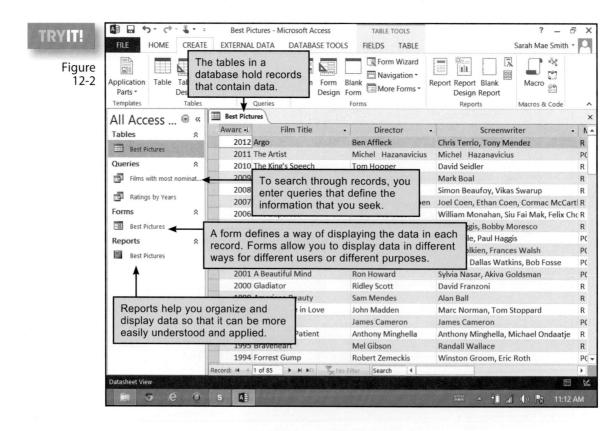

FAQ How do I create a database?

Creating a database consists of two tasks: creating a file structure to hold the data, and adding the data for each record. The specific procedures for these tasks depend on the database software that you've selected, so you can refer to your software documentation for exact instructions.

Suppose you want to create a household inventory in case you need it for an insurance claim. First, you can use your database software to create the **file structure**—a specification for the database fields and their characteristics. You'll need to assign a name to each field, such as Category, Item, Description, Date Purchased, Value, or Photo. Some database software might require you to specify the maximum length of each field. You might also have to specify the **data type** for each field, which indicates whether the field will hold text, numbers, dates, or graphics.

Once you have created the file structure, your database software displays a table with empty fields for entering each household item. You will be able to reliably locate items in your database only if you enter data accurately and consistently. Keep these tips in mind when entering data:

- **Be accurate.** As you enter each record, compare the on-screen data to your original documents to verify its accuracy.

- **Be consistent with grouping terms.** Use the same set of terms for fields that might be used to group your data. Suppose you plan to group your household inventory by categories such as jewelry, furniture, appliances, and electronics. You must then enter "jewelry"—not "jewels"—in the Category field for your diamond ring, for example.

- **Use consistent capitalization.** Most database software is case sensitive. Be aware that if you enter "Microwave oven," case-sensitive database software will not find anything when you later search for "microwave oven."

- **Make sure your spelling is correct.** If you misspell an item—such as "portable Jakuzi"—when you add it to the database, you won't be able to find it if you later search for "portable Jacuzzi."

- **Use abbreviations consistently.** To your database software, "TV" and "T.V." are completely different.

- **Be careful about symbols.** The telephone number (906) 227-1000 is not the same as 906.227.1000.

Click the Try It! button to learn how to create a database using Microsoft Access. You'll find out how to specify field names and select data types.

TRY IT!

Figure 12-3

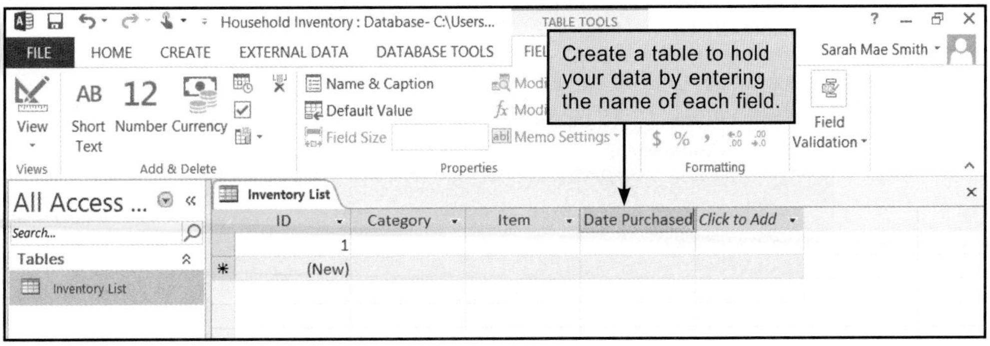

FAQ Can I create databases with spreadsheet software?

You can use most spreadsheet software to create and maintain files of information. However, you cannot use it to join files or tables together and create a relational database.

Spreadsheet software typically has data-handling features that allow you to manipulate the rows and columns of a worksheet as if they were records and fields in a database. You can sort data, search for data that meets specific criteria, and create reports. As a rule of thumb, spreadsheet software can handle any data that you could put on a set of cards in a card file.

When working with Microsoft Excel, use the Sort button located on the DATA tab to arrange the data in a worksheet according to the contents of any field. A household inventory could be arranged by room, for example, or by category. You could also arrange the data by purchase date.

A process called **filtering** (also called extracting) is useful for creating reports that show only selected data. For example, suppose that a faulty power line damaged all of your appliances and electronic equipment. If you want your household inventory worksheet to display only records for damaged devices, you can use "electronics" and "appliances" as the filter criteria. You could then print the filtered version of the worksheet to produce a hard-copy list for your insurance company.

Click the Try It! button for a demonstration of how to use spreadsheet software such as Microsoft Excel to manage data.

Figure
12-4

FAQ What about databases on the Web?

You'll find many databases on the Web that are populated with all sorts of information. For example, you can look for your old roommate in a phone-book-style database that covers the entire country; find a low-cost airfare to Beijing in a database that contains flight schedules for major airlines; look for the author of *Trout Madness* in the U.S. Library of Congress database; check the value of a 1964 Ford Mustang in a digital Kelley Blue Book database; find a definition of the term "CD-R" in a database of technical terms; or sift through your favorite band's music at the iTunes Store.

When you use a browser to access databases on the Web, you'll typically enter a query using an **HTML form**. The form might simply consist of a single text box where you can enter one or more keywords. This type of query is common when searching for specific products at e-commerce sites. When you see a question mark in a URL, such as the one in Figure 12-5, your browser is displaying the results of a database query.

Figure 12-5

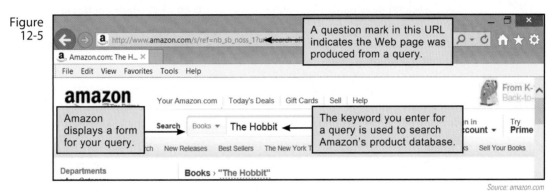

Source: amazon.com

You can also add data to an online database, a process that typically takes place when registering for an account at a Web site or when checking out at an e-commerce site. The data that you entered into a form is collected by a program that runs on the Web site's server. That information is passed along to the database software, which in turn transfers your data into the database itself. Figure 12-6 helps you visualize the setup of databases that work behind the scenes on the Web.

Figure 12-6

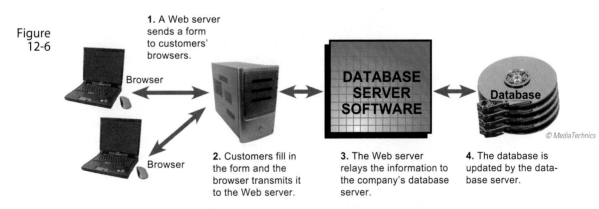

1. A Web server sends a form to customers' browsers.

2. Customers fill in the form and the browser transmits it to the Web server.

3. The Web server relays the information to the company's database server.

4. The database is updated by the database server.

© MediaTechnics

Transferring data from a form to a Web server, then to a database server, and finally to the database might seem like a complex process, but separating the database from public access enhances security. Banking and e-commerce databases would certainly be less secure if consumers were entering their data directly; granting public access to a database would increase the risk of unauthorized changes to the data.

Technology

Tracking devices

Today, location-aware devices and contactless ID cards are everywhere, and their data is often linked to databases. With the increasing popularity of tracking devices come many questions. Can you be tracked without your knowledge? Is tracking data stored in databases without your permission? How many of your devices can track your location? Can these devices track even when they are turned off? To answer these questions, you need to know a little about today's most common tracking technologies: radio, cellular, GPS, and RFID.

Radio. Real-time locating systems are similar to baby monitors. With a range that covers approximately 600 feet, they can be used to keep a virtual eye on children and pets. A tracking device worn by the trackee transmits signals to a nearby base station using radio waves.

Radio tracking devices can be configured to issue an alert when the trackee moves out of a designated area—for example, to alert a parent that a child has wandered out of the backyard. These devices can also be used for surveillance as long as the tracker stays within range of the trackee.

Cellular. Mobile locating (sometimes called mobile triangulation) tracks the position of a cellular device, such as a mobile phone, based on its distance from cell towers. The accuracy of mobile locating depends on the number of nearby towers and the coverage area.

A cell phone tower covers a roughly circular area anywhere from 0.5–30 miles in diameter. In rural areas, for example, a single cell tower might provide service for a five-mile radius. A cellular device can determine its approximate distance from the tower by transmitting a short signal and gauging the time for a response.

Even when your distance from a tower is known, however, a tower with a non-directional antenna cannot determine if you are north, south, east, or west of it. Towers with directional antennas can more accurately pinpoint the direction from which a signal originates; but with a single tower, location cannot be determined with much accuracy.

In a situation where a cellular device is within range of more than one tower, accuracy increases dramatically. Signaling three towers, for example, produces circles for three ranges, and the phone is located where those circles overlap. Triangulation for a phone within range of two or more towers can be as accurate as 50 yards.

Figure 12-7

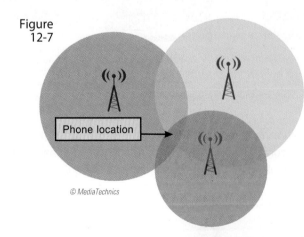

© MediaTechnics

To triangulate its location from a tower, a cellular device must be turned on. Your cell phone cannot be used to track your location when it is off. Whenever your phone is on, however, your cellular carrier has a record of the tower to which your phone is transmitting. Those records are stored in a database and can be accessed by the cellular carrier and by law enforcement personnel.

Technology
(continued)

GPS. **GPS** (Global Positioning System) technology is much more accurate than cellular triangulation. GPS-enabled devices include smartphones, handheld GPSs for outdoor activities (Figure 12-8), dash-mounted GPSs for driving, and GPS loggers for surveillance.

Figure
12-8

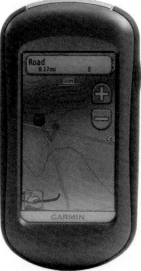

© MediaTechnics

GPS devices receive signals transmitted by a collection of Earth-orbiting satellites. A GPS device must lock on to four satellites to determine a location. That process takes about a minute every time you turn on the device. During the startup process, the device downloads almanac and ephemeris data from the satellites. This data provides current information about the satellites' orbits and locations throughout the day.

Getting a lock requires that the device have a line of sight to the sky. Signals transmitted by GPS satellites can pass through clouds, plastic, and glass, but not through buildings or mountains, which is why GPSs do not work indoors.

Once a GPS device has a satellite lock, its GPS chip continually monitors its location by executing a series of calculations based on its distance from each of the satellites. Consumer-level GPS devices are accurate to about 30 feet.

A basic GPS device has two components: a receiver/antenna to pick up satellite signals, and a GPS chip to perform the calculations necessary to pinpoint its location. These devices know their location but don't broadcast it.

Handheld and dash-mounted GPS units can tell you where you are, but don't transmit that information. GPS satellites are not equipped to receive location data, so any GPS device that sends location data requires additional transmitting capabilities, which are usually supplied by radio or cellular service.

The use of GPS-enabled tracking is exploding. Tiny GPS loggers can be inconspicuously mounted on rental cars, taxis, or trucks to log locations at various intervals. The device can later be retrieved and its database of geographical points uploaded to a computer.

Dedicated GPS tracking devices can also be locked onto a wrist or an elbow, carried in a purse, incorporated in an ID badge, or strapped to a belt. Used for keeping track of kids, elderly parents, pets, employees, and parolees, these devices can monitor the location and moving speed of the person being tracked. Used as a geofence, this type of device can send an alert when the person moves outside of a defined area, and can surreptitiously listen in on conversations. Alerts can be sent as text messages or e-mail. Detailed reports can be stored on the Web and accessed from a browser.

GPS-enabled cell phones can be configured to perform the same functions as dedicated GPS trackers. Software for these applications is available from cellular phone carriers and from independent software publishers. Once installed and running, the software periodically reports the phone's location to a Web server. The tracking map can be viewed by logging in to the Web server with your personal user ID and password.

Technology
(continued)

In addition to intentional tracking set up by the cell phone owner, a cell phone has the potential to determine its location using mobile locating or GPS, and broadcast it without the phone owner's permission or knowledge. Theoretically, such tracking can be done only by the cellular service provider with your permission (in the case of an emergency) or with a court order (in the case of a crime). Tracking is not possible if the phone is turned off or in areas where there is no cell service.

Figure
12-9

Source: Apple

RFID. A third tracking technology, **RFID** (Radio Frequency Identification), is quite different from GPS and mobile locating. RFID is not location aware, and its main capability is transmitting identification information. RFID technology's main use is to identify rather than geolocate. It is incorporated in passports, driver's licenses, credit cards, toll passcards, merchandise labels, and animal ID tags.

An RFID tag is composed of a tiny read-only memory chip and transmitter that are incorporated onto a flexible backing. Each RFID tag includes an antenna that picks up electromagnetic energy beamed from a reader device. The chip uses this energy to send back data from the read-only memory chip. The big advantage of RFID is that tags can be scanned by a remote reader without swiping or making any sort of physical connection.

At the simplest level, an RFID tag stores a unique ID number that can be cross-checked with a database containing additional information. More sophisticated RFID tags contain a fairly extensive set of data, however. RFID credit cards, for example, include account numbers and expiration dates.

Unauthorized access is a potential problem with RFID tags. They can be read right through your clothes, purse, wallet, or backpack without your knowledge or consent. When carried in a wallet inside a purse, RFID cards can be read from a distance of nine feet. An RFID card casually carried in a pocket can be read from a distance of 20 feet. To prevent unauthorized scanning of any RFID cards that you carry, consider keeping them in protective sleeves or shielded wallets. You can find these products on the Web.

Project

Explore databases

Collections of data have existed since long before the term "database" was coined. However, the ability to store these collections electronically and manage them efficiently with database software has become so indispensable to our current lifestyle that it's hard to imagine how we got along without them. In this chapter, you were shown how to design and build databases. You also learned that you can use spreadsheet software to perform basic database functions.

When you have completed the project, you should be able to:

- Create a database.

- Design and build tables.

- Create a report.

Requirements: This project requires Microsoft Windows and database software (such as Microsoft Office Access or LibreOffice Base), or spreadsheet software if database software is not available.

Deliverables:

1. A database containing ten records for books in your collection

2. A report listing book titles, authors, and publishers sorted by title

1. Open your database or spreadsheet software.

2. Suppose you have a personal library containing several books that you like to lend out to friends. To prevent lost or unreturned books, you can keep track of them by creating a simple library database. Create a database as follows:

   a. In Microsoft Access 2013, select *Blank desktop database* from the preliminary screen.

   b. In LibreOffice Base, use the Database Wizard. Select the following options: *Create a new database*, *Do not register the database*, and *Open the database for editing*.

   c. If you're using spreadsheet software, you should have a blank spreadsheet on your screen.

3. Name the database [Your Name] Library and click the Create or Save button. If you're using spreadsheet software, use the Save As option and name the file [Your Name] Library.

• Explore databases (continued)

4. Enter the following field names, data types, and descriptions to create a table. (Hint: If you are using spreadsheet software, simply enter the field names as column headings.)

Field Name	Field Type	Description
Title	Text (Short Text)	The book title
Author	Text (Short Text)	The author(s) of the book
Publisher	Text (Short Text)	The book publisher
Borrower	Text (Short Text)	The person who borrowed the book
Date Out	Date & Time	The date the book was borrowed
E-mail	Text (Short Text)	The borrower's e-mail address

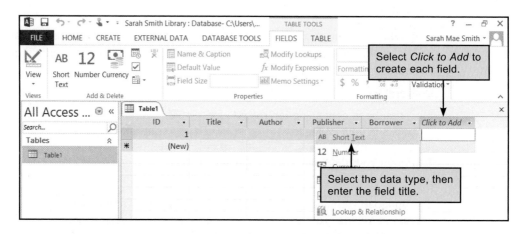

5. A **primary key** is a field that functions as the unique identifier for each record. Access automatically created the ID field when the table was created. In Base, you must add the field to the table; use ID as the field name, select Integer as the field type, and select Yes for AutoValue in the Field Properties section at the bottom of the window.

6. Save the table.

    a. In Access, click the Save button on the Quick Access toolbar, enter Personal Library, then click the OK button.

    b. In Base, close the Design View window, save your changes, then name the table Personal Library. When Design View closes, Select Personal Library to open your completed table.

    c. For a spreadsheet, click the Sheet1 tab and rename it Personal Library.

7. The empty table should now be ready for data entry. Choose ten books that you own and fill in all of the fields except Borrower and E-mail. If you want to change the width of any columns, you can drag the dividing line between field headings. Click the Save button, then close the table.

• Explore databases (continued)

8. Sort your list of books by Author. (Hint: Use the field headings.)

9. Fill in the Borrower, Date Out, and E-mail fields for two of your records.

10. Open the Report Wizard by completing the following steps:
    a. In Access, select the CREATE tab, then select the Report Wizard button.
    b. In LibreOffice Base, close the Personal Library table, select the Report icon, then select the option to use the Report Wizard.
    c. For a spreadsheet, do your best to duplicate the format shown in the screen below.

11. Interact with the Report Wizard to enter the following specifications:

    Include the Title, Author, and Publisher fields only.

    Do not add a grouping level.

    Sort by title.

    Select the Tabular format and use Personal Library as the report title.

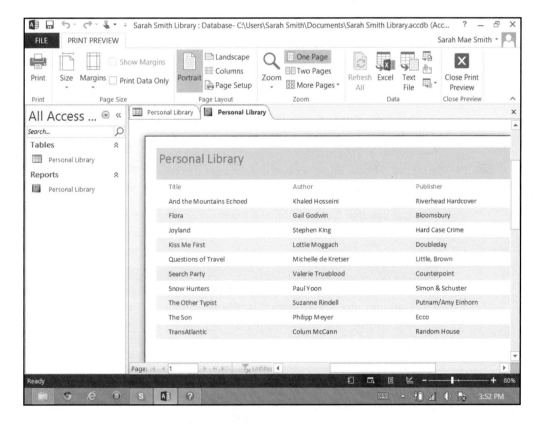

12. Save the table and report before closing your database.

13. Submit your database on a flash drive, as an e-mail attachment, or as a printout according to your instructor's preference.

Issue

Who owns information about me?

There is an astounding amount of information stored about you in computer databases. Your bank has information on your financial status, credit history, and the people, organizations, and businesses to which you write checks. School records indicate something about your ability to learn and the subjects that interest you. Medical records indicate the state of your health.

Credit card companies track the merchants you deal with and what you purchase in person, by mail, or over the Internet. Your phone company stores your phone number, your address, and a list of the phone numbers you dial. The driver's license bureau has your physical description. Your Internet cookies track many of the Web sites that you frequent. Using this data would make it possible to guess some very private things about you, such as your political views or even your sexual orientation.

When records were manually stored on index cards and in file folders, locating and distributing data was a laborious process that required hand transcriptions or photocopies of sheaves of papers. Today, this data exists in electronic format and is easy to access, copy, sell, ship, consolidate, and alter.

Privacy advocates point out the potential for misusing data that has been collected and stored in computer databases. They are encouraging lawmakers to restrict the sale and distribution of information about individuals. One proposal would require your permission before information about you can be distributed.

However, the wisdom of such a proposal has been questioned, and not just by corporate interests. Information about you is not necessarily "yours." Information about you can be collected without your direct input.

For example, suppose you default on your credit card payments. The credit card company has accumulated information on your delinquent status. Shouldn't it have the freedom to distribute this information, for example, to another credit card company? Or suppose a home improvement store keeps a record of the products you purchase. Does that information belong to you or the store?

You can see that the issue of who owns information is not always clear. If you are not the owner of information, you might not have the right to control it.

What do you think?

1. Can you identify an actual incident when you discovered that data about you had been distributed without your approval?   ○ Yes ○ No ○ Not sure

2. Do you accurately fill out all the questionnaires that you encounter on the Web?   ○ Yes ○ No ○ Not sure

3. Do you think that you have a right to be consulted before anyone distributes information about you?   ○ Yes ○ No ○ Not sure

QuickCheck A

1. A(n) [_____] database is able to link the records from two or more tables and treat them as a single unit.

2. True or false? To access databases on the Web, you'll have to purchase database software. [_____]

3. To create your own databases, you must first design the file [_____] by specifying the names for each data field.

4. True or false? The location of a GPS-equipped cell phone can be electronically triangulated even when it is turned off. [_____]

5. A basic [_____] tag stores a unique serial number that can be transmitted to a reader device and cross-checked against a database.

CHECKIT!

QuickCheck B

Carefully examine the entries in the database. Give each record indicated by an arrow an **A** if it meets the criteria described on page 189 for accurate and consistent data. Otherwise, give it an **F**.

1. [____]

2. [____]

3. [____]

4. [____]

5. [____]

	ID	Category	Company	Toll-Free Number	Purchase Date
1. →	1	Computer	Dell	(800) 624-9896	8/30/2012
	2	Printer	Epson	(800) 444-1498	9/1/2009
2. →	3	Sofware	Microsoft	(866) 234-6020	9/10/2012
	4	Printer	Hewlett-Packard	(800) 474-6836	11/16/2007
	5	Computer	IBM	(800) 426-6666	3/27/2012
3. →	6	Printer	I.B.M.	(800) 426-6666	8/12/2008
	7	Computer	IBM	(800) 426-6666	6/28/2009
4. →	8	Computer	dell	(800) 224-9896	7/12/2010
	9	Software	Adobe	(800) 833-6687	6/20/2013
5. →	10	Printers	Epson	(800) 444-1498	9/30/2013
	11	Computer	Compaq	(800) 474-6836	9/1/2009

Equipment

CHECKIT!

GETIT? While using the digital textbook, click the Get It? button to see if you can answer ten randomly selected questions from Chapter 12.

13 Making Presentations

What's inside?

Chapter 13 focuses on creating and delivering computer-supported presentations in settings such as classes, meetings, clubs, committees, and fund-raisers. Using computer software designed for presentations, you can create a compelling and effective visual backdrop that helps your audience pay attention and understand your key points.

What's in the digital book?

Chapter 13 walks you through the key activities for creating computer-supported presentations. In addition, a video shows you how to set up presentation equipment.

FAQ How do I create effective visuals for a presentation?

Presentation software, such as Microsoft PowerPoint and LibreOffice Impress, can help you create the visual backdrop for speeches, lectures, and demonstrations. A presentation consists of slides that can be viewed on a computer monitor, large-screen TV, or projection screen.

A **presentation slide** can contain text, graphics, and audio elements. Each slide usually has a title. A few simple bulleted items can be used to present key concepts. Numbered lists can present the steps in a process. Tables, charts, or graphs can simplify complex ideas and present numerical or statistical data. Diagrams can illustrate processes or devices. Photos add an element of realism. Slides can even contain video and audio clips. When creating a presentation, use the elements that best help your audience understand the information you want to convey.

You can create a presentation simply by generating a series of slides, or you can begin by using the outlining feature of your presentation software to work on the progression of ideas that you want to present. Your outline can then be converted into slides.

Making a slide is easy. Your presentation software offers a variety of **slide layouts** that help you place titles, text, lists, graphs, photos, and other elements. You can easily insert, delete, and rearrange slides until your presentation is just right. Click the Try It! button to find out how to select slide layouts and add elements, such as titles, bulleted lists, and numbered lists.

TRY IT!

Figure 13-1

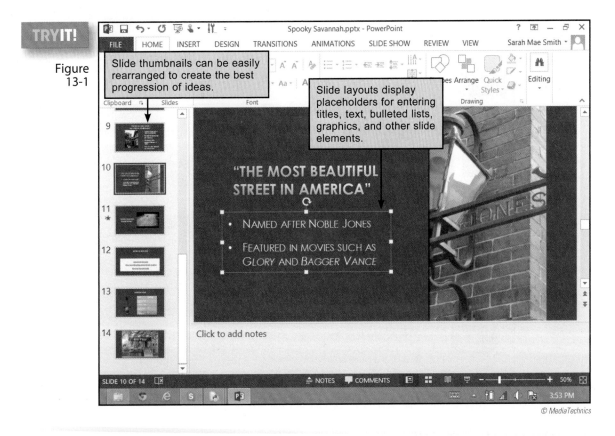

© MediaTechnics

FAQ How do I choose the right colors, graphics, and fonts for my slides?

The slides in a presentation can be unified by colors, formats, and styles. Most presentation software provides a variety of options for the "look" of your slides. These options are called themes, templates, or Quick Styles, depending on the presentation software you're using.

Presentation themes simplify the process of creating a presentation by providing ready-made, professional-looking background graphics, fonts, and other visual elements that are designed to complement each other.

Themes can support the message you want your presentation to communicate. When you select a theme, consider the point you want to make and the image you want to convey. Bright colors and snappy graphics, for example, tend to convey a more casual approach than somber colors. If you don't find a suitable theme, you can create one from scratch or you can modify a predefined theme.

Professionally designed themes are suitable for most presentation venues. You should, however, use a font size that can be easily seen by your audience. When selecting font sizes, consider the size of the room, the size of your presentation screen, and the distance between your audience and the screen. You can select a theme for your slides when you first create a new presentation, or you can apply a theme after you've entered the content of your slides. Click the Try It! button to see how to select a theme when working with Microsoft PowerPoint.

TRY IT!

Figure 13-2

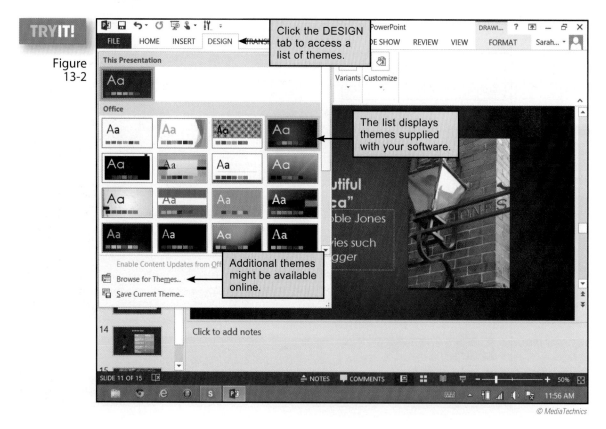

© MediaTechnics

FAQ How should I use transitions and animations?

A **transition effect** specifies how a slide replaces the previous slide during a presentation. Transitions include fades, wipes, and dissolves. You can also select sound effects to accompany a transition. If you do not specify a transition, the current slide simply cuts to a new slide.

An **animation effect** adds motion to slide elements, such as titles or bulleted list items. A frequently used animation effect makes bulleted list items glide onto a slide one by one under the control of the person delivering the presentation. Other effects include enlarging, shrinking, and spinning.

Transitions and animations can be set to occur when you click a mouse button or press a key during a presentation. They can also be set to occur automatically after a specified period of time. Use the automatic settings when a transition or an animation does not have to coordinate with a specific statement you make during the presentation.

It is easy to get carried away with spiffy transitions and animations; but after the fourth slide that spins onto the screen accompanied by blaring trumpets or your favorite rap ring tone, the audience might get a bit irritated. Use transitions and animations sparingly for highlighting the most important points, or for a change of pace during the more lengthy segments of your presentation. Click the Try It! button for a demonstration of handy transitions and animation effects.

Figure 13-3

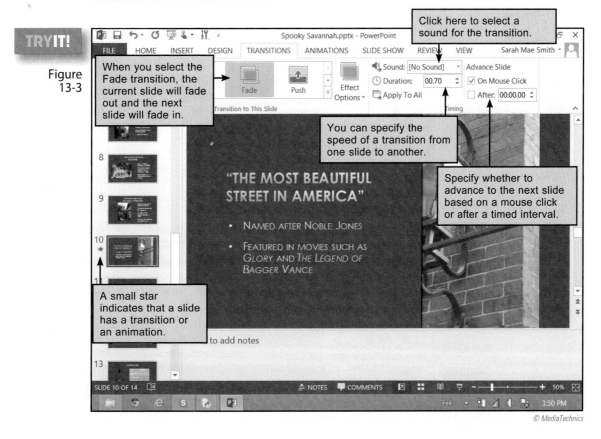

© MediaTechnics

FAQ How do I finalize a presentation?

Presentations are designed for various purposes. Some presentations are intended to convey information, whereas others are designed to convince the audience of your point of view. Avoid pitfalls that will reduce the credibility of your presentation. Make sure you check spelling and grammar on every slide. In addition, check your facts to make sure they are accurate.

The slides in your presentation should reinforce the ideas that you want to present; they are not the script for your presentation. If all you do is read your slides to your audience, your presentation will be very dull. You should plan to embellish your presentation with additional facts and comments. To remember what you want to say, you can add **speaker notes** to each slide.

Your presentation software provides various ways to print speaker notes for reference during a presentation. You can print them in the form of a script. Alternatively, you can print each slide with its corresponding speaker notes.

Your presentation software is also likely to offer a way to show speaker notes on your computer screen, but display the notes-free slides on the projected image that's seen by the audience. To set up dual displays, Windows must be configured to support two monitors. Additional settings might be required from within the presentation software. With PowerPoint, for example, use the Monitors group on the SLIDE SHOW tab to select Presenter View.

Speaker notes not only remind you of what you want to say about a slide; they also help you maintain good rapport with your audience because you don't have to look at the projected slides behind you. The Try It! for Figure 13-4 helps you explore speaker notes.

TRYIT!

Figure 13-4

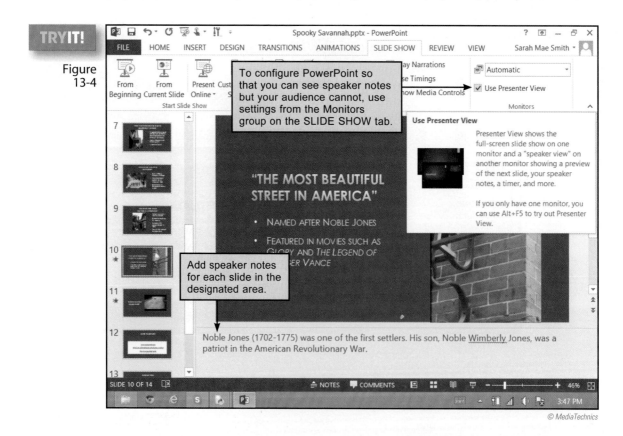

© MediaTechnics

FAQ How do I deliver a presentation?

Typically, you will deliver presentations using your presentation software's slide show view. This view hides the toolbars, ribbons, and other controls you used to create the presentation, and displays each slide at the full size of the screen. You can use the mouse button or arrow keys to move from one slide to the next.

To highlight important information, you can write on slides during the presentation. When using PowerPoint, for example, select a pen or highlighter from the Pointer Options menu by right-clicking the slide. Hold down the left mouse button and drag the pointer to write on the slide.

As an alternative to delivering a presentation to a live audience, you can distribute your presentation in several other ways. You can print your slides on paper and distribute them as handouts. PowerPoint presentations can also be converted into PDF format, which can be viewed on any computer with Adobe Reader installed.

PowerPoint presentations can be displayed using a viewer instead of the full presentation software product. A program called PowerPoint Viewer displays presentations on computers on which PowerPoint is not installed. PowerPoint Viewer can be downloaded for free from the Microsoft Web site. You can package your presentation on a CD along with PowerPoint Viewer for people who cannot attend your live presentation.

Some presentation software converts slides to HTML pages that you can post on the Web, but these pages typically do not incorporate transitions and animations. With PowerPoint 2013, however, you can save the presentation as a video that includes transitions, animations, and sounds. These PowerPoint videos can be posted on the Web. Access the Try It! to find out how to turn a PowerPoint presentation into a video.

TRY IT!

Figure 13-5

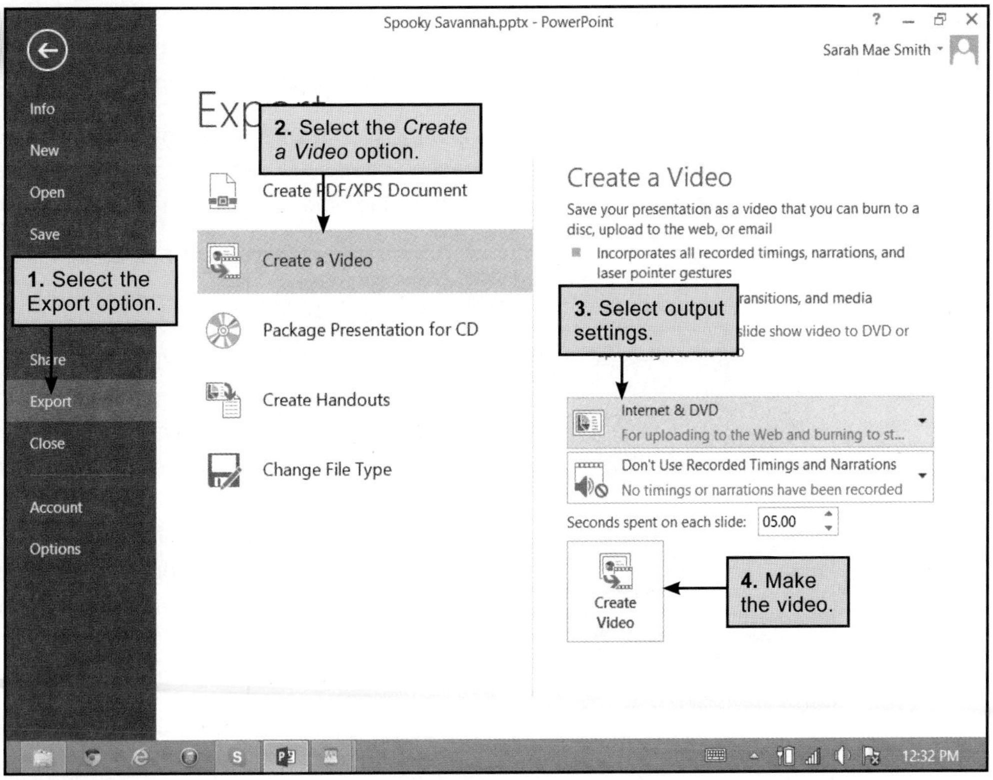

Technology

Computer projection devices

You can display the slides for a presentation on a PC screen for a one-on-one or small group presentation. For large groups, a **computer projection device** can display your slides on a wall screen in a conference room or theater.

Figure
13-6

Source: Dell

Computer projection devices are commonly used in schools, libraries, and businesses. You are likely to have an opportunity to use one—for example, when you pitch a new publicity campaign to your company's best client; when you give an oral report in your anthropology class; when you brief volunteers for the United Way campaign; or even when you're trying to convince the city council to put some effort into urban renewal. Two types of projection devices popular today are LCD projectors and DLP projectors.

An **LCD projector** shines a bright light through a small LCD (liquid crystal display) panel. The LCD contains a matrix of tiny elements that form the colors for an image. Light is projected through the LCD matrix to generate a large image on a wall or screen.

A **DLP projector** shines a bright light onto an array of miniature mirrors. The mirrors rotate to create different colored dots on the projected image. DLP projectors have a reputation for smooth, jitter-free images, with good contrast and less screen-door effect than LCD projectors. **Screen-door effect** refers to the perception that the pixels in an image are surrounded by a thin black border, giving the impression that you are looking through a fine mesh screen. Prices for computer projection devices are $199 and up, with DLP projectors costing a bit more than LCD projectors with similar features.

Projection devices connect to computers, standalone DVD players, and cable television converter boxes. A variety of connecting cables are generally supplied with every projector; the types of cables depend on the type of video signals the projector accepts.

PLAYIT!

Figure
13-7

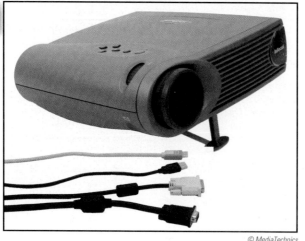

© MediaTechnics

When connecting a projector to your computer, you usually have a choice of using DVI, HDMI, VGA, or Mini DisplayPort connectors. DVI, Mini DisplayPort, and HDMI are digital ports and produce the best quality output. Use digital ports if you have them on your computer and projector. Click the Play It! button to find out how to connect an LCD projector to a laptop PC.

Technology
(continued)

Factors that affect the price of LCD and DLP projectors include brightness, resolution, and portability. The brightness of a projection device is measured in lumens, sometimes expressed as ANSI lumens. Projection devices with higher lumen ratings produce a brighter picture and can be more easily viewed in rooms with ambient light. A projector with less than 2,000 lumens is best used in a dark room.

Image resolution refers to the number of pixels that can be displayed by the projection device. As is the case with most computer screens, higher resolution projection devices typically cost more than those with lower resolutions. Basic computer projection devices support either SVGA (800 x 600), XGA (1024 x 768), or WXGA (1280 x 800) resolution.

As a rule of thumb for PowerPoint presentations, look for a projector that has the same resolution as your computer screen. You can lower the resolution on your computer to match a low-resolution projector; but if your projector resolution is higher than your computer screen resolution, the interpolated image will tend to appear fuzzy.

Smaller and lighter projection devices normally cost more than larger, heavier devices with similar specifications. Many portable projection devices—those designed to be carried from presentation to presentation—weigh less than five pounds. Projectors suitable for portable or fixed applications weigh in at seven to ten pounds. Heavier units are intended for permanent installations.

While many projection devices are used for training and group presentations, video buffs have discovered that LCD or DLP projectors work very well as large-screen projection devices for home theaters. A laptop computer with a DVD drive can serve as the core of a home theater system when connected to a set of large speakers and a projection device. Projectors designed for home theaters have resolutions of 720p (1280 x 720) or 1080p (1920 x 1080).

Computer projection devices can include bells and whistles to enhance presentations, such as built-in speakers, remote controls, and built-in CD/DVD players. Keystone control is available on most projector models. **Keystoning**, the bane of professional speakers and audio-visual specialists, is the tendency of projected images to appear more like trapezoids than true rectangles. It occurs when the projector is not positioned directly in line with the middle of the screen. Because it is often practical to mount the projector on a table that's lower than the screen or on the ceiling above the screen, keystoning is a common artifact of presentations. Keystone control compensates for the position of the projector to produce a professional-looking rectangular image.

Figure
13-8

© MediaTechnics

The projected image has keystoning.   Keystone control squares off the image.

Technology
(continued)

Technology is great—when it works. But it doesn't always work. Occasional problems with your PC can affect your personal productivity, but technology glitches can become very public when you depend on presentation equipment. It's awfully nerve-wracking to stand in front of a group of 100 people while someone tries to track down a replacement bulb for the LCD projector. You can avoid many of the curveballs that technology throws your way if you get serious about planning and preparing for your presentation:

- **Determine whether presentation equipment will be available.** If you plan to use your own laptop computer, make sure it is compatible with the projection device and that the correct connecting cables will be supplied. If you intend to use a computer other than your own, make sure the necessary presentation software has been installed.

- **Check out the equipment ahead of time.** If possible, schedule a trial run the day before your presentation. Connect your computer and then display a few slides so you are certain that everything works.

- **Make sure that your audience will be able to see and hear your presentation.** During your trial run, sit in the back of the room and be certain that the text on your slides is large enough to be easily read.

- **Arrive early.** Allow at least 30 minutes to set up your equipment and connect it to the presentation device.

- **Know how to get technical support.** If you are unfamiliar with any of the equipment, you might request the presence of a technical support person during your trial run or while you set up. Find out how you can contact a technician if you run into problems during the presentation.

- **Be prepared for problems.** Find out what to do if the projector bulb burns out. If you're using a laptop PC with batteries, keep your power cord handy. If this presentation can make or break your career, you might consider printing copies of your most important slides so that you can distribute them to your audience in case of a power failure.

Figure 13-9

© Pavel L Photo and Video/Shutterstock.com

Project

Explore presentation software

Presentation software is optimized to create slides containing text, sound effects, and graphics. You can design your slides from scratch, but you'll also find a good selection of ready-made slide templates that contain professionally designed background graphics and fonts in sizes that are easy to read when projected on a wall screen.

Most office suites include a collection of clip art images that provide eye-catching additions to documents, spreadsheets, and slides. For a true multimedia presentation, you can add sound effects to your slides. You can incorporate even more visual interest by selecting active transition effects between slides, such as fades, wipes, and dissolves.

When you have completed this project, you should be able to:

- Select a slide template to use as the theme for your presentation.
- Create a slide with a bulleted list.
- Add an animation effect for the bulleted list.
- Add an image to a slide.
- Select a transition effect.
- Add speaker notes for your slides.

Requirements: This project requires Microsoft Windows and presentation software, such as Microsoft PowerPoint or LibreOffice Impress.

The deliverable for this project is a three-slide presentation that includes:

1. A title slide
2. A second slide with a bulleted list
3. An animation effect for the bulleted list on the second slide
4. A third slide with clip art
5. A transition effect for all slides
6. Speaker notes for all slides

1. Open your presentation software.

2. Suppose you want to create a presentation that explains why it is important to contribute to a charity such as UNICEF. Begin by choosing an appropriate template or theme for your presentation.

   a. In Microsoft PowerPoint, begin with a blank presentation, then select the DESIGN tab. Rest your pointer on several themes to get a preview of their colors and backgrounds. When you find a theme you like, select it.

   b. In LibreOffice Impress, use the Presentation Wizard. In Step 1 of the Wizard, choose *From template*, click the down-arrow button beside Presentations, then select Presentation Backgrounds. Select one of the options. In Step 2, select Slide for the output medium, then click the Create button. Select the Title Slide layout from the Layouts task pane after the wizard closes. The task pane is located on the right side of the screen.

• Explore presentation software (continued)

3. Enter an appropriate title for your title slide, such as UNICEF. Enter a subtitle, such as The United Nations Children's Fund.

4. Add a new slide containing a title and bulleted list.
   a. In PowerPoint, click the HOME tab, click the New Slide button, then select the *Title and Content* layout.
   b. In Impress, click the Insert menu, then select Slide. When the new slide is displayed, select the *Title, Content* layout from the Layouts task pane.

5. Type a title and enter your bulleted items. Compare your slide to the example below. If you make any mistakes and you want to delete a slide, you can select the slide in the Slides task pane and press the Delete key on the keyboard.

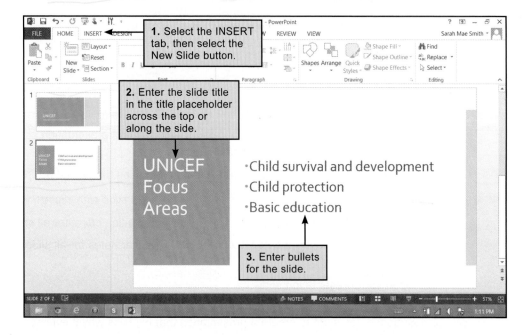

6. Add an animation effect to the bulleted list. (Hint: Be sure the insertion point is positioned within the bulleted list.)
   a. In PowerPoint, click the ANIMATIONS tab. Select the Fly In animation from the Animation Styles list.
   b. In Impress, from the Custom Animation task pane, click the Add button, select the Fly In effect, then click the OK button.

7. Create a new slide containing graphics and text.
   a. In PowerPoint, add a slide with the *Content with Caption* layout. Select the Online Pictures button in the Content area of the slide. Enter children in the search box. Select a cute cartoon, then close the Clip Art task pane.
   b. In Impress, add a slide with the *Title, Content* layout. Double-click the Insert Picture icon. Select an image from your Pictures library.

• Explore presentation software (continued)

8. Resize the graphic as necessary by dragging the sizing handles. **Sizing handles** are small squares or circles at the corners and sides of a graphic used for resizing the graphic.

9. Enter a title for your slide and add appropriate text, as in the example below.

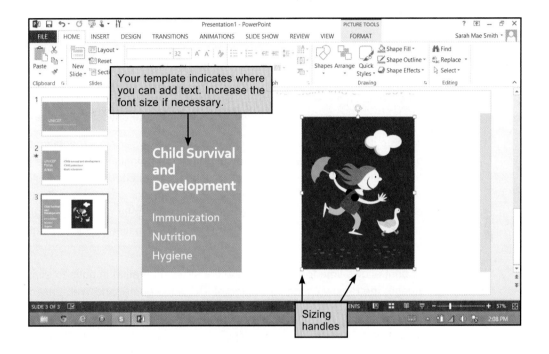

10. Apply a slide transition effect to all your slides.
    a. In PowerPoint, select the TRANSITIONS tab. Select a transition, then select the Apply To All button in the Timing group.
    b. In Impress, select a transition from the Slide Transition pane. Scroll to the bottom of the pane, then select the *Apply to All Slides* button.

11. Add speaker notes to all your slides. In Impress, select the Notes tab above your current slide.

12. View your slide show. In PowerPoint, select the SLIDE SHOW tab, then select the From Beginning button. In Impress, select the first slide, select the Slide Show menu, then select Slide Show.

13. Save your file as Project 13 [Your Name].

14. Submit your presentation file as an e-mail attachment or using any other delivery method specified by your instructor.

Issue

Is it the medium or the message?

A Canadian professor named Marshall McLuhan coined the phrase "the medium is the message" to express the idea that media, such as films, books, and television, have an impact far greater than that of the material they communicate. Suppose you're surfing the Web and you encounter a site with barely readable light pink text. This site might as well carry no message as far as you're concerned. You might skip it because the text is too difficult to read. This is a clear case of the medium (that awful light pink text) becoming the message (don't bother).

"The medium is the message" is not, however, the last word of advice for people who create documents, spreadsheets, and presentations. It would be a miscalculation to believe that your content doesn't matter as long as it is wrapped up in a flashy package. Today's media-savvy audience members might be entertained by bling, but they can quickly bypass the visuals, transitions, and animations to critically examine your ideas.

Growing up in a world of fast-paced multimedia creates certain expectations about the pace and format of information. Some cultural anthropologists hypothesize that today's media mix might affect the evolution of individuals and cultural groups. Children exposed to the fast-paced media blitz of music videos, pop music, and special effects may be developing psychological coping mechanisms that are quite different from those of their parents and grandparents, who spent time with slower-paced media, including printed books, magazines, and newspapers.

While print allows time for reflection and constructing mental images to supplement words on a page, the rapidly changing collage of TV, video game, and Web-based images requires participants to develop quite a different set of mental skills.

Today, effectively conveying a message requires a variety of skills. Good presenters need to understand how to use electronic tools provided by software and digital devices, but they also must consider the perceptions and psychology of their audience.

What do you think?

1. Do you believe that McLuhan was correct in saying that "the medium is the message"?   ◯ Yes ◯ No ◯ Not sure

2. Do you agree that, as a rule of thumb, the time you devote to preparing for a presentation should be divided as 50% research and writing, and 50% designing electronic slides?   ◯ Yes ◯ No ◯ Not sure

3. Do you believe that electronic media can fundamentally change the personality and thought patterns of an entire generation?   ◯ Yes ◯ No ◯ Not sure

QuickCheck A

1. Fades, wipes, and dissolves are examples of [_____] effects, which determine how a slide replaces the previous slide in a presentation.

2. Speaker [_____] that you add to your slides can form the script for your presentation.

3. Most projection devices use either LCD or [_____] technology.

4. True or false? Projectors designed for home theaters have resolutions of 720p or 1080p. [_____]

5. True or false? Selecting the right theme can support the message you want your presentation to communicate. [_____]

CHECKIT!

QuickCheck B

Indicate the letter that correctly matches each description.

1. A slide with an animation effect [____]

2. Speaker notes [____]

3. A sizing handle [____]

4. A sound effect [____]

5. A transition effect [____]

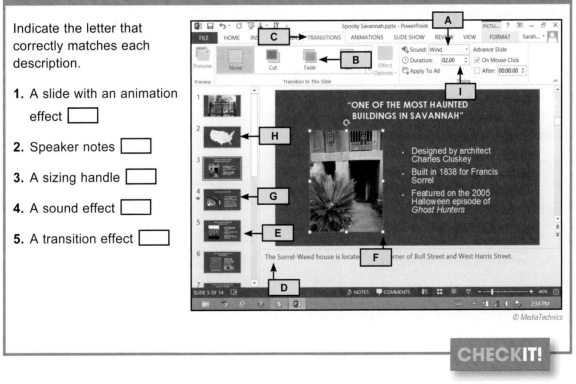

© MediaTechnics

CHECKIT!

 GETIT? While using the digital textbook, click the Get It? button to see if you can answer ten randomly selected questions from Chapter 13.

CHAPTER **14** # Recording and Editing Sound

What's inside?

Music, sound effects, and speech are important features of our environment. Therefore, it seems natural for PCs to have audio capabilities. In Chapter 14, you'll learn how computers generate sound effects, speech, and music, and you'll find out how to incorporate audio in your own projects.

What's in the digital book?

Because sound is the topic of Chapter 14, you'll get the most benefit from the chapter's software tours and videos if your PC is equipped for sound and you have speakers or headphones.

FAQ How does audio capability enhance my PC?

Sound adds dimension to your computing experience. Beeps and other sound effects provide feedback as you use your PC, alerting you to error messages and other important events. Music lovers can connect to their favorite music store on the Web and listen to sample tracks. Sound effects can enliven business presentations. Children can listen while their PCs read stories. Computer game enthusiasts can hear a riot of sound effects as monsters attack, grenades explode, and tanks rumble past war-torn computerscapes. Individuals with visual disabilities can also gain access to computers through technology that reads aloud the content of a PC screen.

Computers work with two general categories of sound: digital audio and synthesized sound. **Digital audio** is a recording of real music, vocals, sound effects, or speech that has been converted into electronic signals, which a computer can then store, manipulate, and transmit. **Synthesized sound** has not been recorded from a live source, but instead has been generated by a machine—such as a computer. Click the Play It! buttons in Figure 14-1 and listen to digital audio and synthesized sound clips. Can you tell the difference?

PLAYIT!

PLAYIT!

Figure 14-1   Digital audio   Synthesized sound   © MediaTechnics

Each category of sound has unique characteristics and applications. The table in Figure 14-2 offers an overview of digital audio and synthesized sound, designed to help you select the one that is most suitable for your projects.

Figure 14-2

	File Type	Characteristics	Popular Uses
Digital Audio	AAC and M4P	Good sound quality, small files	iTunes
	MP3	Good sound quality, small files	Digital music players; music downloads
	WAV	Good sound quality, but large files; supported in browsers without a plug-in	Background music for Web pages, recording your voice on your PC, ring tones
	WMA	Good sound quality, small files	Commonly used on Windows computers for recording and playback; Xbox Music downloads
	Ogg (Vorbis)	Free, open standard; supported by some browsers	Free music, Creative Commons files for Wikipedia
Synthesized Sound	MIDI	Synthesized sound, very small files	Digital instruments, background music for Web pages, movie and game sound effects, ring tones

© MediaTechnics

FAQ What are the best sources for digital music?

Today, a dwindling amount of digital music is distributed on audio CDs. Most music is now distributed by Internet-based music services. These services use two distribution models: downloading and streaming.

Downloading music. The files that contain digital music can be downloaded from an Internet-based server to your desktop computer, laptop, tablet, smartphone, or digital music player. Popular online music stores include iTunes, Google Play, 7digital, and Amazon MP3. Music download and playback are usually aided by an app or a browser plug-in. A **plug-in** is a software component that adds functionality to a browser, such as the ability to play MP3 music. Music download services commonly charge by the song, though some services offer free music and a few allow unlimited downloads for a monthly subscription.

Downloaded files from some services are protected by **digital rights management** (DRM) that limits copying and sharing. Music that is not protected by DRM, however, is still copyrighted, so read the download site's usage policy to find out if copying and sharing are allowed.

Streaming music. Streaming is a digital delivery process that transmits a music file as a stream of data in real time as you listen to it. The process is similar to listening to a radio broadcast because you listen as the music is transmitted, and the music is not permanently stored on your computer.

Popular music streaming services include Spotify, iTunes Radio, Pandora, Rdio, Rhapsody, and Slacker. Some of these services allow subscribers to select songs and create custom playlists, whereas other services provide preselected music in the form of "radio stations" that offer various music genres such as rock, rap, classical, and jazz. Streaming music services are typically subscription-based. A free version of the service might be available with advertising, whereas a paid subscription might be ad-free.

Streaming music requires a player compatible with the music file format. If your browser already has the required plug-in, you'll not need to download anything. If the music is supplied in a specialized format, then you might have to download a player or an app. Apps might also offer extra features, such as displaying song lyrics and album reviews.

Figure
14-3

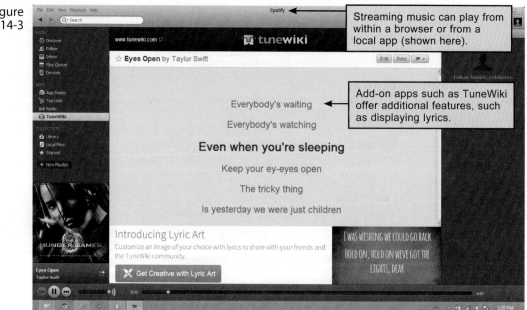

Streaming music can play from within a browser or from a local app (shown here).

Add-on apps such as TuneWiki offer additional features, such as displaying lyrics.

Source: Spotify

FAQ What do I need to know about converting music files?

Music and other audio files are stored in various formats, and those formats might not play on all of your devices. You can, however, convert music files from one format to another. For example, suppose you find a cool MIDI ring tone on the Web. It won't work on your iPhone unless you convert it into an MP3. And what about the songs on your favorite audio CD? If you want to listen to them on your iPod, you'll have to rip the tracks into MP3 or AAC format.

Ripping is a slang term that refers to the process of importing tracks from an audio CD to your computer's hard disk. The technical term for ripping is **digital audio extraction**. Ripping is handy if you have a CD and you'd like to move one or more tracks to your computer hard disk or a portable device, such as an iPod. You can also import ripped tracks to your iTunes collection.

Music is stored on CDs in a digital format called **CD-DA** (Compact Disc Digital Audio). The format offers high fidelity; but as with WAV files, one minute of CD-DA music requires in excess of 10 MB of storage space. During the ripping process, music in CD-DA format is converted into a compressed format such as MP3, AAC, or WMA to reduce file size.

Many software tools are available for ripping CD tracks. One of the most versatile tools is Apple iTunes software. Windows Media Player, distributed with Microsoft Windows, also includes ripping routines.

In the United States, ripping music for personal use is controversial. Consumer advocates argue that it is acceptable "fair use," whereas representatives of the music industry maintain that ripping without permission is not legal. You are most likely acting legally if you rip tracks only from CDs that you have purchased, and keep the ripped versions for your own use. Click the Try It! button to learn how to rip tracks from a CD using iTunes software.

TRY IT!

Figure
14-4

Source: Apple

FAQ What should I know about MIDI?

MIDI (Musical Instrument Digital Interface) specifies a standard way to store music data for synthesizers, electronic MIDI instruments, and computers. Unlike digital audio files, which contain digitized recordings of real music and voices, MIDI files contain a set of instructions—called **MIDI messages**—for synthesizing music based on the pitch, volume, and duration of each note made by each instrument. MIDI music is like a player piano roll that produces notes based on the position of punched holes, whereas digital audio is analogous to a tape recording.

To translate MIDI messages into music, most PCs use wavetable synthesis technology. **Wavetable synthesis** generates music by patching together a set of sounds that were prerecorded as individual notes from actual instruments. This set of sounds is sometimes referred to as a **patch set**. The larger the patch set, the more realistic the sound.

MIDI is suitable for instrumental music but not for vocals because of the complexity of synthesizing the human voice singing lyrics. MIDI's advantage lies in its ability to store a lengthy musical sequence in a very small file. One minute of MIDI music might require only 10 KB of disk space, compared to 500 KB for one minute of MP3 music.

MIDI is a key component of techno dance music with its signature beat, and MIDI is commonly used as backup instrumentation in a wide variety of music styles. Sound effects for movies and computer games are usually generated using MIDI.

You can use **sequencer software**, such as Cakewalk SONAR, FL Studio, and Steinberg Cubase, to capture musical themes from a MIDI instrument, or you can enter the notes of your composition on a musical staff. You can then edit your composition by assigning the notes to different instruments, adding harmony, and inserting a percussion track. To find out what it's like to compose MIDI music, click the Try It! button.

TRYIT!

Figure 14-5

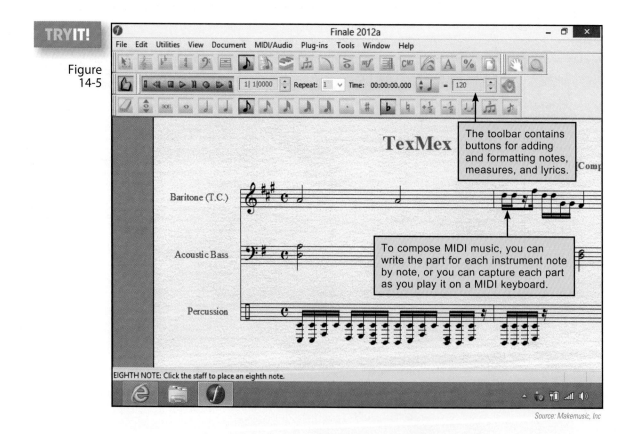

Source: Makemusic, Inc

FAQ How do computers recognize and generate speech?

Computers can accept and process spoken input using a process called **speech recognition**. Speech recognition software can be integrated with word processing software so that you can enter text simply by speaking into a microphone. Going beyond word processing, speech recognition can be used to activate Windows controls instead of using a mouse, and it can be used with a browser to "voice surf" the Web.

Speech synthesis is the process by which machines, such as computers, produce sound that resembles spoken words. Most speech synthesizers string together basic sound units called **phonemes**. For example, the phonemes "reh" and "gay" would produce the word "reggae."

A speech synthesis system typically includes text-to-speech software and synthesizing hardware. **Text-to-speech software** examines the text stored in a file, displayed on the screen, or entered from the keyboard, and then breaks it down into a series of sounds that can be output. **Synthesizing hardware** consists of electronic circuitry that can generate speech or musical sounds. PC-based speech synthesis uses the computer's built-in audio circuitry as synthesizing hardware.

Unlike digitized speech, synthesized speech can theoretically produce any words or phrases—not just those that you have recorded. Synthesized speech is ideal for applications that require a computer to generate spoken responses to typed or voice input. It provides the underlying technology for voice-response systems, such as telephone directory assistance, and the voices you hear on NOAA Weather Radio.

Text-to-speech systems also make it possible to phone your voice mail system and hear not only your voice mail messages, but also your computer e-mail. Perhaps most importantly, a speech synthesizer's ability to read a computer screen aloud is the key that unlocks access to PCs and to the Internet for individuals with visual disabilities. Windows includes a text-to-speech module called Narrator. Use the Try It! button to see and hear how it works.

TRY IT!

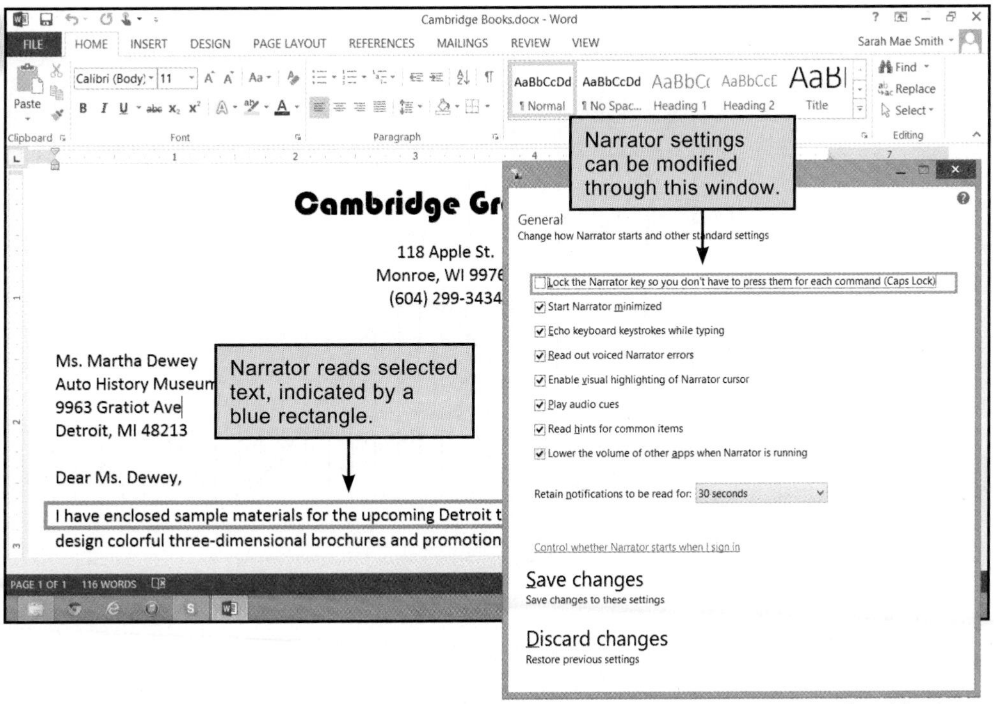

Figure 14-6

Source: Microsoft.com

Technology
Sampling

To create digital audio, you need a microphone and sound software, such as Windows Sound Recorder or open source Audacity. After you start the software, simply point the microphone at the sound source, then click the software's record button.

You probably know that a sound consists of energy waves, which your ears and brain detect as voices, music, and assorted sound effects. A sound wave provides information about a sound. The height of a wave indicates volume, which technically is called **amplitude**. The time between wave peaks indicates the sound's **frequency**—that is, whether it is a high note or a low note.

To digitally capture a sound wave, your PC periodically records a **sample** of the wave's amplitude as a binary number. A sequence of samples is stored as an audio file. The more samples your PC takes per second, the more accurately it can reproduce the wave.

Sampling rates are measured in kHz (kilohertz), where 1 kHz is 1,000 samples per second. An 11 kHz sampling rate produces fairly realistic digitized human speech. However, music requires sampling rates of 22 kHz or 44 kHz for good fidelity.

At higher sampling rates, digital audio samples (shown in green below) more closely follow the shape of the sound wave (shown in purple below). Click the Try It! buttons to compare the audio quality at each sampling rate.

Figure 14-7

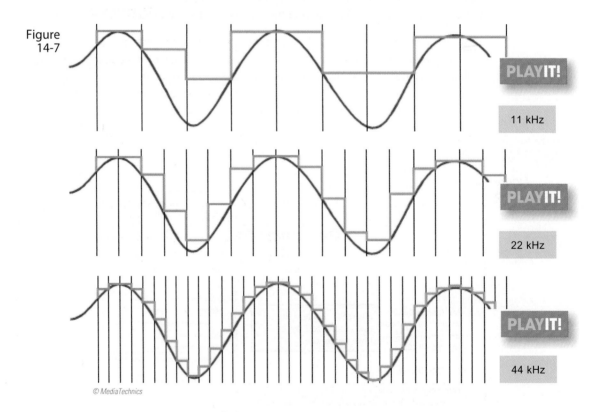

PLAYIT!

11 kHz

PLAYIT!

22 kHz

PLAYIT!

44 kHz

© MediaTechnics

Technology
(continued)

Sampling creates big files. One minute of digitally recorded music requires about 10 MB of storage space when stored in WAV format, a popular "raw" or non-compressed audio file type. Files stored in other non-compressed formats such as AIFF, AU, and PCM produce files of similar sizes.

To shrink files to more manageable sizes, they can be converted into compressed audio formats. As with compression of other media types, audio files can be compressed using lossless or lossy compression. Lossless compression retains the quality of the original audio and provides compression ratios of 2:1.

A **data compression ratio** compares the uncompressed size of a file to its compressed size using the notation *uncompressed size:compressed size*. For example, music that originally requires 80 MB of storage space might be compressed to 40 MB. The compression ratio is 80:40, or 2:1.

Lossless compression maxes out at a 2:1 compression ratio by compressing files to half their original size. Lossless audio formats include FLAC, M4A, and MPEG-4.

© MediaTechnics

Figure
14-8

Lossy compression sacrifices some audio quality, but files are usually smaller than those compressed with lossless techniques. Lossy compression ratios can exceed 10:1. For example, a 10 MB WAV file converted to MP3 shrinks to only 1 MB. Lossy compression formats include MP3, Vorbis, AAC, and WMA. Compressed audio files have a slight loss of quality, but they are certainly more convenient for downloading and require far less storage space than non-compressed audio. That efficiency means your smartphone can hold lots more music files when stored in lossy formats.

Although compression ratios offer a way of quantifying the difference between original and compressed file sizes, compression is more commonly expressed in bit rates.

Bit rate is a measurement of how many bits of data are sent to the processor during a one-second time span. Bit rates for audio files are expressed as kbps or kbit/s. Lower bit rates indicate more compression but lower audio quality. When working with audio files, you might have to choose a bit rate for compression. The table in Figure 14-9 can help you select a bit rate that is appropriate for a project.

Figure
14-9

Bit rate	Equivalent	Uses
32 kbps	4 kHz	Minimum acceptable quality for speech and narrations
96 kbps	11 kHz	Good quality for speech and narrations
128 kbps	18 kHz	Mid-range music quality
192 kbps	24 kHz	Typical compressed audio bit rate
320 kbps	40 kHz	High-quality audio, but large file size

© MediaTechnics

Technology
(continued)

Your computer's **sound card** is responsible for transforming the data stored in an audio file into music, sound effects, and narrations. Most sound cards can play digital audio files containing music and narrations, deliver 3D audio for computer game soundtracks, and produce surround sound when you play DVD movies.

Initially, sound cards were small circuit boards that plugged into an expansion slot inside a computer's system unit. These cards contained audio processing circuitry plus a variety of input and output jacks for speakers, microphones, and headphones.

Today, you can still purchase expansion cards for desktop computers; but in many computers, audio circuitry is built into the system board and called **integrated audio**. Laptops, tablets, and smartphones have integrated audio because manufacturers save space by incorporating audio circuitry into the system board.

Audio circuitry is typically equipped to accept input from a microphone and send output to speakers or headphones. For processing digital audio files, a sound card contains two types of circuitry. A digital-to-analog converter (DAC) transforms digital bits into analog waves when you play an audio file. An analog-to-digital converter (ADC) samples live sounds and converts them into digital data.

To play a digitally recorded sound, the data from an audio file is transferred to your computer's sound card, where it is converted into signals that can be output to speakers or a headset.

When you speak into your computer's microphone while Skyping or recording the narration for a soundtrack, the analog-to-digital converter samples the sound many times per second to create a list of digital values that represent the sound wave. Figure 14-10 illustrates the input and output from a sound card.

Figure
14-10

Analog audio signals

Analog audio signals

A sound card's ADC converts analog audio into digital data that the computer can store and process.

A sound card's DAC converts digital audio into analog signals that can be output to speakers or earbuds.

© MediaTechnics

Digital audio signals

Digital audio signals

Project

Explore digital sound

Imagine playing a fast-paced video game or watching an Alfred Hitchcock thriller on your PC with the speaker volume set to mute. Somehow, the suspense is watered down without appropriate music and sound effects. Sound, whether it's digitized or synthesized, plays a critical role in providing the ultimate multimedia experience. In this project, you will explore the array of sounds that Windows uses with program events and activities, such as testing speaker volume. You will also learn to use software, such as Windows Media Player, that is designed to handle audio files in various formats.

When you have completed the project, you should be able to:

• Customize the Windows sound scheme.

• Compare and contrast different audio formats.

• Rip tracks from a CD and create a playlist.

Requirements: This project requires Microsoft Windows, Paint, Windows Media Player, and one or two music CDs.

Deliverables:

1 A screenshot of your modified Windows sound scheme

2 A screenshot showing the Project 14 playlist

Source: Microsoft.com

1. Windows uses a **sound scheme**, which is a set of sounds that accompanies events in Windows and applications. To hear an example, do the following:

   Go to the Windows desktop and select the speaker icon.

   Move the slider up or down and listen to the chime sound.

2. Access the sound scheme settings by completing the following steps:

   Open the Control Panel. In the *Large icons* view, select the Sound icon.

   Select the Sounds tab.

   Scroll down the list in the Program Events windows to get an idea of sound scheme elements. Note that any event with an associated sound is marked with a ◀ symbol.

3. Modify the Default Beep sound by completing the following steps:

   Locate and select the Default Beep.

   In the Sounds box, notice that the Default Beep uses Windows Background.wav.

   Sounds:

   | Windows Background.wav ⌄ | ▶ Test |

   Source: Microsoft Corporation

   Select the Test button to hear the sound.

   Select the down-arrow for the Sounds box.

   Select any one of the sounds from the list.

   Select the Test button to hear the sound.

• Explore digital sound (continued)

4. Save your modified sound scheme by selecting the Save As button near the top of the Sound dialog box and entering [Your Name] as the name of your sound scheme. Click the OK button.

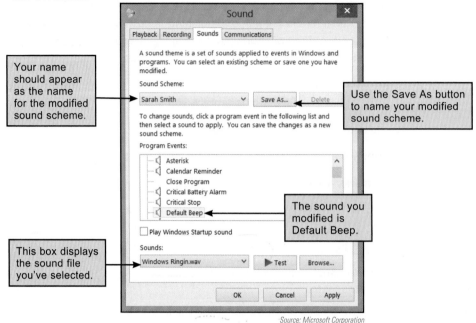

Your name should appear as the name for the modified sound scheme.

Use the Save As button to name your modified sound scheme.

The sound you modified is Default Beep.

This box displays the sound file you've selected.

Source: Microsoft Corporation

5. Take a screenshot of the Sound window and save it as Project 14A [Your Name].

6. If you are using a lab computer, return the Sound Scheme setting to Windows Default. Close all windows.

7. Suppose you have several favorite songs that are on a CD and you want to transfer them to your computer. Find a music CD and then complete these steps:

Insert the music CD in your computer's CD/DVD drive. (If your computer has no CD drive, connect an external CD drive to your computer's USB port.)

If the AutoPlay window appears, close it.

At the Start screen, open Windows Media Player.

Select your CD from the Navigation pane.

Press the Alt key on your keyboard to display the menu.

Select Tools, then select Options.

Select the Rip Music tab.

8. Before you rip tracks, you must select an audio format. To do so:

Click the down-arrow button as shown at right.

Select each format and look at the resulting slider-bar settings to see which formats require the least space.

Rip settings

Format:

Windows Media Audio Pro ⌄

Windows Media Audio
Windows Media Audio Pro
Windows Media Audio (Variable Bit Rate)
Windows Media Audio Lossless
MP3
WAV (Lossless)

☐ Eject CD after ripping

1. Select the down-arrow, then select a format.

...opy protection

Audio quality:

Smallest Size ————————▯————— Best Quality

Uses about 28 MB per CD (64 Kbps).

2. Find out which format creates the smallest files.

Source: Microsoft Corporation

• Explore digital sound (continued)

9. Select the MP3 format as shown in the example below, then click OK.

Source: Microsoft Corporation

10. Uncheck all tracks except for three that you'd like to rip. Click the Rip CD button on the toolbar.

11. Rip three more tracks from a second CD. Alternatively, you can rip three more tracks from the first CD.

12. Combine the six tracks that you've ripped into a playlist by clicking *Create playlist* on the toolbar. Enter Project 14 as the name of the playlist. Scroll through your Music library and drag all six tracks to Project 14.

13. Select the playlist. Take a screenshot and save it as Project 14B [Your Name].

Source: Microsoft Corporation

14. Follow your instructor's directions to submit your project deliverables.

Issue

Can I copy it?

Until 1971, no U.S. law protected recorded music. So-called "record pirates" legally copied and distributed hit songs. When an amendment to copyright law finally protected digital music, Congress did not intend to prevent individuals from recording broadcasts from tapes or records. It was perfectly legal to purchase, say, an Elvis Presley record and make a recording of it onto cassette tape for your own use.

Digital music put the home recording concept to the test. An online music sharing system called Napster allowed people to freely share and copy music in MP3 format. Millions of music lovers took advantage of Napster to build extensive collections of popular, copyrighted music. However, the Recording Industry Association of America determined it was losing millions of dollars in revenue; and as a result, music today is often distributed with digital rights management (DRM) that physically prevents copying, sharing, and other unapproved distribution.

Circumventing DRM is possible; however, the Digital Millennium Copyright Act makes it illegal to circumvent any technological measure that controls access to a work. Breaking into a copy-protected song is illegal. Even distributing instructions on how to break copy protection is illegal.

The current status of DRM seems to conflict with consumer expectations for manipulating and copying music, video, and other digital content. According to a Reuters survey, more than two-thirds of consumers believe that once they purchase media content, it should be theirs to use, copy, or share.

If you purchase a CD, for example, you might expect to be able to copy your favorite songs to your computer, your mobile phone, or your portable audio player. If the CD is protected by DRM, however, copies of the music might be deliberately distorted with buzzes and pops. Music files purchased from an online music store might be encoded with restrictions on the number of copies you can make.

DRM technologies are still evolving, as are copyright laws. The Digital Millennium Copyright Act undergoes a formal review every three years, but so far music label lobbyists have been successful in preventing any relaxation of the rules. Relief for consumers has come primarily from Apple CEO Steve Jobs, who removed DRM from iTunes music in 2009.

What do you think?

1. When you purchase a music CD, do you believe that you should have the right to convert it into any format (such as WMA or MP3) for your own use?　　　　　　○ Yes ○ No ○ Not sure

2. Do you think the Digital Millennium Copyright Act should be revised to allow people to circumvent DRM for music that they have purchased legitimately?　　　○ Yes ○ No ○ Not sure

3. Have you ever been prevented from copying music by some type of DRM technology?　　○ Yes ○ No ○ Not sure

QuickCheck A

1. For the clearest, most realistic digital recording, you should use a sampling rate of [_____] kHz.

2. Digital audio is analogous to a tape recording, whereas [_____] music is more like a player piano roll.

3. [_____]-to-speech is the underlying technology for NOAA Weather Radio and computer screen readers.

4. The process of importing tracks from an audio CD to your computer's hard disk is called [_____] .

5. True or false? MP3 is a lossy compressed digital sound format. [_____]

CHECK**IT!**

QuickCheck B

Click the Sound buttons to listen to each sound, then match it with the correct description below:

1. Synthesized voice [_____]

2. Digitized voice at 11 kHz sampling rate [_____]

3. Digitized voice at 44 kHz sampling rate [_____]

4. Digital audio [_____]

5. MIDI music [_____]

Sound
A

Sound
B

Sound
C

Sound
D

Sound
E

To use this QuickCheck, your PC must be equipped with a sound card and speakers (or headphones).

CHECK**IT!**

 GETIT?   While using the digital textbook, click the Get It? button to see if you can answer ten randomly selected questions from Chapter 14.

15 Working with Graphics

What's inside?

You live in a world filled with strong visual images—kaleidoscopic MTV videos, photo-rich magazines, and lavishly illustrated Web sites. It is more important than ever to learn how to work with graphical images that you incorporate in documents, add to presentations, and post on social media sites. Chapter 15 will get you started.

What's in the digital book?

Chapter 15's videos and screen tours show you how to work with basic tools for creating and manipulating digital graphics.

FAQ What kinds of graphics can I work with on my PC?

The pictures that you can create, modify, store, download, and transmit using your PC are referred to as **graphics** or **images**. Graphics add visual interest to documents, worksheets, presentations, and Web pages.

If you're artistic, you'll probably enjoy creating artwork and illustrations using your PC. However, you don't have to be an artist to spice up your projects with graphics. You can obtain ready-made images from a variety of sources. Clip art and stock photo collections distributed on the Web contain thousands of professionally designed images. Old photos can be converted into computer-compatible formats. New photos taken with a digital camera can be transferred to a computer or uploaded directly to social media sites.

You can use a scanner to convert pictures from books and magazines into image files that can be stored, edited, and displayed on your PC. A **scanner** is essentially a photocopier that produces digital files instead of paper copies. Scanners can be standalone devices or they can be incorporated into a multifunction printer. When using images that someone else has created, always be sure to cite the source and adhere to any applicable copyright laws or licensing restrictions.

You'll typically work with two types of graphics: bitmap graphics and vector graphics. Understanding the difference between the two allows you to select the type of graphic that is best suited for a project. The rest of the FAQs in this chapter provide the basic information that you need to work with bitmap and vector graphics.

A bitmap graphics image (upper left) has a distinctly different appearance than a vector graphics image (lower right).

Figure
15-1

© MediaTechnics

FAQ When should I use bitmap graphics?

Bitmap graphics, sometimes called raster graphics, represent an image as a grid of colored dots. Each dot in the grid is referred to as a pixel. On your computer screen, each dot is represented by a tiny liquid crystal or LED light. On a printout, a pixel is represented by a drop of ink.

Because bitmap graphics produce photograph-like images, they are used for photos, for images added to Web pages, and for art converted from paper to computer format. To create and manipulate bitmap graphics, you can use **paint software**, such as Adobe Photoshop, Corel Painter, open source GIMP, or Microsoft Paint. The Web also offers a variety of graphics tools, such as pixlr, PicMonkey, and Photoshop Express.

The quality of an image depends on its resolution and color depth. **Image resolution** is expressed as the width and height of the grid that holds the dots. For example, an image with 1024 X 768 resolution is formed from a grid 1,024 dots wide and 768 dots high. High-resolution images exhibit details more clearly than low-resolution images.

Each dot in an image is assigned a code number for its color. The number of bits required to store the color number is referred to as **color depth** and determines the number of colors that the image contains. A 1-bit color depth produces an image containing only two colors: black and white. An 8-bit color depth produces 256 colors. A 24-bit color depth produces 16.7 million colors, sometimes referred to as **true color**. The more colors an image contains, the more realistic it appears.

Windows includes basic bitmap graphics software called Paint that you can access from the Accessories folder. Click the Try It! button to find out how to use Paint to create and modify bitmap graphics.

TRY IT!

Figure 15-2

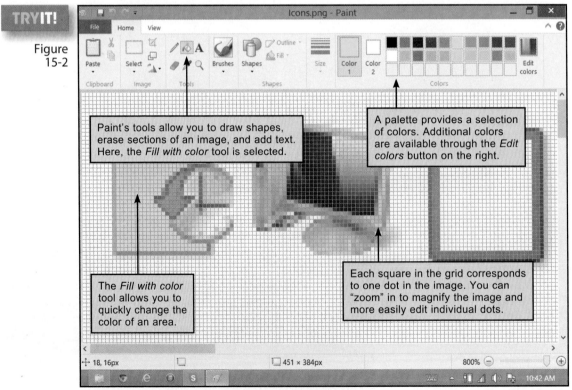

Paint's tools allow you to draw shapes, erase sections of an image, and add text. Here, the *Fill with color* tool is selected.

A palette provides a selection of colors. Additional colors are available through the *Edit colors* button on the right.

The *Fill with color* tool allows you to quickly change the color of an area.

Each square in the grid corresponds to one dot in the image. You can "zoom" in to magnify the image and more easily edit individual dots.

Source: Microsoft Corporation

FAQ How do I choose a bitmap format?

Bitmap graphics are most commonly stored in JPEG, TIF, BMP, PNG, GIF, and RAW files. The file type used to store an image is often referred to as its format. The format you choose for a graphic depends on how you plan to use it. For printed publications, you should use a format that retains high resolution and 24-bit color depth. Images for social media sites should be stored in a format supported by browsers. Web graphics and e-mail attachments should be stored in compact formats so they can be transmitted quickly over the Internet. You can decrease file size by shrinking the physical dimensions of an image, saving it in a compressed file format, or reducing its color depth.

Reduce dimensions. Shrinking the physical dimensions of an image allows you to reduce its file size. A 2" x 2" image can be stored in a file that is one-quarter the size of the same image at 4" x 4". Most graphics software provides a tool to resize an image.

Apply compression. You can use compression techniques to decrease image file size. Some file formats provide built-in compression that reduces file size simply by using a more effective storage technique. For example, when stored in non-compressed BMP or TIF format, an image might require about 950 KB of storage space. Using JPEG format with built-in compression, the file size can be reduced to 48 KB.

As you learned in an earlier chapter, images can be compressed using lossy or lossless compression. PNG and GIF formats are lossless. JPEG uses lossy compression. Be careful when working with JPEG images because lossy compression discards data every time you save the image. This **generation loss** can lead to images becoming increasingly blurrier with successive saves.

Reduce color depth. A true-color graphic requires 24 bits for each dot of color in an image, whereas a 256-color graphic requires only 8 bits. Therefore, by reducing the color depth from true color to 256 color, the image file shrinks to one-third of its original size. When combined with compression techniques, color reduction can significantly shrink file size. Unfortunately, reducing color depth can reduce image quality. You'll have to view the converted image to evaluate if it is acceptable.

Figure 15-3

File Type	Characteristics	Uses
BMP	Windows native bitmap graphics file format; not compressed; large files	Graphical elements, such as buttons and other controls used in computer programs
JPG (JPEG)	User-selectable compression; generation loss can reduce image quality; supported by most browsers	Photographic or scanned images for desktop publishing, Web page images, e-mail attachments
PNG	An open-source graphical format that compresses images without losing data; supported by most browsers	An alternative to GIF for Web graphics; better than JPEG for storing images containing text
TIF	Versatile format that can be compressed; supported by many digital cameras	High-resolution images of photos or line art for desktop publishing and printouts from photo printers
RAW	Unprocessed data captured directly from a digital camera's sensor array; very large files	RAW images must be converted into other formats before they can be edited or printed
GIF	Supported by most Web browsers; limited to 256 colors; lossy compression	Most commonly used for Web page graphics, but not for digital photography

© MediaTechnics

FAQ When should I use vector graphics?

A **vector graphic** consists of a set of points, lines, arcs, and other geometrical shapes. Each shape is defined as a series of line segments called vectors, and attributes such as line width and fill color. A list of these vectors and attributes becomes essentially a set of instructions for redrawing the image. Vector graphics are ideal for diagrams, line drawings, typesetting, graphs, corporate logos, road signs, sequential art, and organizational charts. They are also associated with **computer-aided design** (CAD), the process of creating technical drawings and blueprints on a PC.

Vector graphics do not look like photographic images. Two-dimensional vector graphics typically have large flat areas of color and more closely resemble cartoons than photos. Vector graphics have three advantages over bitmaps. First, vector files tend to be small because the vectors and attributes describing a shape can be stored very efficiently. Second, vector graphics can shrink or expand with no loss of quality. Third, the shapes in a vector graphic exist as individual objects that you can modify independently without affecting other parts of the image.

Drawing software provides tools to create and manipulate vector graphics. Popular packages include Adobe Illustrator, LibreOffice Draw, and CorelDRAW. **CAD software** includes AutoCAD, CADopia, IntelliCAD, and TurboCAD. You'll find many Web-based vector graphics files stored in SVG (Scalable Vector Graphics) format. Graphic designers make extensive use of Adobe Illustrator (AI) and EPS (Encapsulated PostScript) formats. Windows clip art is usually stored as WMFs (Windows Metafiles). Popular CAD formats include DXF, DWG, and DS4.

Vector graphics are designed to work with layers of shapes. For example, the sun, clouds, sky, rocks, and grass in Figure 15-4 are defined by their shapes, position, colors, and layers. Click the Try It! button to discover how to work with vector graphics.

TRYIT!

Figure
15-4

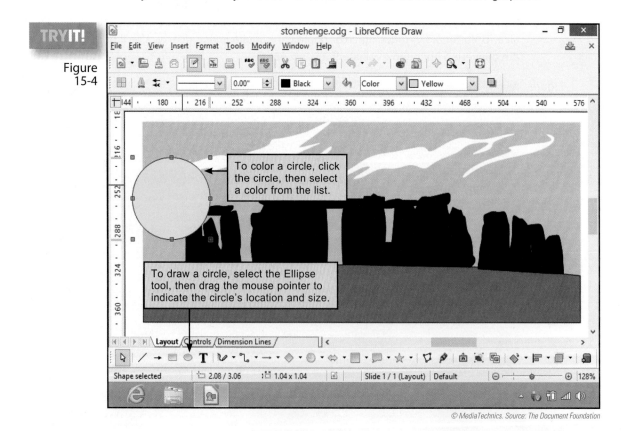

FAQ How do I create 3D graphics?

You can create **3D graphics** containing objects that appear to be three-dimensional. Objects in a 3D graphic not only look three-dimensional, but also include the data necessary to display, rotate, and view them from any angle, viewpoint, or perspective. Composed of vectors, 3D objects are typically created using the same drawing and CAD software as two-dimensional vector graphics.

To create a 3D object, the first step is to produce a line drawing called a **wireframe** by outlining every surface on the front, back, and inside of the object. Once the wireframe is complete, you can define the texture, transparency, and color for each of its surfaces. The process of applying surfaces to a wireframe and producing a 2D image is called **rendering**. This process is similar to draping a nylon tent covering over its frame and then snapping a photo of it.

As part of the rendering process, you can specify a light source and your PC automatically determines where to put highlights and shadows. This part of the rendering process is called **ray tracing** because your computer essentially traces the rays of light from the light source to the object.

Rendering is a complex activity that requires your PC to carry out extensive calculations. Today's high-speed processors render action figures and scenery for computer games in real time as you play the game. For more complex images, such as movie special effects, the rendering process can take minutes or hours, depending on the complexity of the objects, the computer processing speed, and the resolution of the completed image.

Rendered 3D graphics have a new-car-brochure look that's sometimes referred to as "super-realistic." Objects within the image are perfectly shaped and highly defined. Surfaces appear unflawed and brilliantly highlighted. Click the Try It! button to learn how to construct a wireframe, render a 3D object, and apply ray tracing.

TRYIT!

Figure 15-5

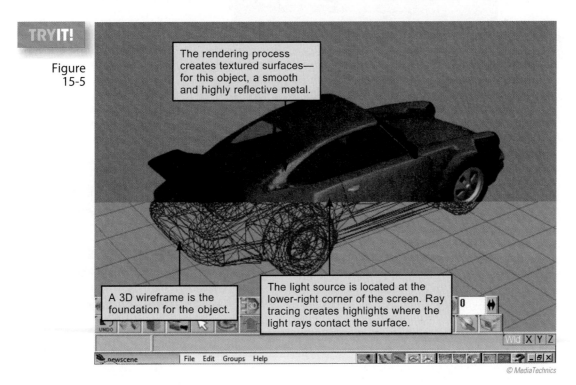

The rendering process creates textured surfaces—for this object, a smooth and highly reflective metal.

A 3D wireframe is the foundation for the object.

The light source is located at the lower-right corner of the screen. Ray tracing creates highlights where the light rays contact the surface.

© MediaTechnics

Technology

Digital cameras

A **digital camera** takes photographs or video footage by capturing images on an electronic image sensor. Digital cameras are available as standalone devices or they can be incorporated into other devices, such as cell phones, computer monitors, automobiles, and security systems.

Still images for photographs are captured with a single exposure and then stored. To create video footage, a camera takes many pictures every second. These pictures, sometimes referred to as frames, are stored as one file. During playback, the frames are shown sequentially to give the impression of movement.

To capture an image, a camera's lens focuses light onto a small image sensor called a **charge-coupled device** (CCD). A CCD contains a grid of tiny light-sensitive diodes called **photosites**. CCDs vary in size from 0.5" to 2.5". A one-half-inch square CCD can contain up to 500,000 photosites. Each photosite detects the brightness and color for its tiny piece of the total image.

A CCD's photosites correspond to pixels. The more pixels used to capture an image, the higher its resolution, and the better the resulting picture. Cameras with large CCDs produce high-quality images. Some cameras contain multiple CCDs, which enhance the color quality of a camera's output. Play the video for Figure 15-6 to learn more about CCDs.

Figure
15-6

A camera's CCD captures light on an array of photosites.

All © MediaTechnics

Close-up view of a CCD

Technology
(continued)

Camera prices depend on several factors. One of these factors is the camera's resolution, which is typically measured in megapixels. A **megapixel** is a million pixels, calculated by multiplying the number of horizontal pixels by the number of vertical pixels. To arrive at the total number of pixels, simply multiply the number of horizontal pixels by the number of vertical pixels. A camera with 3872 x 2592 pixels, for example, stores 10,036,224 pixels for each photo and would be advertised as a 10-megapixel camera.

The quality of digital photos has increased dramatically over the past few years, while prices of digital cameras have plummeted.

Compact cameras. Cameras with a built-in lens are referred to as compact cameras. Ranging from inexpensive, basic models to costly prosumer models, compact cameras are easy to carry and use. Basic compact cameras are suitable for capturing good-quality snapshots for use on the Web and in personal photo albums. Prosumer compacts are a good choice for photo enthusiasts. The lens in a compact camera is slightly offset from the viewfinder, so the image you see in the viewfinder is framed slightly differently than the actual photo. The LCD panel of a compact camera, however, shows exactly what is captured by the lens, so the LCD can be used for accurate framing.

SLRs. An SLR (single lens reflex) is a large-body camera with a viewfinder that shows the exact image captured by the lens. This feature is important to professional photographers who are concerned with precise framing and composition. SLR camera bodies accept interchangeable lenses, too, so photographers can select a lens best for lighting conditions and focal distance.

Smartphone cameras. Smartphones commonly include one or two digital cameras that can be used for point-and-shoot photography and short video segments. Smartphone camera resolutions are equivalent to mid-range compact cameras. Most exceed 10 megapixels.

Digital video cameras. Video cameras are dedicated to capturing video footage. Their use has decreased rapidly as cameras in other classifications have gained the ability to shoot and store video. Professional movie makers still use professional-grade digital video cameras, but most consumers rely on their smartphones or compact cameras for shooting video.

Webcams. A Webcam streams live video directly to a computer's storage device. These cameras are commonly built into computer screens. They can also be purchased as standalone units that connect to a computer with a USB cable. Webcams are used primarily for Skyping, video chatting, and video conferencing.

Technology
(continued)

Digital photos and videos are stored on removable memory cards inside the camera body. A **memory card** (or flash card) is a small, re-recordable solid state storage device that can retain its contents without a constant supply of power. Storage capacities range from 16 MB to 256 GB.

The most popular memory cards for digital cameras are SD (Secure Digital) cards, which are available in several physical sizes and speed classes. An SD card's speed dictates how fast information can be recorded. Speed class 2 is suitable for recording basic video, whereas class 4 is required for HD video. Figure 15-7 shows you where to find the speed class on an SD card.

Figure
15-7

Speed class: ⑩   © MediaTechnics

After finishing a photo or video shoot, there are several ways to transfer data from the camera to a computer, photoprinter, or Web site. If your computer includes slots that accept the type of memory card used in your camera, you can remove the card from your camera and insert it into the memory slot of your PC. Alternatively, you might be able to plug your camera into your computer's USB port. Photos and videos taken with a smartphone can be e-mailed to yourself, uploaded directly to a photo sharing site, or posted to a social networking site. Photos can be transferred directly to a photoprinter that accepts SD cards.

The process of transferring images from your camera to the hard disk drive of your PC can take several minutes, depending on the number of photos or videos you've taken and their size. As the images are transferred, they're stored as files on your PC. You can open these image files using most paint or photo editing software.

Click the Play It! button to learn how to produce your own digital photos. This video takes you through the entire process. You'll find out how to take the photo, transfer it from your camera to your PC, save it, and print it.

PLAYIT!

Figure
15-8

© MediaTechnics

Project

Explore digital photos

Photo editing software is a specialized type of paint software that provides a set of tools for manipulating and retouching digital photographs. Even with the simplest photo editing software, you can rescue pictures that are washed out, too dark, too bright, or out of focus. You can even eliminate those poltergeist-like red eyes caused by your camera's flash.

You can use photo editing software to have some fun with your photographs. For example, you can turn current photos into old-fashioned tintypes. With more sophisticated photo editing software, you can go for a "Pleasantville" look by hand-coloring parts of black-and-white photos. You can also delete unwanted objects from a photo or create an entirely new reality by superimposing objects on backgrounds—like pasting your dog on a lunar landscape.

When you have completed this project, you should be able to:

- Adjust the lighting and sharpen a photo image.

- Touch up a photo to remove red eye, whiten teeth, or airbrush out blemishes.

- Create a black-and-white version of a color photo.

- Crop a photo.

- Resize a photo.

Requirements: This project requires Microsoft Windows, and browser software such as Internet Explorer, Netscape, Safari, Chrome, or Firefox.

The deliverable for Project 15 is an e-mail message that includes the following:

1. A zipped attachment named Project 15 containing the following photos:

   a. Your original photo

   b. A version of your photo with the exposure and color improved

   c. A version of your photo in black and white

   d. A version of your photo cropped to a single subject

   e. A version of your photo that has been resized

2. A comparison of the file sizes of the original and edited photos

1. Open File Explorer and select a photo that's stored on your computer. You will be submitting this photo to your instructor, so make sure it is not offensive. You'll achieve the best results if you select a photo that has a person or an animal as its subject.

2. Make a note of the file size for the photo that you select. Also note its name and whether it is a PNG, BMP, or JPEG.

3. Open your browser and connect to a photo editing site, such as pixlr or PicMonkey.

• Explore digital photos (continued)

4.   Follow instructions at the photo editing site to upload your photo.

5.   Adjust your photo for the optimum lighting and sharpness. To complete this step, look for an AutoFix or Auto Adjust option in your photo editing software.

6.   Experiment with various effects to improve the photo. Consider eliminating red eye, smoothing out blemishes, or whitening the subject's teeth.

7.   Save a copy of your photo as [File Name] Adjusted. If you are given compression options, save at 100% to retain maximum quality.

Flat Albert with Fire Engine   Flat Albert with Fire Engine Adjusted

8.   Create a black-and-white version of your photo. To complete this step, look for a black-and-white effect option.

9.   Save the black-and-white version as [File Name] B&W.

Flat Albert with Fire Engine B&W   *All © MediaTechnics*

• Explore digital photos (continued)

10. Undo the black-and-white effect.

11. Crop the photo so that it features a single subject.

12. Save this photo as [File Name] Cropped.

© MediaTechnics

Flat Albert with Fire Engine
Cropped

13. Undo the crop so that the photo is its original size.

14. Resize the photo by reducing its width and height by half. For example, if the original width is 4000 pixels and the height is 3000 pixels, resize the photo to a width of 2000 pixels and a height of 1500 pixels.

15. Save the resized photo as [File Name] Small.

16. Close the photo editing app and close your browser.

17. Open File Explorer and navigate to the folder where you stored the photos.

18. Start an e-mail message to your instructor that lists the five files and their sizes.

19. Create a zipped folder containing all the edited photos. To complete this step:
    Select all five files.
    Select the Share tab.
    Select the Zip button.
    Enter Project 15 [Your Name] as the name of the zipped folder.

20. Attach the zipped folder to the e-mail message and send it to your instructor.

Issue

Is that really a UFO?

The highly publicized O. J. Simpson murder trial was followed by an equally high-profile wrongful-death suit. Introduced into evidence were a bloody footprint from the crime scene made by a size 12 designer shoe, and a photo of Mr. Simpson wearing such a shoe. Conclusive evidence of guilt? Not according to the defense attorney, who raised doubts about the photo's authenticity.

Faked photos are not a product of the digital age. Long before the first digital cameras, tabloid newspapers in supermarket checkout lanes carried blurry photos depicting UFOs, the Loch Ness monster, and other images of dubious authenticity. In those days, most people had confidence that experts could detect photos doctored by amateurs or even by professionals. The deception could be discovered by a missing shadow, an obvious trace of cut and paste, or inconsistencies in color.

In today's digital world, however, it is possible to alter the individual dots in a photo. When done carefully, these alterations can be difficult or even impossible to detect. Sure, it can be innocent fun, like when you digitally paste your roommate's head onto a picture of Bart Simpson. Unfortunately, it also introduces a note of uncertainty into the evidence we rely on to form opinions of everyday events and life-and-death situations, such as a murder trial or war crimes investigation.

Even videotapes, once virtually impossible to alter, can be digitized and doctored today. In the film *Forrest Gump*, digital editing techniques were used to paste the star, Tom Hanks, into authentic newsreels of past events—Forrest Gump meets with President Kennedy and history appears to be changed.

In *Simone*, Al Pacino portrays a desperate director who uses a computer-generated actress as his leading lady. Adoring fans think Simone ("Simulation One") is a real star. Pacino's character quips, "Our ability to manufacture fraud now exceeds our ability to detect it." Living in a digital world, it is important to consider how you can responsibly evaluate the images that you see in newspapers, on television, and at the movies.

What do you think?

1. In your opinion, should photos and videotapes be allowed as evidence in civil and criminal trials?   ◯Yes ◯ No ◯ Not sure

2. Do you think that it would be possible for someone to use doctored photos and videotapes to convince people that a fake event actually took place?   ◯ Yes ◯ No ◯ Not sure

3. Do you have a set of criteria for judging the authenticity of newspaper and TV images?   ◯ Yes ◯ No ◯ Not sure

QuickCheck A

1. An image formed by a grid of colored pixels is referred to as a(n) [＿＿＿＿＿＿] graphic.

2. True or false? To prepare an image for Web use, you should store it in true-color BMP format. [＿＿＿＿]

3. [＿＿＿＿＿＿＿] graphics are stored as a set of instructions for recreating the shapes and attributes of an image.

4. Architects often use [＿＿＿＿＿＿＿] software to create 3D graphics.

5. The part of the rendering process that creates highlights and shadows for a 3D object is called [＿＿＿＿＿＿＿] . (Hint: The answer contains two words.)

CHECKIT!

QuickCheck B

There is only one way to correctly match the five objects pictured on the right to the five descriptions below. Indicate the correct letter for each description.

1. A wireframe [＿＿＿]

2. A vector graphic [＿＿＿]

3. A bitmap graphic [＿＿＿]

4. A rendered image [＿＿＿]

5. An image produced by a 1-bit color depth [＿＿＿]

A

B

C

D

E

All © MediaTechnics

CHECKIT!

While using the digital textbook, click the Get It? button to see if you can answer ten randomly selected questions from Chapter 15.

16 Creating Digital Video and Animation

What's inside?

Today, videos are everywhere. You see them at news sites, social media sites, and YouTube. This chapter helps you understand digital video formats and software so that you can efficiently create, modify, and view your own videos and videos created by others.

What's in the digital book?

Wear your director's beret and ascot for Chapter 16. When you've completed the screen tours and videos, you'll be shouting, "Lights! Camera! Action!"

FAQ What are the advantages of digital video?

A video is a series of still frames projected at a rate fast enough to fool the human eye into perceiving continuous motion. **Digital video** uses bits to store color and brightness data for each pixel in a video frame. Digital video technology is used for most of today's films, YouTube videos, video conferencing, video phones, and television programs.

Digital video makes it easy to post, view, and download videos from the Web at news sites, video sharing sites, and online video stores. Unlike analog video stored on VHS tapes, digital video retains image quality no matter how many times it is copied. When you make a copy of a DVD movie in case the original is damaged, the copy preserves the same quality as the original.

Videos in digital format can be easily manipulated on a personal computer, putting the world of movie-making at your fingertips. You can shoot digital video footage with just about any digital camera and use your computer to edit this footage into videos suitable for a variety of personal and professional uses, such as video wedding albums, product sales videos, training videos, and video scrapbooks. These videos can be stored on a hard disk or distributed on DVDs, memory cards, social media sites, or photo sharing sites.

Digital videos can be displayed on a computer screen with popular video player software and browser plug-ins, such as Adobe Flash Player, Microsoft Windows Media Player, or Apple QuickTime Player. Click the Try It! button to find out how to use Windows Media Player to view videos on your PC.

© MediaTechnics

TRYIT!

Figure 16-1

Buttons similar to those on a standalone DVD player allow you to control video playback.

© MediaTechnics

FAQ How do I transfer video footage to my computer?

Webcam video and video that you download from the Web or receive as an e-mail attachment is stored directly on your computer, but footage from external devices must be transferred to your hard disk if you want to view it on the screen and edit it. Footage from analog sources, such as videotapes, must be digitized as it is being transferred. The following points summarize the transfer process for the most popular video sources.

Digital camera. Transfer a memory card from your camera to your computer or connect your camera to your computer with a cable, and use your video editing software to control the data transfer.

VHS tape, analog video camera, or television broadcast. The data on VHS tapes, analog digital cameras, and television broadcasts is in analog format, so it must be converted into a digital data stream. You can use an external **video capture device**, which is available as an expansion card that you install inside a computer system unit or as a standalone device that can be attached to a computer with a cable. You can also use an import routine provided by software such as Windows Movie Maker.

DVDs. DVD movies are stored in a format that most video editing software cannot directly manipulate. DVD data might also be encrypted to protect it from illegal copying. DVD ripping and decryption software can convert and decrypt data from any DVD you insert into your computer's DVD drive, and then copy it to your computer's hard disk. In some countries, video decryption is illegal, so make sure your activities conform to local laws.

Cell phone. If your cell phone can sync with your computer using a cable, then you can probably transfer videos using such a setup. Otherwise, you can e-mail the video from your phone to your computer. When the video arrives as an e-mail attachment, you can save it as a standalone file. Most mobile phone videos can be viewed with a standard media player, such as QuickTime or Windows Movie Player.

Click the Play It! button to learn more about shooting video footage and transferring it to your PC.

PLAYIT!

Figure
16-2

© MediaTechnics

FAQ How do I edit a digital video?

The process of transferring or capturing raw video footage produces a file on your computer's hard disk that you can edit using software tools. **Video editing software** helps you cut out unwanted frames, add special effects, arrange segments, overlay a soundtrack, and designate transitions from one segment to the next.

Popular consumer-level video editing software includes Adobe Premiere Elements, Corel VideoStudio Pro, Windows Movie Maker, and Cyberlink PowerDirector. Online offerings include YouTube Video Editor, Pixorial, Rapt Media, Magisto, and Loopster. Video editing apps are also available for tablets and smartphones.

More expensive video editing offerings, such as Apple Final Cut Pro and Avid Media Composer, are designed for professional film editors and have been used to produce feature-length films, such as *Cold Mountain*, *Corpse Bride*, *Where the Wild Things Are*, *The Girl with the Dragon Tattoo*, and *Napoleon Dynamite*.

To begin the editing process, open your video editing software and import any files that contain photos, video footage, or audio clips for the final video. Once imported, you can drag these elements onto a storyboard that represents the video stream. Your video editing software also allows you to insert predefined transition effects that control the way one clip blends into another—for example, by fading, flipping, overlaying, or simply cutting to the next scene. To complete your video, you can add titles and other special effects.

Click the Try It! button to learn the basic steps of video editing: importing video and sound clips, arranging the clips in sequence, selecting transition effects, and previewing the final masterpiece.

Figure
16-3

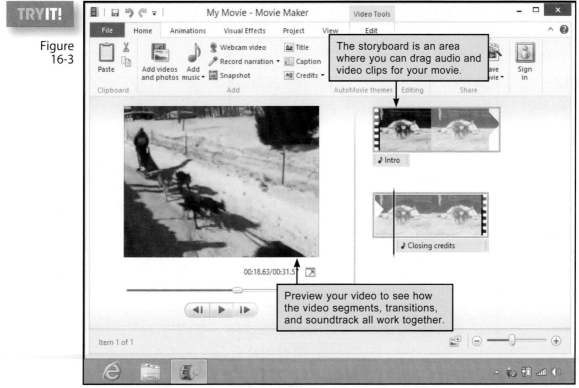

© MediaTechnics; Microsoft Corporation

FAQ How do I finalize a video for DVDs, Web sites, and other uses?

Video editing software allows you to preview your entire video production, complete with soundtrack and transitions. When you're satisfied with your work, the next step is to specify output settings. The settings you select for your video depend on its intended use.

Video files that you plan to distribute on DVDs and play in standalone DVD players must be laid out in a specific format called DVD-Video. If your video editing software does not offer DVD output, you can use DVD authoring software to add an opening menu, specify a scene selection menu, and add special features just like on a professional DVD.

Some entry-level video editing software allows you simply to select a use for your video, such as sending it as an e-mail attachment, posting it on the Web, publishing it on YouTube, or viewing it from your local hard disk. Alternatively, your software might give you the option of selecting a maximum file size. For example, if you are planning to send a video as an e-mail attachment, you might limit the size to 1 MB.

If your software doesn't offer automated settings, you can manually select settings for aspect ratio, display size, frames per second, and file format. **Aspect ratio** refers to the relative width and height of the video frame; widescreen is 16:9 and fullscreen is 4:3. **Display size** corresponds to the resolution of the video window. A typical display size for desktop and Web video is 320 x 240. DVD video has a resolution of 720 x 480. High-definition video has a resolution of 1920 x 1080. **Frame rate** is the number of frames displayed per second (fps). Standard frame rates for digital videos range between 24 and 30 fps.

Figure 16-4 illustrates two methods for selecting video output settings: by selecting the playback device, or by choosing settings manually. Both are offered by Windows Movie Maker. The second option provides information on the size of the final file.

Figure 16-4

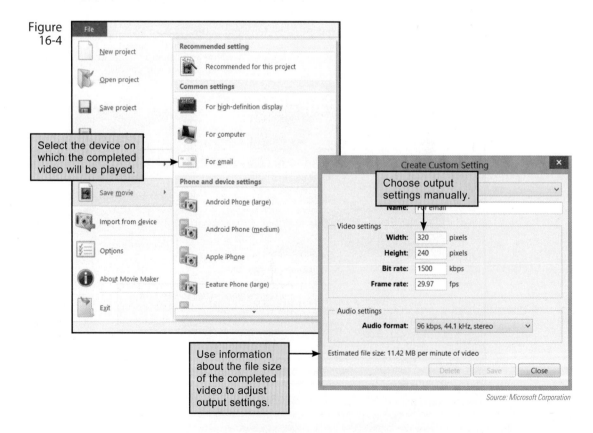

Select the device on which the completed video will be played.

Choose output settings manually.

Use information about the file size of the completed video to adjust output settings.

Source: Microsoft Corporation

FAQ What are the most popular video formats?

There is no single, standard file format for digital video. The files posted on YouTube are stored in a different type of file than videos posted at the iTunes Store. You can think of the files that store digital videos as containers because they can hold video and audio streams. Digital video file formats are sometimes referred to as **container formats** because they are essentially a receptacle for the elements of a video.

Video player software deals with one or more video file formats. By looking at the file extension or file type, you can determine a video's format and the appropriate software necessary to play it. Popular video container formats include the following:

QuickTime Movie (MOV) is a popular container format that packages media in files with .mov extensions. Use Apple's QuickTime Player to play these files.

Advanced Systems Format (ASF) containers hold Windows Media Video (WMV) files and are usually identified by .wmv extensions. Windows Media Player is designed to work with these files.

Audio Video Interleave (AVI) containers were one of the original video file formats, and are still popular with file-sharing communities because of the availability of open source players.

MPEG offers a variety of container formats, most notably .mp4 and .m4v files, used by Apple's iTunes Store for distributing movies, television shows, and podcasts. Apple iTunes software can be used to play videos stored in these formats.

Flash Video (FLV) is a proprietary video format popular for video distributed on YouTube, CNN.com, and other Web sites. These files can be identified by their .flv or .swf extensions. They can be played using the standalone Adobe Flash Player or the Flash browser plug-in.

Video Object File (VOB) is the standard format for videos distributed on commercial DVDs. Files are stored with .vob, .ifo, and .bup extensions.

Ogg is an open source container that produces video files with .ogv extensions. Built-in browser support for playing Web-based Ogg files is included in Mozilla Firefox, Google Chrome, and Opera. Helix is a popular standalone player for Ogg videos.

WebM is a free container format that plays videos in Firefox and Chrome without additional plug-ins. It works with the HTML5 video tag to easily display videos on the Web at sites such as YouTube and for Skype video.

Digital videos can be converted from one file format to another through a process called **transcoding**. If you want to move a video into a different file format, you can check to see if your video editing software offers a conversion, export, or transcoding option. If not, you can find transcoding software on the Web.

Transcoding is quite common. For example, YouTube, a popular video sharing Web site, accepts videos in a variety of formats, but it automatically transcodes them into Flash video and WebM so that all the clips are of uniform quality and can be viewed with standard browsers. Transcoding can cause loss of quality, so avoid transcoding an already transcoded video file.

FAQ What is a codec?

You might have encountered video files that don't play on your computer even though the files seem to be in standard formats with .wmv or .mov file extensions. To successfully play a video on your computer, however, your media player must be equipped to deal not only with the container format that holds the video, but also with the codec used to compress the video. A **codec** (compressor/decompressor) is the software that compresses a video stream when a video is stored, and decompresses the file when the video is played.

The codec used to compress a video also must be used to decompress the video when it is played. If you don't have the right codec, your computer cannot play the video. Windows Media Player automatically attempts to locate missing codecs and installs them when needed. When using other software, you might see a message such as "A codec is needed to play this file." You can manually search for the codec on the Web, download it, and install it. Popular codecs include MPEG, VP8, VP9, DivX, H.264, Theora, and Windows Media Video.

When creating your own videos, you should use one of the codecs included in popular video players. Each codec uses a unique algorithm to shrink the size of a video file. A compression ratio indicates the ratio of compressed data to non-compressed data. A video file with a high compression ratio, such as 35:1, has more compression, a smaller file size, and lower image quality than a file with a smaller compression ratio, such as 5:1. You might have to experiment with compression ratios a bit to find the best balance between file size and image quality.

As with audio compression, video compression can be expressed as a bit rate that refers to the amount of data transferred per second as a video plays. Non-compressed video files contain a huge number of bits per frame, so smooth playback requires a high bit rate, such as 340 Kbps. Compressed files contain fewer bits per frame and play back more smoothly at lower bit rates, such as 38 Kbps, offered by slower Internet connections. If you are asked to select a bit rate, realize that selecting a low bit rate produces a file that requires less storage space but is lower quality than a video output at a high bit rate. Click the Play It! buttons to compare video and audio quality produced by different compression settings.

Figure
16-5

© MediaTechnics

 File type: WMV
Frame rate: 10
Bit rate: 90 Kbps
File size: 359 KB

 File type: WMV
Frame rate: 15
Bit rate: 448 Kbps
File size: 1177 KB

PLAY**IT!** File type: WMV
Frame rate: 30
Bit rate: 928 Kbps
File size: 2448 KB

FAQ What about animation?

Computer animation, sometimes referred to as **CGI** (computer-generated imagery), generates moving images from 2D or 3D objects. Animated special effects for movies, animated game characters, and environments for 3D computer games begin as a sequence of 3D images, in which one or more objects are moved or otherwise changed between each frame.

In traditional hand-drawn animation, a chief artist draws **keyframes**, and then assistants create each of the in-between images—24 of these images for each second of animation. For 3D computer animation, a computer creates in-between images by moving objects and producing a series of new images. All the images are then combined into a single file, essentially creating a digital movie.

Graphics design companies, such as Pixar Animation Studios and DreamWorks, use 3D animation techniques to produce feature films as well as special effects. The first full-length animated 3D movie was *Toy Story*, released in 1995 by Walt Disney Studios and Pixar. Since then, digitally animated films have become increasingly sophisticated.

You can create 3D animations on a standard PC with commercially available software. However, professional 3D software—such as Autodesk Maya and Autodesk 3ds Max—is expensive and has a steep learning curve. If you want to dabble in 3D animation before making an expensive software investment, you might try Smith Micro Poser, DAZ Studio, or open source Blender.

Animation software provides tools to create shapes and move them along a specified track. Simple 3D objects like the ball in Figure 16-6 can be animated in real time. More complex scenes require a considerable amount of render time to transform wireframe objects into the final animation sequence.

Figure 16-6

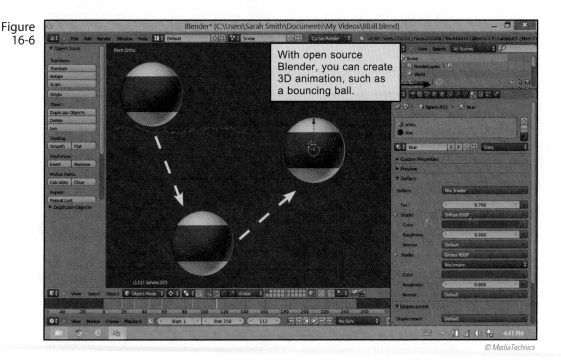

With open source Blender, you can create 3D animation, such as a bouncing ball.

© MediaTechnics

Technology

Optical discs

Today, with the proliferation of cloud storage, streaming music, and movie downloads, it is easy to regard local storage as outdated technology. However, long after data is removed from the cloud, music and movies stored on optical discs will remain accessible. **Optical storage technology** records data as microscopic light and dark spots on a layer beneath the surface of a specially coated disc. The dark spots are called **pits**. The lighter, nonpitted surface areas of the disc are called **lands**. An optical drive rotates the disc over a laser lens. The laser directs a beam of light toward the underside of the disc to read the differences in reflected light from the dark pits and light lands (Figure 16-7).

Figure
16-7

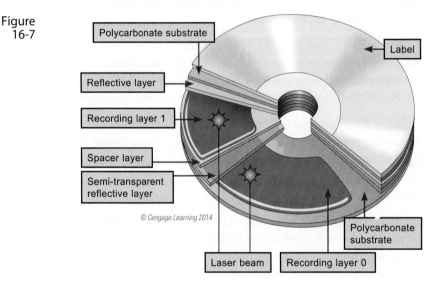

© Cengage Learning 2014

Optical discs are quite durable and less susceptible to environmental damage than hard disks and other magnetic media because optical data is stored under a clear, protective surface. An optical disc is not affected by humidity, fingerprints, dust, magnets, or spilled soft drinks. Data stored on an optical disc is estimated to last at least 30 years.

Optical media include CDs, DVDs, and Blu-ray discs. The term **CD** first referred to audio compact discs that contained music albums. Computer CDs were originally called CD-ROMs to distinguish them from audio CDs. The term **CD-ROM** is an abbreviation of "compact disc read-only memory," a reference to the fact that CD-ROMs are preloaded with data that can be "read" by your computer, but cannot be used to store additional data.

An optical drive, however, stores data on CD-R and CD-RW discs. **CD-R** (CD-recordable) technology allows you to create your own music CDs and data discs. Data on a CD-R cannot be changed once it is recorded.

A variation of CD technology, **CD-RW** (CD-rewritable), allows you to write data to CD-RW discs, and later change the data that they contain. Blank CD-RWs are a bit more expensive than CD-Rs and the recording process takes longer. Some computers have trouble reading CD-RWs created on other machines, so CD-Rs are considered more dependable than CD-RWs. A typical CD-R or CD-RW holds 650–700 MB of data.

Technology
(continued)

DVD (digital video disc) is a storage technology originally designed to replace VHS videotape. A basic DVD has more than enough storage capacity for an entire feature-length film; up to 3 hours of high-resolution video or 8 hours of CD-quality audio. DVDs can also store computer data. Although it is the same physical size as a CD, a DVD can hold far more data. Data can be stored on a DVD using one of four formats, as shown in Figure 16-8. DVD storage capacity depends on whether data is stored on one or two sides of the disc, and how many layers of data each side contains.

Figure 16-8

Number of Sides	Number of Layers	Storage Capacity
1	1	4.7 GB
1	2	8.5 GB
2	1	9.4 GB
2	2	17.0 GB

© MediaTechnics

As with CDs, DVDs are available in read-only, recordable, and rewritable formats. The read-only format used for distributing movies and videos is called DVD-ROM. DVD-R and DVD+R are recordable technologies that allow you to record data but not change it. DVD-RW and DVD+RW are rewritable technologies that allow you to write data and later change it.

A **Blu-ray disc** (sometimes referred to as a BD) offers high-capacity storage for high-definition video and computer data. BD capacity offers 25 GB per layer. A single-layer BD can store about 4.5 hours of high-definition video or 11 hours of standard video.

Devices that play CDs, DVDs, and Blu-ray discs are commonly referred to as "players." If the devices can also record data on discs, they are referred to as "burners." The speed of an optical drive is denoted by X values, but the X-value scale differs for CD, DVD, and Blu-ray drives. The table in Figure 16-9 helps you compare the speed designations for optical drives.

Figure 16-9

Speed Designation	Data Transfer Rate (per second)		
	CDs	DVDs	Blu-ray
Single-speed	150 KB	1350 KB	4500 KB
2X	300 KB	2700 KB	9000 KB
4X	600 KB	5400 KB	18000 KB
8X	1200 KB	1030 KB	36000 KB
16X	2400 KB	2160 KB	72000 KB
24X	3600 KB	3240 KB	
32X	4800 KB		
48X	7200 KB		
56X	8400 KB		

© MediaTechnics

Technology
(continued)

Today's optical drives can work with CDs, DVDs, and Blu-ray discs. If your computer does not include an optical drive, you can temporarily connect one using a USB cable. Connecting an external optical drive gives your computer the ability to load software that is distributed on CDs, rip music from audio CDs, and play DVD movies. You can also use an optical drive to make archival copies of important documents and photographs. Although you might think that your Facebook photos will remain on the Web for all of posterity, when you migrate to a new social media platform, there's no telling what will happen to the memorabilia left on the sites you abandon. Archiving to optical storage is one way to preserve your personal content.

File Explorer makes it easy to burn a CD, DVD, or Blu-ray disc. Simply select the files you want to copy. You can decide whether you want to burn the disc so that it works like a USB flash drive or with a CD/DVD player. The option that works like a USB flash drive is sometimes called the Live File System. The files on these discs can be modified at any time. You can leave one of these discs in your optical burner and store files on it whenever you want. These discs reliably work in computers running Windows but do not work in standalone players.

The CD/DVD player option creates mastered discs, which can only be recorded in a single session, after which they are closed so that files cannot be added or changed. These discs work in standalone CD, DVD, and Blu-ray players, such as those in home theater systems. Click the Try It! button in Figure 16-10 to learn more about your options for burning CDs, DVDs, and Blu-ray discs.

Figure
16-10

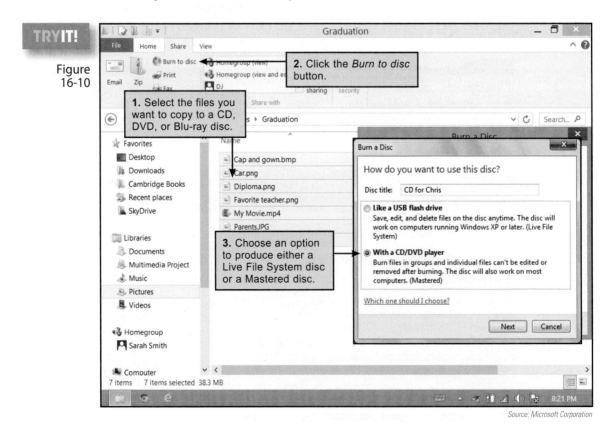

Source: Microsoft Corporation

Project

Explore video editing

The vast selection of video editing and DVD authoring software makes it fairly simple to create your own movies by combining video clips and pictures with music, narration, transition effects, and animated titles. Digital home movies are easy to share via the Web, e-mail, and CDs or DVDs. In this project, you'll use the YouTube Video Editor to create a movie that combines three video clips.

When you have completed this project, you should be able to:

- Upload video footage to YouTube.
- Combine footage from several video and audio clips into a project.
- Crop clips and add special effects.
- Add transitions and titles.

Requirements: This project requires Microsoft Windows and a browser.

Deliverable:

1. An e-mail message containing a link to your completed video

COPY IT!   1. Click the Copy It! button to copy the Prj16.zip file to your Videos folder.

2. Use the Start menu's Search box to open Prj16.zip. Click the *Extract all files* button on the toolbar. By default, the extracted files will be placed in a folder called Prj16. Select your Videos library as the location for the folder.

3. Start your browser and navigate to the YouTube Video Editor.

4. Log in using your Google account. If you don't have an account, create one.

5. Be sure that YouTube is set for a new project. To do so, select the Project button, select *New project*, then name the project Sports Shorts.

| Project ▼ | Sports Shorts | ✕ |

6. Upload the three videos by completing the following steps:

Select the YouTube Upload button.

Click or tap *Select files to upload*.

Navigate to the Videos library on your local computer.

Open the Prj16 folder.

Hold the Shift key down while you select all three files: Biking, Luge, and Skiing.

Select the Open button.

Wait for the files to be uploaded.

• Explore video editing (continued)

7. For each video, make sure the privacy setting is set to Unlisted by completing the following steps:

Select the 👥 privacy icon.

Change the Public setting to Unlisted.

Select the Save Changes button.

Choose the ↰ *Back to Video Manager* button.

Use your browser's Back button to go back to the YouTube Video Editor.

8. Drag the video clips to the time line in this order: Luge, Skiing, Biking.

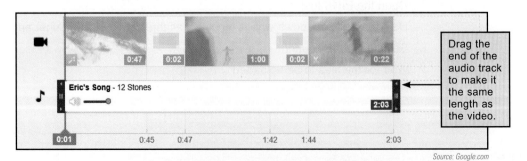

9. The action in the Biking video happens midway through the clip. Crop the beginning and end of the clip by completing the following steps:

Select the Biking video clip.

Drag the black crop bar at the beginning of the clip to the 24-seconds mark.

Drag the black crop bar at the end of the clip to the 22-seconds mark.

Source: Google.com

10. Add a transition between each clip by completing the following steps:

Select the ►◄ Transitions button.

Drag the Crossfade transition to the time line between each clip.

11. Add a music track by completing the following steps:

Select the ♪ Audio button.

Drag one of the audio tracks to the time line.

Drag the end of the audio clip so it is about the same length as the video clips.

Drag the end of the audio track to make it the same length as the video.

Source: Google.com

• Explore video editing (continued)

12. Experiment with effects by completing the following steps:

    Select the Luge clip.

    Select the Effects tool.

    Try selecting various effects, such as Orton-ish, Old-Fashioned, and Thermal.

    (Hint: Deselect each effect before you try another one.)

    Click the Done button when you are satisfied with an effect.

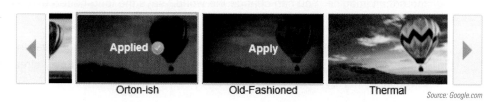

Orton-ish   Old-Fashioned   Thermal

Source: Google.com

13. Add a title at the beginning of the video by completing the following steps:

    Select the Text button from the main YouTube toolbar.

Text button

    Drag the *Centered fade* title to the beginning of the video time line.

    Extend the duration of the title clip to four seconds.

    Select the title clip.

    Enter Sports Shorts as the title.

    Select the Bold button and increase the size of the font to Large.

    Select the Done button.

14. Create a second title by using the Text button again and dragging the *Centered fade* title to the time line. Add your name to this title.

15. Adjust the audio track so that it extends through the entire video.

16. Preview your video and make any other adjustments necessary to finish it to your satisfaction.

17. Select the Publish button to process your video and save it on YouTube.

18. When the video processing is complete, send the link for the video to your instructor by following these steps:

    Click the Share link.

    Right-click the URL, then select Copy.

    Open your e-mail program, address a message to your instructor, then paste the URL into it. Send the e-mail message.

Issue

Can dead celebrities come back to life?

John Lennon appears in a 2009 commercial promoting One Laptop per Child. A young Audrey Hepburn flashes her famous smile in a 2013 ad for Galaxy Chocolate. Paula Abdul dances with Groucho Marx (d. 1977) and flirts with Cary Grant (d. 1986) in a Diet Coke commercial. And Gene Kelly (d. 1996) trades in his 1950s moves and breakdances in a Volkswagen ad. How? Through technological wizardry, of course.

By digitally manipulating the voice and image of John Lennon, he appears to endorse a project that did not yet exist at the time of his death. "You can give a child a laptop and more than imagine. You can change the world," says the long-haired ex-Beatle, wearing his signature wire-framed glasses.

For the Volkswagen ad, Gene Kelly's face is digitally superimposed over the face of dancer David Bernal. But it certainly looks like Gene Kelly doing funky street-wise breakdance moves.

The use of dead celebrities is an eerie trend in show business and marketing. In heavily photoshopped ads, deceased movie stars and singers have been digitally resurrected to sell everything from beer to vacuum cleaners to concert tickets. Celebrities including John Wayne, Fred Astaire, Marilyn Monroe, and Lucille Ball have appeared posthumously in TV commercials.

Some countries have enacted "right of publicity" laws that prohibit unlicensed exploitation of deceased celebrities. However, the application of these laws to digital technology has not yet been fully explored in the courts. Outstanding issues include whether a multimedia developer has a right to create a digital image of a deceased celebrity, even if there is no intent to use the image for commercial gain. Furthermore, would the laws that prohibit using the image of a deceased celebrity also prohibit the use of a digital character that was created from the image of a celebrity look-alike?

The issue becomes even more hazy when you consider that a digital character could combine the traits of several celebrities. In the music industry, it is a violation of copyright law to create mashups from other artists' compositions without permission. Would similar restrictions prevent a developer from creating a digital actor who is a composite of Humphrey Bogart, Clark Gable, and Michael Jackson?

What do you think?

1. Have you seen deceased celebrities featured in any recent TV ads or films?　　○ Yes　○ No　○ Not sure

2. Do you think that multimedia developers should have the right to create a digital character by digitizing a celebrity look-alike?　　○ Yes　○ No　○ Not sure

3. Should laws prohibit the creation of digital characters based on the composite traits of several deceased celebrities?　　○ Yes　○ No　○ Not sure

QuickCheck A

1. Digital video file formats, such as MPEG and QuickTime Movie, are also called [   ] formats because they can hold video and sound clips.

2. True or false? When you make a copy of a digital video, the copy typically does not have the same quality as the original. [   ]

3. Selecting a(n) [   ] such as 128 bps affects the quality of a video and its file size.

4. The software that compresses a video stream when a video is stored and decompresses the file when the video is played is called a(n) [   ] .

5. Optical storage media records data as a series of pits and [   ] on the disc surface.

CHECKIT!

QuickCheck B

For each task described below, indicate the letter of the appropriate tool.

1. Add opening and scene selection menus to a video [   ]

2. Digitize a video from a camcorder or VCR [   ]

3. Compress a video [   ]

4. Archive photos on optical media [   ]

5. Create a video [   ]

Video capture device   DVD   Codec
A   B   C

DVD authoring software
D

Video editing software
E

© MediaTechnics; DivX; Source: Microsoft Corporation

CHECKIT!

GETIT?   While using the digital textbook, click the Get It? button to see if you can answer ten randomly selected questions from Chapter 16.

What's inside?

How does your computer's performance compare? Is it an awesome machine, or just an average performer? Chapter 17 gets into the nuts and bolts—more specifically, the chips and circuits—of computers. You'll find out what goes on inside the system unit and discover various ways to rate your computer's performance.

What's in the digital book?

It's impossible to actually see what's happening inside the chips on your PC's system board, so Chapter 17 contains animated tours to help you visualize the way computers work.

FAQ How does a computer work?

A computer works by manipulating data in various ways. Technically, "data" refers to the symbols that describe people, events, things, and ideas. A computer works with data in four ways: (1) accepting input data, (2) processing data, (3) producing output data, and (4) storing data.

Input is the data that goes into a computer. A computer gets input from many sources, including the keyboard, disk drives, and external devices. What happens to this input? The computer puts it in RAM. Recall from Chapter 1 that RAM (random access memory) is a temporary holding area for data. You might think of it as a lounge area for computer data—a place for it to "hang out" until it is processed, stored, or displayed.

How does a computer know what to do with the data that's in RAM? In addition to data, RAM holds instructions that originate from the software that's running. These instructions tell the computer what to do. A computer's processing circuitry "reads" the instructions, then processes the data according to those instructions. **Processing data** means manipulating it in some way, such as by performing a calculation, sorting a list, or changing the color of the pixels in an image.

Sometimes an instruction indicates that the computer should transfer data from RAM to an external device, such as a printer, router, or display screen. The data sent to these devices is called **output**. Other instructions might direct the computer to transfer data from RAM to a storage device, such as a hard disk drive. This process of **storing data** moves it from the temporary RAM "lounge area" to a more permanent destination.

Data is processed in the microprocessor, which has three important components. The **control unit** fetches instructions generated by computer software. **Registers** hold data that is being processed. The **ALU** (arithmetic logic unit) performs arithmetic operations, such as addition and subtraction, as well as comparison operations that enable the processor to work with text data. Even the simplest processing tasks require many steps. The diagram and Play It! in Figure 17-1 can help you visualize what happens in a microprocessor when it performs the simple calculation 4+5.

PLAY**IT!**

Figure
17-1

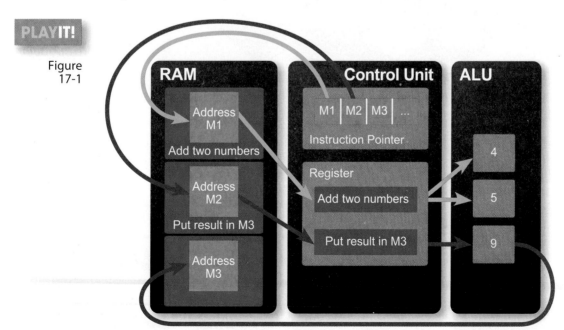

FAQ What do RAM and processing circuitry look like?

RAM and processing circuitry are contained in "chips" inside your PC's system unit. **Chip** is a nickname for an integrated circuit (sometimes called a microchip). An **integrated circuit** is a thin slice of silicon that has been etched with microscopic circuitry.

Different kinds of chips are designed to perform various tasks. For example, a microprocessor chip carries out most of the processing work that takes place in your PC. RAM chips temporarily hold data. One or more ROM chips (read-only memory chips) hold the instructions that your PC uses to boot up. Other chips perform support activities to move data efficiently to and from input devices, the processor, output devices, and storage devices.

A chip is housed in a small, black, rectangular **chip carrier**. Thin wire "feet," which extend from the carrier, can be soldered directly to a circuit board or plugged into a chip socket on a circuit board. A **circuit board** contains electrical pathways that allow data to travel between chips. In a typical PC, a circuit board called the **system board** houses the microprocessor chip, ROM chips, and a variety of support chips. The system board is also referred to as a motherboard or mainboard.

© MediaTechnics

In a desktop computer, a system board is fairly large and includes numerous expansion slots. Laptop, tablet, and smartphone system boards are much smaller and lack expansion capabilities because all the components are soldered onto the board. Figure 17-2 illustrates the difference between desktop system boards and the boards in portable devices. Click the Play It! button to learn more about the chips on your PC's system board.

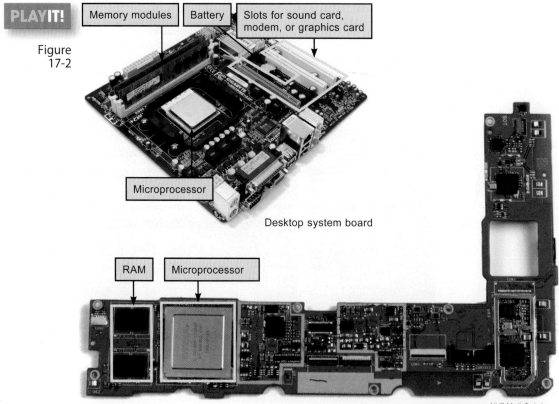

Figure 17-2

PLAY**IT!**

Memory modules   Battery   Slots for sound card, modem, or graphics card

Microprocessor

Desktop system board

RAM   Microprocessor

Tablet system board (enlarged)

All © MediaTechnics

FAQ How does data get into chips?

Your intuition probably tells you that miniature letters, pictures, and other kinds of data don't somehow squirt through the electronic circuitry inside your PC. Instead, your PC works with data that has been converted into a code and then into electronic signals, which can easily travel through circuits that are within chips and circuit boards. This treatment of computer data is similar to the way Morse code converts the letters of a message into a series of dots and dashes that can be represented by the flashing of a signal light. However, keep in mind that "code" in this context simply means converting data from one form to another and has nothing to do with secret codes, security codes, or encryption.

Computers do not use Morse code, but instead use special computer codes that are based on ones (1s) and zeros (0s). For example, a lowercase "y" might be coded as 01111001. Each 1 or 0 is referred to as a bit (short for binary digit). Eight bits form a byte, the unit of measurement for data storage.

Figure 17-3

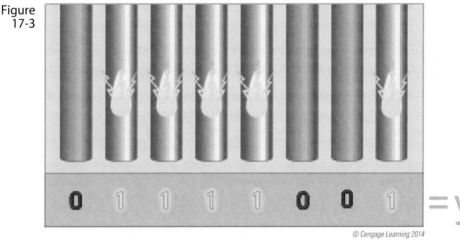

© Cengage Learning 2014

The smallest unit of information in a computer is a bit. A bit can be 0 or 1. The electronic circuits in your PC represent a 1 bit as a pulse of electricity.

A series of eight bits is called a byte and typically represents one character. For example, the eight bits shown here represent the letter "y."

Once data has been coded, it is a relatively easy task to convert the 1s and 0s into a form that can be stored or transmitted electronically. When data is stored in memory, a 1 is represented by the presence of an electrical charge in a miniature electronic circuit; a 0 is represented by the absence of a charge. On a disk, 1s and 0s are represented by metallic particles with different magnetic polarities. On a CD, 1s and 0s are represented by nonreflective pits and reflective surfaces called lands. When data is transmitted to printers or display devices, the 1s and 0s can be represented by different voltages.

As data is gathered, processed, stored, and transmitted, it is constantly converted from one type of signal to another. Special **controller chips** that convert data into various styles of signals are found on the system board, graphics card, sound card, and modem of your PC. For example, a controller chip on the system board converts each key that you press on the keyboard into a corresponding electronic code.

FAQ Does a computer use the same code for all types of data?

Computers use different codes for different types of data. The codes used for text differ from those used for graphics. The coding method for graphics differs from that used for sound. Although many methods for coding computer data exist, all of the computer codes that your PC uses share certain characteristics:

- **Digital.** A digit is a single character in a numbering system. To say a code is digital means that it converts data into a finite set of numbers, rather than an infinite set of analog values.

- **Binary.** The binary number system uses only two digits: 0 and 1. Binary coding allows computers to represent all kinds of complex graphical, sound, text, and numeric data using two simple signals: "off" and "on."

- **Fixed length.** The length of a computer code is measured by the number of 1s and 0s required to represent each data item. Codes that are fixed length use the same number of bits to represent each data item. For example, a code that represents the letter "A" using a string of eight bits also represents a "B" and every other letter of the alphabet using the same number of bits.

Knowing some basic concepts about computer codes helps you understand why some file formats store data in small, efficient files, whereas other data requires large files.

Text. The letters of the alphabet, symbols, and punctuation marks are stored using ASCII, Extended ASCII, and Unicode. **ASCII** (American Standard Code for Information Interchange) uses 7 bits to represent a single character. **Extended ASCII** uses 8 bits to represent characters and an extended set of symbols. **Unicode** uses up to 32 bits to represent thousands of characters, including those used in most modern writing systems, such as Cyrillic (Russian), Greek, and Arabic.

By looking at the Extended ASCII codes in Figure 17-4, you can see that the underlying code is digital, binary, and fixed length. Just for fun, try using codes in the table to write your name.

Figure 17-4

0	00110000	C	01000011	V	01010110	i	01101001
1	00110001	D	01000100	W	01010111	j	01101010
2	00110010	E	01000101	X	01011000	k	01101011
3	00110011	F	01000110	Y	01011001	l	01101100
4	00110100	G	01000111	Z	01011010	m	01101101
5	00110101	H	01001000	[	01011011	n	01101110
6	00110110	I	01001001	\	01011100	o	01101111
7	00110111	J	01001010	]	01011101	p	01110000
8	00111000	K	01001011	^	01011110	q	01110001
9	00111001	L	01001100	_	01011111	r	01110010
:	00111010	M	01001101	`	01100000	s	01110011
;	00111011	N	01001110	a	01100001	t	01110100
<	00111100	O	01001111	b	01100010	u	01110101
=	00111101	P	01010000	c	01100011	v	01110110
>	00111110	Q	01010001	d	01100100	w	01110111
?	00111111	R	01010010	e	01100101	x	01111000
@	01000000	S	01010011	f	01100110	y	01111001
A	01000001	T	01010100	g	01100111	z	01111010
B	01000010	U	01010101	h	01101000		

• Does a computer use the same code for all types of data? (continued)

Numbers. Computers have two classifications for numbers: those that are used for calculations and those that are not. The dialing sequence you enter into a telephone, for example, is not used for calculations. We can call those digits "numerals." Calculations, however, are based on numeric values. We can refer to those values as numbers.

Computers code numerals using character coding schemes such as ASCII, Extended ASCII, and Unicode. Refer back to Figure 17-4 and notice that there are ASCII codes for numerals 0 through 9. A telephone number would be represented by those ASCII codes.

Numbers used for calculations are usually coded using the binary number system. The binary number system has only two digits: 0 and 1. No "2" exists in this system, so counting from one to three in binary consists of 1, 01, and 10. This number system is perfect for a digital device that works with binary data, using "on" and "off" signals.

Bitmap images. Computers code bitmap image data using a binary color code for each pixel in the image. There are many methods for coding colors, but the simplest code uses three bytes of data for each pixel. The first byte defines the amount of red that is in the color. The remaining bytes define the amounts of green and blue. Each color can have up to 256 values. With 256 possible values for red, another 256 for blue, and another 256 for green, a computer can represents millions of colors.

In Figure 17-5, the color values are shown as numbers using base 10. When translated into binary numbers, the lilac color would be 11010010 10010001 11101110.

Figure 17-5

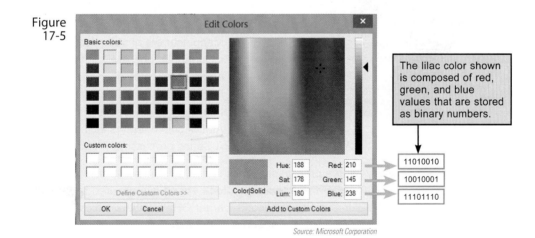

The lilac color shown is composed of red, green, and blue values that are stored as binary numbers.

11010010
10010001
11101110

Source: Microsoft Corporation

Figure 17-6

The height of this sample is 160, which would be stored in binary as 1010000.

Digital audio. Data for digital audio is coded using a binary number to represent the height of each wave sample. The height of each sample is stored as an 8-bit number for radio-quality recordings or as a 16-bit number for high-fidelity recordings. High-fidelity stereo requires two 16-bit numbers for each sample. You can do a little math to determine how much data is required to store one second of stereo using a 44.1 kHz sampling rate. Multiply 32 by 44,100. No wonder we use MP3 to compress our music files!

© Cengage Learning 2014

Technology

Microprocessors

A microprocessor is an integrated circuit that is the main processing device in your PC. The type of microprocessor that's inside a computer indicates its age, dictates the types of programs it can run, affects how fast it can perform computing tasks, and relates to the amount of power it uses.

Low-power mobile chips are designed for portable devices, such as tablet computers, enabling them to run longer on battery power. Chips for desktop computers can blaze away at higher speeds, but typically consume more power.

Chipmakers have produced many microprocessor models. Historically, the first PCs contained Intel 8088 and 8086 processors. That was back in 1981. New chips come out every few years and can be used as a fairly accurate indicator of a computer's age.

Most of today's popular computers contain x86 microprocessors. The term **x86** refers to a design standard for a family of chips that trace their ancestry back to the first generation of PCs. New x86 processors, though faster and more capable, can still run software designed for the first generation of x86 processors.

Figure 17-7

Source: Intel Corporation

Figure 17-8

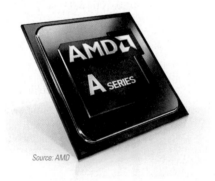

Source: AMD

Manufacturers of x86 microprocessors include Intel and AMD. Intel is the original x86 chipmaker and still the largest. Its current flagship chip is the Intel Core i7 processor (Figure 17-7). AMD's chip offerings include the A Series processors (Figure 17-8).

Computer ads typically hype a processor's clock speed, which is one of several factors that contribute to overall system performance. **Clock speed** is measured in **gigahertz** (GHz). One GHz is 1 billion cycles per second. Larger GHz numbers indicate faster clock speeds. For example, a 3.0 GHz clock speed is faster than a 2.4 GHz clock speed.

Clock speed is analogous to how fast you pedal when you ride a bike. Usually, the faster you pedal, the faster you move. During each clock cycle, the processor executes instructions. The faster the clock speed, the more instructions your microprocessor can carry out in each second. If a 2.4 GHz processor executes one instruction for each clock cycle, it performs 2.4 billion instructions per second!

Clock speed is not the only factor that affects processor performance, and it is becoming a much less important indicator of microprocessor performance than it was in the past. For example, two microprocessors could both be rated at 2.4 GHz. However, one processor might deliver only three-quarters of the performance. What could account for this difference?

Technology
(continued)

Think again about the bike analogy. Your speed depends not just on how fast you pedal, but also on other factors related to the design of your bike, such as gearing and tire size. For example, if your bike allows you to gear down, you can pedal more slowly but still maintain your speed. If you have a bicycle built for two, you can go faster with less effort. Likewise, several factors related to the design of a microprocessor can affect the speed at which it processes instructions.

Instructions per clock cycle. Suppose that during each clock cycle, a processor could perform three instructions instead of one. It would perform three times as much work in the same amount of time. Processors that execute multiple instructions per clock cycle are referred to as **superscalar**.

CPU cache. Before processing can take place, data and instructions exist in RAM chips located several inches away from the processor on the system board of your PC. Even traveling at the speed of light, data can require several clock cycles to move from RAM to the processor. A **CPU cache** (pronounced "cash") is data-holding circuitry from which instructions and data can be accessed faster than from RAM. Typically, cache is measured by its storage capacity in kilobytes (KB) and by the number of cache areas or levels. Most of today's microprocessors have multi-level caches, so you might see references to L1 (Level 1), L2, or L3 caches in advertising materials.

Accelerated front side bus. The circuitry that transports data to the microprocessor is called the **front side bus** (FSB). A fast front side bus moves data quickly and allows the processor to work at full capacity. Processor manufacturers use a variety of techniques, such as HyperTransport and QuickPath, to accelerate the rate at which data travels to the processor.

Extended instruction sets. All x86 processors have a core set of instructions. However, some processors have extended instruction sets that speed up certain types of processing, such as video or photo processing.

Figure 17-9

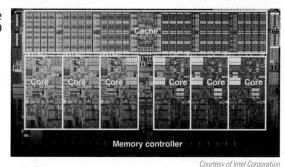

Courtesy of Intel Corporation

Multi-core architecture. A **multi-core processor** is a single microprocessor chip with circuitry that allows it to process more than one instruction at a time. For example, the Intel Core i7 chip in Figure 17-9 contains four processing cores, which theoretically allow the i7 to process instructions four times as fast as a single-core processor. In practice, however, a multi-core processor offers maximum performance only when your computer's operating system and application software are optimized for multi-core processing. Windows supports multi-core processing, as do some games and graphics software.

Word size. Microprocessors work with instructions and data composed of bits. **Word size** refers to the number of bits that a microprocessor can manipulate at one time. Word size is based on the size of registers in the processor and the capacity of circuits that lead to those registers. Today's personal computers typically contain **64-bit processors** that have 64-bit registers and process 64 bits at a time. A few **32-bit processors** are still in use, primarily for tablet computers. Processors with a larger word size can process more data during each processor cycle—a factor that leads to increased performance.

Technology
(continued)

If clock speed doesn't tell you the whole story about processor performance, how can you gauge the performance of this key computer component? Rather than relying on clock speed ratings, you can get a better picture of processor performance from the results of benchmark tests. A **benchmark test** is a set of standard processing tasks that measure the performance of computer hardware or software.

Microprocessor benchmark tests measure the speed at which a processor performs a set of tasks. Computer manufacturers and independent test labs publish the results of benchmark tests in computer magazines and on Web sites. If you're interested in finding out how your own PC stacks up, you can download benchmark testing software from the Web.

Many benchmark tests are available today, and each measures a slightly different aspect of processor performance. To make sense of the results, it is useful to have some idea of how a test relates to what your computer does in real life. For convenience, you can group processor benchmark tests into three categories:

- **Multimedia benchmarks** measure processor performance when processing graphics, video, digitized sound, and other multimedia data.

- **Integer benchmarks** measure processing efficiency for integer data, which includes the words and numbers that you manipulate when using spreadsheet, word processing, presentation, and database applications.

- **Floating-point benchmarks** measure processor performance for numbers stored in "floating-point" format that includes decimal places. Good floating-point performance is required for 3D graphics, computer-aided design, and many computer games.

Although processor performance is important, it is only one factor that affects overall PC performance. Your computer is only as fast as its slowest component. Just as you can pedal fast on an icy road but not make much headway, a processor can spin its wheels while it waits for data from a slow disk drive or Internet connection. Getting an overall picture of your computer's performance requires more than processor benchmarks.

The Windows Experience Index provides a set of scores that indicate how well your computer performs various tasks, based on the speed of the processor, memory, graphics circuitry, and disk access. Figure 17-10 explains the scores.

Five components are tested for performance.

Each component is scored on a scale of 1 (low) to 7.9 (high).

Figure 17-10

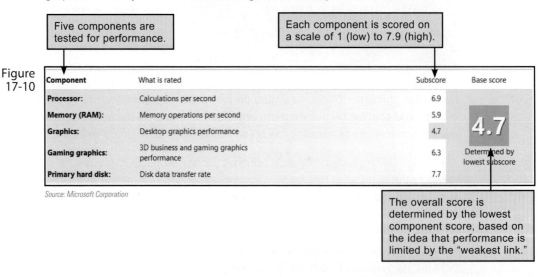

Component	What is rated	Subscore	Base score
Processor:	Calculations per second	6.9	
Memory (RAM):	Memory operations per second	5.9	
Graphics:	Desktop graphics performance	4.7	**4.7**
Gaming graphics:	3D business and gaming graphics performance	6.3	Determined by lowest subscore
Primary hard disk:	Disk data transfer rate	7.7	

Source: Microsoft Corporation

The overall score is determined by the lowest component score, based on the idea that performance is limited by the "weakest link."

Project

Find the technical specifications for your PC

Which processor is in your PC? How fast is it? How much RAM is installed on your PC's system board? The type, capacity, and speed of various components in your PC are called **system specifications**. These specifications are important when you purchase software, upgrade components in your PC, or seek technical support.

When you have completed this project, you should be able to:

- Discover your computer's Windows Experience Index score.

- Access detailed system information.

- Use Task Manager to monitor CPU and RAM activity.

Requirements: This project requires Microsoft Windows, word processing software, and Paint.

The deliverable for this project is a document that contains the following:

1. A list of your computer's scores on the Windows Experience Index

2. A list of your computer's system information

3. A screenshot of Task Manager showing performance statistics for all cores of your computer's processor

1. Access the Windows Experience Index and record your computer's scores. To complete this step:

   At the Start screen, type experience and then select Settings.

   Select the option *Use tools to improve performance*.

   Open your word processing application, and in a new document record each subscore and your computer's base (overall) score.

Source: Microsoft Corporation

2. Record your computer's system information by completing the following steps:

   Below the performance score, select the link *View and print detailed performance and system information*.

   In your word processing document, add the following information about your computer:

   Processor specifications

   RAM capacity

   Graphics specification

   Gaming graphics specification

   Hard disk (total capacity)

   Computer manufacturer and model

   System type (32-bit or 64-bit)

• Find the technical specifications for your PC (continued)

3. Open Task Manager by completing the following steps:

At the Start screen, type Task and then select Task Manager.

(Hint: If you see an option for *More details*, select it.)

Select the Performance tab.

Select the CPU option in the Navigation pane on the left side of the screen.

Drag the borders of the window so it looks like the one below.

4. Use Task Manager to view real-time performance statistics by completing the following steps:

With the Performance tab still selected, select the Options menu and make sure that a checkmark appears next to *Always on Top* so that the Task Manager window remains visible.

Watch the graph for a few moments; if your computer is idle, the graph representing CPU usage should flatline.

5. Open your browser and watch for changes in CPU usage.

6. Open File Explorer and watch for changes in CPU usage.

7. Select the Memory option in Task Manager's Navigation pane.

8. Try opening and closing several applications and watch how those activities affect memory statistics.

9. Select the Disk option in Task Manager's Navigation pane.

10. Open and close several applications and watch how those activities affect disk statistics.

• Find the technical specifications for your PC (continued)

11. In your word processing document, write a paragraph discussing the following question: Do various applications require equivalent performance from the processor, memory, and disk storage?

12. Select the CPU option in the Navigation pane so that you can again view CPU statistics.

13. Change the Task Manager setting so that you can see the performance of each processor core by completing the following steps:

    Right-click the graph.

    Select *Change graph to*.

    Select *Logical processors*.

14. Take a screenshot of Task Manager showing activity on all the processor cores.

Source: Microsoft Corporation

15. Paste the screenshot directly into your word processing document. Adjust the size so the screenshot fits on the page. Save your document as Project 17 [Your Name], then close the document.

16. Close your browser and Task Manager.

17. Submit the Project 17 [Your Name] document as an e-mail attachment, as a printout, or in any other format specified by your instructor.

Issue

Who pays for e-waste?

Environmentally friendly recycling can be a complex and costly process in which a device is disassembled and its plastics, metals, and glass are separated and safely processed. The expense of environmentally sound disposal has created a corrupt international e-waste market that has alarmed environmentalists and human rights activists.

Computers and electronic devices that consumers deliver to recycling centers are sometimes sold and shipped to scrap dealers in developing countries. There, workers who recover copper and other scrap materials from mountains of e-waste are paid pennies per hour and are not protected from toxic components. When the valuable bits have been removed, the remaining e-waste is openly burned, dumped into rivers, or soaked in acid baths, releasing toxic materials into the air, ground, and water.

Proponents of e-waste transshipping point out that processing e-waste in developing countries provides much needed jobs and offers consumers in developed countries a less costly way to dispose of unwanted gear. The environmental and human costs of unregulated disposal practices have triggered a search for a different solution to e-waste disposal.

A basic question regarding the issue of reducing electronic waste is "Who pays?" Should it be the taxpayer, the individual consumer, the retailer, or the manufacturer? When Californians were faced with the prospect of tax hikes to deal with electronic waste disposal, activists questioned if tax increases were fair to individual taxpayers who generate very little electronic waste. Now, consumers buying computers in California must pay a recycling fee at the time of purchase.

Some states have adopted laws that require electronics manufacturers to subsidize e-waste disposal or offer take-back services. The economics of take-back programs can increase product costs, however, if manufacturers pass recycling costs on to consumers.

The Environmental Protection Agency (EPA) advocates a national plan in which consumers, retailers, and manufacturers cooperate to reduce electronic waste, suggesting that because recycling laws differ from state to state, consumers are often confused about how to dispose of their unwanted gear. Some consumers worry that such a plan would lead to additional federal bureaucracy and costs that raise taxes.

What do you think?

1. Have you ever thrown an unwanted electronic
   device into the garbage?   ○ Yes ○ No   ○ Not sure

2. Are you aware of recycling options in your
   local area?   ○ Yes ○ No   ○ Not sure

3. Would you be willing to pay a $10 recycling fee
   for any electronic product you purchase?   ○ Yes ○ No   ○ Not sure

4. Do you think that national recycling laws are
   needed?   ○ Yes ○ No   ○ Not sure

QuickCheck A

1. A computer accepts input, produces output, stores data, and [_____] data.

2. An integrated [_____] is housed inside a chip carrier.

3. True or false? Computer codes are binary because it is a relatively easy task to convert coded 1s and 0s into electronic signals. [_____]

4. A microprocessor includes several components, including a(n) [_____] that performs calculations and comparisons. (Hint: Use the acronym.)

5. True or false? Processors that execute multiple instructions per clock cycle are referred to as multiscalar. [_____]

CHECKIT!

QuickCheck B

Match the letter of each image to its correct description:

1. Benchmark [____]

2. Microprocessor [____]

3. Chip carriers [____]

4. Task Manager [____]

5. ASCII code [____]

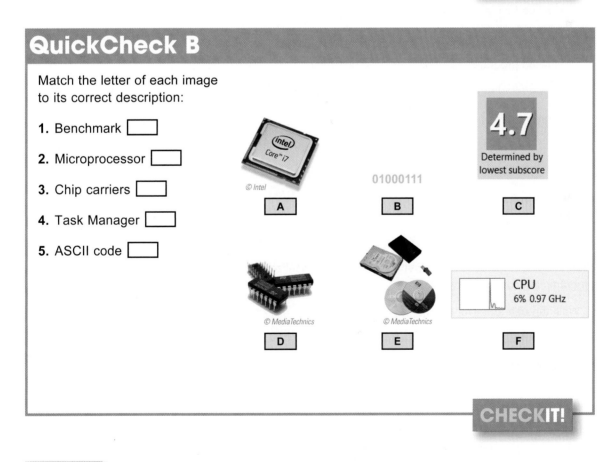

CHECKIT!

GETIT? While using the digital textbook, click the Get It? button to see if you can answer ten randomly selected questions from Chapter 17.

18 Computer Programming

What's inside?

Mobile apps. Productivity software. Games. Music players. All the goodies on digital devices are powered by computer programs. Chapter 18 gives you a taste of what computer programming is all about.

What's in the digital book?

Programming requires thinking, but it also helps to visualize. The tours in Chapter 18 bring programming concepts down to earth.

FAQ What should I know about computer programs?

Software is simply a collection of one or more computer programs or "program modules" containing a list of instructions for the microprocessor. The process of writing computer programs is called **computer programming** and the people who write programs are referred to as **programmers**.

Programming is sometimes referred to as "coding" and program instructions can be referred to as "code." This terminology may have originated with computer programmers who programmed first-generation computers by entering instructions as 0s and 1s referred to as binary code.

Today, program code is written using a computer **programming language**, such as BASIC, Python, PHP, Alice, Java, or C++. These languages consist of English-like command words such as print, while, if, and else. Programs written for commercial application software and operating systems contain many millions of lines of code, but you can get an idea of a very short program from the Adventure Game example in Figure 18-1. Use the Try It! button to see how it works.

TRYIT!

Figure 18-1

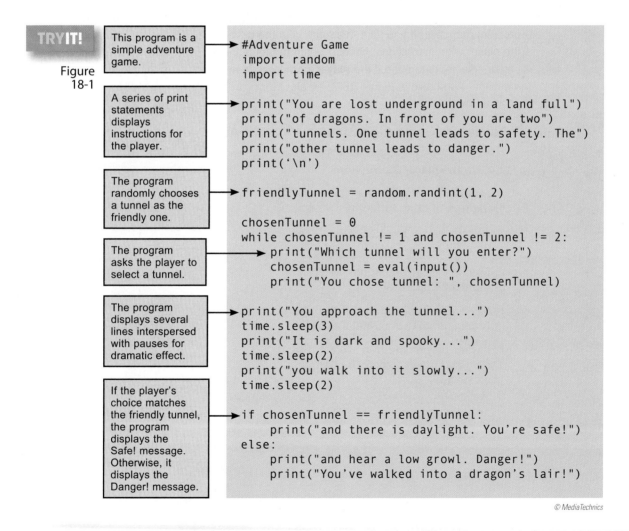

This program is a simple adventure game.

```
#Adventure Game
import random
import time
```

A series of print statements displays instructions for the player.

```
print("You are lost underground in a land full")
print("of dragons. In front of you are two")
print("tunnels. One tunnel leads to safety. The")
print("other tunnel leads to danger.")
print('\n')
```

The program randomly chooses a tunnel as the friendly one.

```
friendlyTunnel = random.randint(1, 2)
```

The program asks the player to select a tunnel.

```
chosenTunnel = 0
while chosenTunnel != 1 and chosenTunnel != 2:
    print("Which tunnel will you enter?")
    chosenTunnel = eval(input())
    print("You chose tunnel: ", chosenTunnel)
```

The program displays several lines interspersed with pauses for dramatic effect.

```
print("You approach the tunnel...")
time.sleep(3)
print("It is dark and spooky...")
time.sleep(2)
print("you walk into it slowly...")
time.sleep(2)
```

If the player's choice matches the friendly tunnel, the program displays the Safe! message. Otherwise, it displays the Danger! message.

```
if chosenTunnel == friendlyTunnel:
    print("and there is daylight. You're safe!")
else:
    print("and hear a low growl. Danger!")
    print("You've walked into a dragon's lair!")
```

FAQ What is an algorithm?

An **algorithm** is a set of steps for carrying out a task that can be written down and implemented. For example, the algorithm for making a batch of macaroni and cheese is a set of steps that includes boiling water, cooking the macaroni in the water, and making a cheese sauce.

An algorithm for a computer program is a set of steps that explains how to begin with known information, how to collect additional information as the program runs, and how to manipulate that information to arrive at a solution. Algorithms are used when planning and designing programs. They help programmers formulate a method for solving problems and carrying out tasks that are performed by the programs they create.

Algorithms are usually written in a format that is not specific to a particular programming language. This approach allows programmers to focus on formulating a correct algorithm without becoming distracted by the detailed syntax of a computer programming language. In a later phase of the software development process, the algorithm is coded into instructions written in a programming language so that a computer can implement it.

To design an algorithm, you might begin by recording the steps required to solve the problem manually. If you take this route with the adventure game, you would provide the player with instructions, choose which tunnel is friendly, find out which tunnel the player selects, determine if the player's tunnel is friendly, and then display the concluding message. As shown in Figure 18-2, an algorithm can be expressed as a set of statements or as a flowchart.

Figure 18-2

Adventure Game Algorithm

1. Give the player instructions.

2. Randomly generate the number of the tunnel that is friendly.

3. Ask the player to select tunnel 1 or tunnel 2.

4. Find out if the player has selected the friendly tunnel.

5. If the player selected the friendly tunnel, display the Safe! message.

6. If the player did not select the friendly tunnel, display the Danger! message.

Adventure Game Flowchart

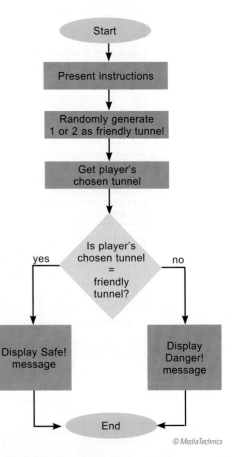

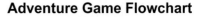

© MediaTechnics

FAQ How do I code a program?

There are many programming languages, and each one requires a unique set of techniques to code a program. You'll learn more about programming languages in the Technology section. In the meantime, let's look at programming with the Python language that is widely used for creating Web services and mobile apps. Python was first released in 1989 and is named after the television show, *Monty Python's Flying Circus*.

A Python program consists of a series of instructions. Just as a sentence is constructed from various words and punctuation marks that follow a set of grammar rules, program instructions are constructed from a set of keywords and parameters that conform to the grammar rules, or syntax, of the programming language.

The vocabulary of a programming language contains a limited number of words. A **keyword**, or command, is a word that has a specific meaning and action. For example, the keyword `print` means to display text on the screen. Python keywords are listed in Figure 18-3.

Figure 18-3

and	elif	from	lambda	return	break	else	global	not	try
class	except	if	or	while	continue	exec	import	pass	def
finally	in	print	del	for	is	raise			

© MediaTechnics

Keywords are combined with additional parameters that provide more specifics pertaining to the instruction. The following instruction displays a message on the screen:

```
print("Which tunnel will you enter?")
```

Programmers also use variables to hold values and text that a program will manipulate. A **variable** represents a value that can change. In the adventure game, `chosenTunnel` is a variable because the player can enter 1 or 2 to select a tunnel. You can think of variables as boxes in the computer memory where a program stores numbers or words. Figure 18-4 illustrates what happens to the variable `chosenTunnel` when the adventure game runs.

Figure 18-4

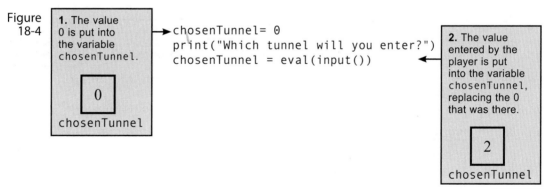

© MediaTechnics

A key concept about programming is the use of variables. A programmer can create variables, put values and text in them, and change their contents. Variables that hold values can be used in calculations. Variables that hold text can be manipulated to combine words, sort lists, change uppercase to lowercase, and find specific letters in a string of text. Knowing that the variable `chosenTunnel` contains 2, what do you think is produced by the following Python statement?

```
print("You chose tunnel: ", chosenTunnel)
```

FAQ How do programs carry out logical operations?

Computer programs must handle many scenarios. The adventure game program includes one scenario in which the player selects the friendly tunnel, and another scenario in which the player selects the dangerous tunnel. Based on the selected tunnel, the program decides whether to display the Safe! message or the Danger! message. That decision is represented by a diamond-shaped branch on the program flowchart.

Figure
18-5

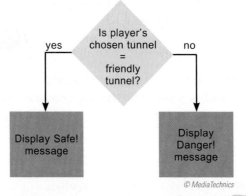

© MediaTechnics

A statement that requires a program to branch is called a **selection control structure** because the program selects a path based on a specified condition. The condition is often defined by the contents of variables. In the adventure game, the condition is based on the values in the two variables: chosenTunnel and friendlyTunnel.

The variable chosenTunnel contains 1 or 2, representing the player's choice of tunnel 1 or tunnel 2. The variable friendlyTunnel contains a 1 or 2 depending on which of those two numbers was randomly selected by the computer. The program tells the computer to compare the values in those two variables to find out if the player has selected the friendly tunnel.

Python uses if and else as the keywords for a selection control structure. Figure 18-6 explains how it works.

Figure
18-6

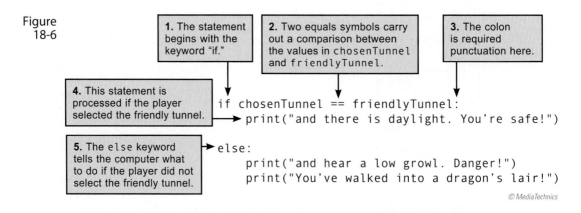

© MediaTechnics

Now suppose that you are a computer executing the control structure above. The variable friendlyTunnel holds 2 and the variable chosenTunnel holds 1. Which message will be displayed?

Answer to previous page: The Python statement print("You chose tunnel: ", chosenTunnel) displays the following: You chose tunnel: 2

FAQ How do programs carry out repetitive operations?

Computers often perform repetitive tasks. For example, when you log in to Facebook, a program asks you to enter your user ID and password. If you don't enter them correctly, the program repeats and asks you to try again until you enter the correct credentials.

As another example, when you enter a telephone number on your cell phone, the phone's software collects the first number you enter, then it collects the next number, and the next number, and so on until you touch the Call button.

A **repetition control structure** directs the computer to repeat one or more instructions until a certain condition is met. The section of code that repeats is referred to as a **loop**. Python uses the `while` command to designate a repetition control. Usually a variable is used to control the number of times the loop repeats. For example, a programmer might define a variable called `loopCount` to keep count of the repetitions.

Remember Dorothy in *The Wizard of Oz*? She clicks her heels together and repeats three times, "There's no place like home." The flowchart in Figure 18-7 illustrates how a repetition control structure directs a program to repeat a phrase three times.

The flowchart contains a decision point in the diamond shape that checks to see if the loop has been executed a specified number of times. To make additional repetitions, the computer program must backtrack to the beginning of the loop. The repetition control structure handles that task.

Figure
18-7

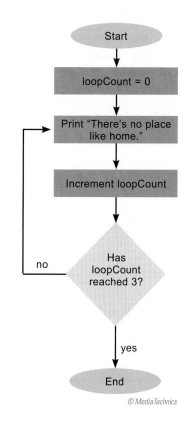

© MediaTechnics

Answer to previous page: The friendly tunnel is 2, but the player chose tunnel 1. Therefore, the program prints the following two lines:

```
print("and hear a low growl. Danger!")
print("You've walked into a dragon's lair!")
```

• How do programs carry out repetitive operations? (continued)

To get a better idea of how a loop works, imagine that you're the computer executing the instructions below. You can use the box labeled loopCount at the bottom of the page as a variable. Use the Screen Output box for writing the output. Now, walk through the loop.

```
loopCount = 1

while (loopCount <= 3):

    print("There's no place like home.")

    loopCount = loopCount + 1
```

1. As the computer, the instruction loopCount = 1 directs you to set the loopCount variable to 1. To do so, write 1 in the loopCount box at the bottom of the page.

2. Next, the instruction while (loopCount <= 3): tells you that you can proceed only when the value in the loopCount box is less than or equal to 3. Look at loopCount. It is 1, so you can continue to the next instruction.

3. Execute the instruction print("There's no place like home."). To do so, write the phrase "There's no place like home." in the Screen Output box. (Hint: Write small; you'll be adding more text to this box as you proceed.)

4. The next instruction loopCount = loopCount + 1 means to add 1 to the value in loopCount, so change that number to 2.

5. Now, loop back to the instruction while (loopCount <= 3): and check if the value in the loopCount box is less than or equal to 3. It is, so go to the next instruction, which is print("There's no place like home."). Write this sentence again in the Screen Output box.

6. Moving on, you reach the loopCount = loopCount + 1 statement again, so add 1 to the value in the loopCount box.

7. Continue back to the instruction while (loopCount <= 3): and check the loopCount box to make sure it does not contain a value greater than 3. It doesn't, so continue.

8. The next line is print("There's no place like home.") Write this sentence again in the Screen Output box.

9. Now, add 1 to the loopCount box.

10. The next statement is while (loopCount <= 3): so check the value in the loopCount box. It is greater than 3, so the loop is complete.

11. When the program is complete, the loopCount box should contain the number 4, and the Screen Output box should contain three lines of "There's no place like home."

Screen Output	loopCount

FAQ How does a programmer know if a program works?

A computer program must be tested to ensure that it works correctly. Basic testing consists of running the program and entering test data to see whether the program produces correct results. If testing does not produce the expected results, the program contains an error, sometimes called a bug. This error must be corrected, and then the program must be tested again and again until it runs error-free.

When a program doesn't work correctly, it is usually the result of a syntax, runtime, or logic error.

Syntax errors. A **syntax error** occurs when an instruction does not follow the syntax rules, or grammar, of the programming language. For example, leaving off the colon in the statement while (loopCount <= 3): would produce a syntax error because the colon is required to set off the loop control from the statements that are executed within the loop. Syntax errors are easy to make, but they are usually also easy to detect and correct. Figure 18-8 lists some common syntax errors.

Figure 18-8

Omitting a keyword, such as THEN

Misspelling a keyword, as when mistakenly typing PIRNT instead of PRINT

Omitting required punctuation, such as a colon or parentheses

Using incorrect punctuation, such as a semicolon where a colon is required

Forgetting to close parentheses

© MediaTechnics

Runtime errors. An error that is detected as a program runs is referred to as a **runtime error**. Some runtime errors result from instructions that the computer can't execute. The Python instruction loopCount = heelClicks/0 produces a runtime error because dividing by 0 is a mathematically impossible operation that the computer cannot perform.

Logic errors. A **logic error** is a type of runtime error that is caused by a fault in the logic or design of a program. In the Wizard of Oz code, using while (loopCount < 3): would produce a logic error because the program would print "There's no place like home." only two times instead of three times. The correct code (loopCount <= 3): differs from the incorrect code by the addition of an = symbol. Logic errors can be caused by an inadequate definition of the problem or an incorrect formula for a calculation, and are usually more difficult to identify than syntax errors.

Programmers can locate errors in a program by reading through lines of code, much like a proofreader. They can also use a tool called a **debugger** to step through a program and monitor the status of variables, input, and output. A debugger is sometimes packaged with a programming language or can be obtained as an add-on.

Technology

Programming tools

In the search for one perfect language to use for programming computers, computer scientists have invented thousands of programming languages. Wikipedia lists about 600 mainstream languages, but there are dialects of these languages and a vast collection of esoteric languages that were created as experiments to push the boundaries of language theory.

An esoteric language called reMorse produces program statements that look like Morse code. A language called Whitespace uses only whitespace characters—tab, linefeed, and space—as program keywords. Such languages are not designed for practical programming projects, but they are not much wackier than the original method for programming computers. Back in 1946, one of the first computers was programmed by manually setting switches and cables within the CPU.

Figure 18-9

Courtesy of U.S. Army Photo

Programming languages can be divided into two major categories: low-level languages and high-level languages.

Low-level languages. A **low-level language** is based on commands specific to a particular CPU or microprocessor family. Programs written with these languages run directly on the hardware without any preprocessing. Low-level languages include machine code and assembly languages.

Machine code consists of 1s and 0s that can be directly executed by the computer. Imagine a computer program that consists of pages and pages of 1s and 0s. Machine code is difficult to read and debug. It is rarely used by programmers to code programs. However, all programs are eventually converted into machine code so that they can be executed by the microprocessor.

Assembly languages are one step above machine code in ease of use. An **assembly language** uses short op codes as keywords. For example, the op code `mov` moves a value from memory to a register in the microprocessor. The op code `add` adds the contents of two registers in the microprocessor.

Remember the statement `loopCount = loopCount + 1` in the Wizard of Oz program ? That statement added 1 to the value in the variable called `loopCount`. In assembly language, this statement would be `inc LC`.

Assembly languages are used in limited and very specific situations. They are used to code device drivers, malware, parts of computer games, flight navigation systems, and other applications that require fast execution time and minimal program size.

Technology
(continued)

High-level languages. A **high-level language** uses command words and grammar based on human languages to provide what computer scientists call a level of abstraction that hides the underlying low-level assembly or machine language. These languages are used to develop applications, games, Web apps, and most other software.

High-level languages, such as BASIC, Java, Python, and C, make the programming process easier by replacing unintelligible strings of 1s and 0s or cryptic assembly commands with understandable commands, such as PRINT and IF.

As you learned in Chapter 3, the overhead with high-level languages is that they must be converted into machine code before they can be executed by the microprocessor. Although the conversion from high-level code into machine code is carried out by the computer, the process takes time, either while the program is being developed or while the program is executing.

As you learned in chapter 3, the human-readable version of a program created in a high-level language by a programmer is called source code. The procedure for converting source code into 0s and 1s can be accomplished by a compiler or an interpreter.

A **compiler** converts all the statements in a program in a single batch, and the resulting collection of instructions, called **object code**, is placed in a new file. Most of the program files distributed as software applications contain object code that is ready for the processor to execute. These files usually have .exe or .com file extensions. Because the conversion to machine code takes place before the program runs, compiled programs execute quite quickly.

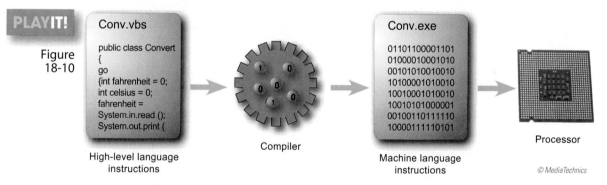

PLAYIT!

Figure 18-10

Conv.vbs

public class Convert
{
go
{int fahrenheit = 0;
int celsius = 0;
fahrenheit =
System.in.read ();
System.out.print (

High-level language instructions

Compiler

Conv.exe

01101100001101
01000010001010
00101010010010
10100001010010
10010001010010
10010101000001
00100110111110
10000111110101

Machine language instructions

Processor

© MediaTechnics

As an alternative to a compiler, an **interpreter** converts and executes one statement at a time while the program is running. After a statement is executed, the interpreter converts and executes the next statement, and so on. Because interpreters do their work at runtime, interpreted programs execute more slowly than compiled programs.

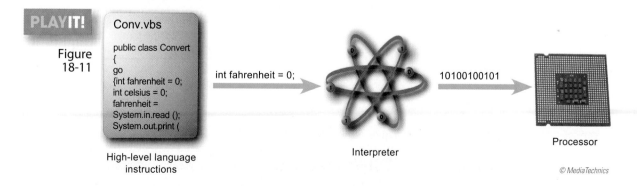

PLAYIT!

Figure 18-11

Conv.vbs

public class Convert
{
go
{int fahrenheit = 0;
int celsius = 0;
fahrenheit =
System.in.read ();
System.out.print (

High-level language instructions

int fahrenheit = 0;

Interpreter

10100100101

Processor

© MediaTechnics

Technology
(continued)

Back in the days of the Apple II and the IBM PC, every computer included a programming language, such as BASIC, which made it easy to experiment with programming. Today's computers include a very rudimentary batch processing language that can be used to enter a sequence of operating system commands. That language cannot be used for more general programming, however.

To experiment with a full-featured programming language, you need a program editor to write the code, and you need a language-specific compiler or an interpreter to run and test the programs you create. You can use an online programming environment (Figure 18-12 top) or download programming tools and install them locally (Figure 18-12 bottom). You'll have a chance to work with an online environment when you complete the project for this chapter.

TRYIT!

Figure 18-12

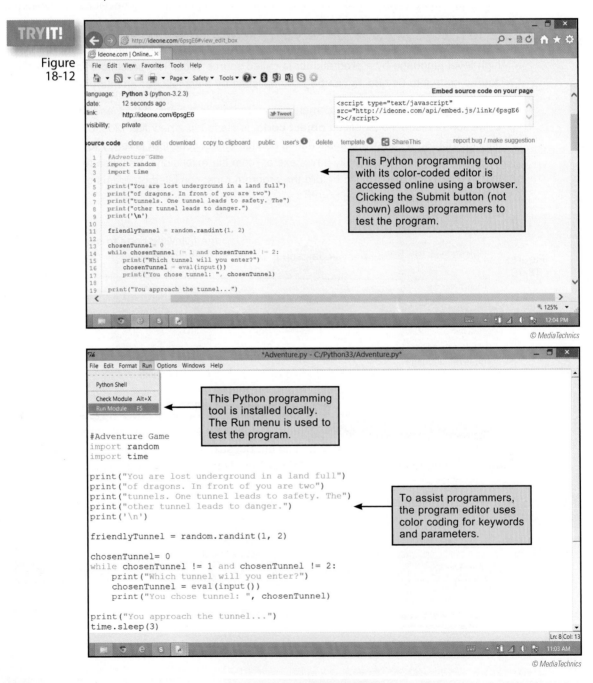

© MediaTechnics

© MediaTechnics

Project

Get started with programming

In this chapter, you were acquainted with the basic process of computer programming, from designing algorithms to coding short Python programs. Programming is fascinating because you work within a defined system that provides instant feedback when you try to run your program. Your goal is to write a program that runs without errors. You know you've succeeded when the program produces the correct output.

In this project, you'll try your hand at a few activities designed to give you a taste of the challenges and the rewards of computer programming.

When you have completed this project, you should be able to:

- Walk through a program to determine its output.

- Debug a program by finding a logic error.

- Use an online Python programming environment.

- Modify a program and run it without errors.

Requirements: This project requires Microsoft Windows and a browser.

The deliverable is an e-mail message containing the following:

1. The output of the Python program in Step 1

2. An explanation of the logic error in Step 2

3. The output from the two scenarios for the program in Step 3

4. The output from Step 5

5. The revised program you create in Step 6

1. Play the role of the computer and walk through the following code to see if it produces the lyrics to a Beatles song. To complete the walk-through, use the loopCount and Screen Output boxes. Start an e-mail message to your instructor for this project and add your results to it.

```python
loopCount = 1
while loopCount <= 2:
    print("All you need is love, ")
    loopCount = loopCount + 1
print("love")
print("Love is all you need.")
```

Screen Output

loopCount

• Get started with programming (continued)

2. Play the role of the computer and walk through the following code to find out why it doesn't work. The program is supposed to ask for a password and allow access only if the password entered is the correct one. Add your results to your project e-mail message. (Hint: The syntax is correct; look for a logic error.)

```
windowsID = "Sarah Smith"
windowsPassword = "ticket2ride"
print("Login as "), windowsID
print("Enter your password: ")
passwordEntered = input()
print(passwordEntered)
if windowsID == windowsPassword:
    print("Welcome "), windowsID
else:
    print("Access denied.")
```

3. Here's a program that could be played in Las Vegas. What happens when you roll 5 and 2? What happens when you roll 3 and 3? Add your answers to your project e-mail.

```
#Roll the Dice!
import random
die1 = random.randint(1,6)
die2 = random.randint(1,6)
print("You rolled ", die1, die2)
print("You win $", die1 + die2)
if die1 == die2:
    print("No wait! Make that $", (die1 + die2)*2)
```

4. Locate an online Python programming environment. You can find one by conducting a Google search for Python online. If the site requires registration, go ahead and register. (Hint: Use a site that offers Python 3.0 or above. The syntax is slightly different from Python 1.0 and 2.0.)

5. Enter the following Python code and then run the program to make sure it works. Copy the output to your project e-mail message. (Hint: Some online programming environments require you to enter your input before you test your code. If an input area is supplied, type your input there.)

Use the exact case. →
```
print("How many text messages have you sent this month? ")
messages = eval(input())   ← Include all parentheses.
print(messages)
if messages >= 500:
```
Indent four spaces. →
```
    print("You've exceeded your limit.")
else:
    print("You can send ", 500-messages, "more texts.")
```

• Get started with programming (continued)

COPY IT!

6. Enter and test the Adventure Game program by completing the following steps:

Click the Copy It! button to download a file containing the Adventure Game program.

Open the file in Notepad.

Copy the program into your online Python programming environment.

(Hint: If you are unable to download the program by using the Copy It! button, type the code below into your online Python programming environment.)

Run the program to make sure it works.

```python
#Adventure Game
import random

print("You are lost underground in a land full")
print("of dragons. In front of you are two")
print("tunnels. One tunnel leads to safety. The")
print("other tunnel leads to danger.")
print('\n')

friendlyTunnel = random.randint(1, 2)

chosenTunnel = 0
while chosenTunnel != 1 and chosenTunnel != 2:
    print("Which tunnel will you enter?")
    chosenTunnel = eval(input())
    print("You chose tunnel: ", chosenTunnel)

print("You approach the tunnel...")
print("It is dark and spooky...")
print("you walk into it slowly...")

if chosenTunnel == friendlyTunnel:
    print("and there is daylight. You're safe!")
else:
    print("and hear a low growl. Danger!")
    print("You've walked into a dragon's lair!")
```

7. Modify the program to create your own game. Instead of selecting a tunnel, for example, you might want to ask the user to select a cave. The friendly cave might contain a treasure. You can change the dragon to a troll, or make other improvements to the game.

8. Submit your game according to your instructor's guidelines. You may be able to send a link to your program, or you might be required to copy your program code and paste it into an e-mail message.

Issue

Who invented the first electronic digital computer?

In a 1973 lawsuit, a computer manufacturing company called Sperry Rand claimed to hold a patent on the technology for electronic digital computers. If the courts upheld this claim, then no company would have been able to manufacture computers without obtaining a license from and paying royalties to Sperry Rand.

Historically, the first inventor to produce a binary digital computer was probably Konrad Zuse, an engineer in Germany who, in 1938, completed work on a computer called the Z1. World War II made collaboration on technology projects difficult, so Zuse's work was not widely known until after the war. More significantly, Zuse did not file for a U.S. patent.

About the same time that Zuse was building the Z1, John Mauchly and J. Presper Eckert began work in Pennsylvania on a computer called the ENIAC, which became operational in 1946. Mauchly and Eckert obtained a patent for digital computer technology and then formed a computer company. Their company and patent were eventually acquired by Sperry Rand.

At the time of the 1973 lawsuit, Sperry Rand appeared to have a clear claim on digital computer technology. However, a seemingly insignificant meeting dating back to 1941 between Mauchly and a mathematician named John Atanasoff had far-reaching consequences on the Sperry Rand patent case. In this meeting and in subsequent correspondence, Atanasoff shared his ideas on computer design with Mauchly. Atanasoff had been constructing a computer of his own, but had never filed for a patent. Mauchly and Eckert subsequently incorporated several of Atanasoff's ideas to build the ENIAC computer.

When these events became known during the 1973 patent dispute, the judge ruled that "Eckert and Mauchly did not themselves first invent the automatic electronic digital computer, but instead derived that subject matter from one Dr. John Vincent Atanasoff." The Sperry Rand patent was declared invalid.

What do you think?	
1. Does it appear to you that the judge made the right decision, despite the fact that Atanasoff never filed for a patent?	○ Yes ○ No ○ Not sure
2. Do you think that Zuse, instead of Atanasoff, should be declared the inventor of the first electronic digital computer?	○ Yes ○ No ○ Not sure
3. Do you think that the computer industry would be different today if Sperry Rand had won its patent case?	○ Yes ○ No ○ Not sure

QuickCheck A

1. A(n) [_____] is a set of steps for carrying out a task that can be written out and implemented.

2. In the Adventure Game program, `chosenTunnel` is a(n) [_____] .

3. The [_____] control structure is associated with the Python command `if`.

4. The keyword `while` is used to control [_____] .

5. Forgetting the colon at the end of a `while` statement is a(n) [_____] error.

CHECKIT!

QuickCheck B

This program code contains a few errors. For each item, enter E if it is an error, or N if it is not.

A. [____]

B. [____]

C. [____]

D. [____]

E. [____]

© MediaTechnics

```
#Roll the Dice!
imp[A]random
die1 = random.randint(1,6)
die2 = random.randin[B]6)
print("You rolled ", die, die2)
print "You win $" die1 + die2 ←[C]
if die1 == die2:←[D]          [E]
        print("No wait! Make that $", (die1 + die2) X 2)
```

CHECKIT!

GETIT? While using the digital textbook, click the Get It? button to see if you can answer ten randomly selected questions from Chapter 18.

Index